Digital Currencies and the New Global Financial System

This book analyses the current debate around Central Bank Digital Currencies (CBDCs) and the future of New Global Financial System. It offers deep insight into the global monetary policy in the context of digital and cryptocurrencies and examines both the opportunities and challenges to come.

The book draws a clear distinction between digital and cryptocurrencies and answers several research questions, such as what the consequences of forming CBDCs and their impact on the financial markets, in both advanced and developing economies, might be. Another question refers to whether the role of monetary policy easing has led to the rise of the virtual currency market, while still others relate to the impact of the pandemic on international settlements. The book also discusses the issue of investment in cryptocurrencies, and the related risks, whether this is a profitable investment vehicle, and how the digital banking system evaluates such investments. Further, the book also highlights the post-pandemic challenges for central banks, such as future monetary policy. It includes a complex review of the literature and presents elaborate econometric models of digital currencies and cryptocurrencies. The book has a wide geographic focus, examining these aspects from the perspective of several countries, including China, India and the US.

The primary audience for the book is researchers, scholars and students of international finance and economics, but it also appeals to practitioners concerned with the digitalisation of financial systems, policymakers and regulatory agencies.

Ranjan Aneja is Professor and Head of the Department of Economics, Central University of Haryana, Mahendergarh, Haryana, India.

Robert Dygas is Assistant Professor in the Department of East Asian Economic Studies, SGH Warsaw School of Economics, Warsaw, Poland.

Routledge International Studies in Money and Banking

Finance and Sustainable Development
Designing Sustainable Financial Systems
Edited by Magdalena Ziolo

The Financialized Economy
Alexander Styhre

Financialization, Financial Literacy, and Social Education
Edited by Thomas A. Lucey

Moral Hazard
A Financial, Legal, and Economic Perspective
Edited by Juan Flores Zendejas, Norbert Gaillard and Rick Michalek

Mergers, Acquisitions, and International Financial Regulation
Analysing Special Purpose Acquisition Companies
Daniele D'Alvia

Pension Fund Capitalism
The Privatization of Pensions in Developed and Developing Countries
Leokadia Oręziak

Central Banks in Organizational Networks
Entangled Market Actors
Christoph F-D. Wu

Responsible Finance and Digitalization
Implications and Developments
Edited by Panu Kalmi, Tommi Auvinen and Marko Järvenpää

Digital Currencies and the New Global Financial System
Edited by Ranjan Aneja and Robert Dygas

For more information about this series, please visit: www.routledge.com/Routledge-International-Studies-in-Money-and-Banking/book-series/SE0403

Digital Currencies and the New Global Financial System

Edited by Ranjan Aneja and Robert Dygas

SGH
Szkoła Główna Handlowa w Warszawie

110 1906 2016
WITH HERITAGE TO PROGRESS

Routledge
Taylor & Francis Group
LONDON AND NEW YORK

First published 2023
by Routledge
4 Park Square, Milton Park, Abingdon, Oxon OX14 4RN

and by Routledge
605 Third Avenue, New York, NY 10158

Routledge is an imprint of the Taylor & Francis Group, an informa business

British Library Cataloguing-in-Publication Data
A catalogue record for this book is available from the British Library

Library of Congress Cataloging-in-Publication Data
Names: Aneja, Ranjan, editor. | Dygas, Robert, editor.
Title: Digital currencies and the new global financial system / edited by Ranjan Aneja and Robert Dygas.
Description: Abingdon, Oxon ; New York, NY : Routledge, 2023. | Series: Routledge international studies in money and banking | Includes bibliographical references and index.
Identifiers: LCCN 2022024744 (print) | LCCN 2022024745 (ebook) | ISBN 9781032315720 (hardback) | ISBN 9781032315737 (paperback) | ISBN 9781003310365 (ebook)
Subjects: LCSH: Cryptocurrencies. | Digital currency. | Finance—Technological innovations.
Classification: LCC HG1710.3 .D54 2023 (print) | LCC HG1710.3 (ebook) | DDC 332.4—dc23/eng/20220805
LC record available at https://lccn.loc.gov/2022024744
LC ebook record available at https://lccn.loc.gov/2022024745

ISBN: 978-1-032-31572-0 (hbk)
ISBN: 978-1-032-31573-7 (pbk)
ISBN: 978-1-003-31036-5 (ebk)

DOI: 10.4324/9781003310365

Typeset in Times New Roman
by Apex CoVantage, LLC

Contents

Figures

Tables

Contributors

Ranjan Aneja, Professor, Department of Economics, Central University of Haryana, India

Andreas Bielig, Associate Professor, SGH Warsaw School of Economics

Robert Dygas, Assistant Professor, World Economy Research Institute, SGH Warsaw School of Economics, Warsaw, Poland

Piotr Filipiak, Consulting Director, Financial Services at Comarch SA, Poland

Aneta Hryckiewicz, Associate Professor, Koźmiński University, Poland

Meelis Kitsing, Rector, Professor of Political Economy, Estonian Business School, Estonia

Aleksandra Kopeć, Silesian University, Poland

Magdalena Kozińska, Assistant Professor, Collegium of Socio-Economic Banking Institute Department of Banking Safety Net, SGH Warsaw School of Economics, Expert at Bank Guarantee Fund, Poland

Łukasz Kurowski, Assistant Professor, SGH Warsaw School of Economics, also expert in National Bank of Poland

Waldemar Milewicz, Assistant Professor, SGH Warsaw School of Economics, Poland

Krzysztof Piech, Lazarski University, Poland

Paweł Pisany, Assistant Professor, Institute of Economics, Polish Academy of Sciences, Poland

Vishal Sarin, Professor, Mittal School of Business, Lovely Professional University, India

Smita Shukla, Professor, Alkesh Dinesh Mody Institute for Financial and Management Studies, University of Mumbai, India

Paweł Smaga, Professor, SGH Warsaw School of Economics, also expert in National Bank of Poland

Grzegorz Sobiecki, Warsaw School of Economics, Poland

Manish Talwar, Alkesh Dinesh Mody Institute for Financial and Management Studies, India

Shalini Talwar, Associate Professor, S. P. Jain Institute of Management and Research, Mumbai, India

Artur Tomeczek, Assistant Professor, Global Economic Interdependence Unit, SGH Warsaw School of Economics, Poland

Marta Tomeczek, District Court of Katowice, Poland

Preface

This book is the result of a joint effort of academic professional authors from European and Asian universities to review the digital currencies and New Global Financial System, which includes Eurosystem and other financial systems operating in the US and Asia which are also based on digital money and cryptocurrencies. The concept of the digital currencies has attracted the attention of researchers worldwide and a large number of papers address the emergence of digital currencies. There are also some papers that discuss the New Global Financial System, but quite a few of them linked the cryptocurrencies with the New Global Financial System. That can be treated as the research gap. A few attempts have been made to analyse the characteristics of digital currencies and its future prospectus with the help of econometric and statistics techniques. This monograph has the character of a textbook introducing the subject of digital currencies in selected countries. Individual cases in each chapter by the authors give interesting insight and a variety of concepts and outcomes in the global economy. The main research questions raised in this book is what the New Global Financial System will look like and how it will be implemented. The New Global Financial System, with its digital and crypto currencies, seemed to be a core element of the future world economy. Rapid changes and a strong push for security and sustainability of the world development require the new financial model for international transactions. Digital currencies is a new concept which is promoted by the international organizations such as International Monetary Fund (IMF), European Commission and financial elite represented by the multinational companies like Facebook or SpaceX that is working on new system with the support of the space industry. The main aim of the authors is to ordering knowledge in this area and presents the meaning and the role of digital and cryptocurrencies in the New Global Financial System. There are several research questions answered by this monograph. One of them is indicating potential consequences by forming the central bank digital currencies (CBDCs) and its impact on global financial system in advanced and developing economies. A question refers to the role of monetary policy easing lead to the rise of the virtual currency market. Other research questions relate to COVID-19 impact on the international settlements which are the important pillar of the New Global Financial System. It also discusses the post-pandemic challenges for central banks, such as monetary future policy. There is a complex review of the literature regarding this subject including elaborated econometric models of digital currencies and cryptocurrencies. It has to be a clear distinction between digital currency which is electronic form of fiat money and cryptocurrencies which is a store value secured by encryption. Recently the concept of investing in cryptocurrencies such as Bitcoin made lot of investors worldwide to consider this option of the investment as very interesting and lucrative option forms the perspective of potential profits. The book discusses that issue if investment in cryptocurrencies is really profitable and how the digital banking system is evaluating such investments. There are also risks related to any investment so the same is with cryptocurrencies. One of the benefits for the reader of the book is to understand such risks before considering any serious investment in cryptocurrencies. Other benefits are related to understanding of creation of New Global Financial System which can be based on the digital and cryptocurrencies as well. This is just a part of the New Global Financial System. The book discusses IMF activities and regulations in creating such system. Some countries like China very advanced in a digital currency was able to include this into Social Credit Screening System to stimulate also internal demand through imposing expiration date on the digital yuan (e-CNY). The audience of this book is mainly professionals who are interested in digitalisation of financial systems but also policy makers who are trying to set up the rules which limit the risk of investment in cryptocurrencies. The book is a very good source of information for international finance students doing their MA and PhD in finance and accounting. The book is also written by the active professionals working in the banking sector and national institutions such as national banks and guarantee funds. The book uses all available material regarding investing in cryptocurrencies and also recent documents of IMF regarding digital currencies, settlements and regulations for CBDC.

The book is also about a coming future of financial world where new technology and digitalization of social life trigger internal demand for product and services. The authors are looking on digital currencies from different perspective such as alternative investment opportunity or inequality and poverty. The book is describing a New Global Financial System which is not described deeply in the literature. It gives also a complex so far literature review and trying to investigate quantitative models which relate to global financial system. This book contains 12 chapters with different perspective views on the analysed subject. Although the concept of new global financial system was not fully documented and defined from academic perspective, this review is complex with the look on period of 2000–2021. **Chapter 1** refers to academic and scientific papers and monographs describing that subject. The authors also study IMF's directives and recommendations regarding international settlements and new global financial system. Besides that, a summary of quantitative approaches/models and results of researches are also presented in this chapter as the starting point for the further investigation upon New Global Financial system and how it can be implemented. In March 2020, when the measures needed to contain COVID-19 led to a near-standstill of large parts of the economy and global supply chains, the global financial system was on the verge of collapse. **Chapter 2** concentrates on concerted action by leading central banks on an unprecedented scale to save the financial system from collapse. Both the statistical dimension of this process at global level and its impact on individual economies were presented. Although these monetary policy measures led to the destabilization of the system, it remains in an extremely precarious state in which euphoric highs alternate with depressive price falls at short intervals. **Chapter 3** shows that the results of the analysis of the responses collected through some one-on-one in-depth interviews with retail investors revealed that they are hesitant to invest in cryptos despite being aware of and interested in them. The common theme that emerged from the interviews was that despite all the hype and visibility, there is no clarity about how to choose the right ones from the different cryptos available, what percentage of the portfolio should be devoted to cryptos, what are the valuation challenges, and what are the potential risks associated with investing in them. As far as economics go, many aspects of cryptocurrencies remain relatively unexplored. Their forecasting is extremely difficult due to the unpredictability. There are many motives for buying cryptocurrencies, like speculative investment or safeguarding against inflation. **Chapter 4** aims to establish the relationship between economic inequality and poverty and cryptocurrency use. Inequalities are one of the most important aspects of modern economies, both developed and developing ones. Although the cryptocurrencies have emerged recently as result of digitalization of different economic spheres, the debate over costs and benefits of cryptocurrencies can be placed into a wider context on the nature of money and exchange rates. **Chapter 5** argues that cryptocurrencies can have emerging elements of complex semi-public goods by relying on theories of exchange rate governance. **Chapter 6** investigates whether the monetary easing and the consequent increase in the worldwide money supply have contributed to the rapid development of the virtual currency market. To extend this, this chapter further analyses the effect of money supply measured by M2 in 16 countries on several virtual market indicators such as: Bitcoin capitalization, Bitcoin price, Google trends and the number of transactions over the period 2008–2019. The main outcome of this chapter is that quantitative easing has spurred the development of virtual currency market; however, there are significant differences in contributions of individual countries to this effect. **Chapter 7** contains the analysis of four most important challenges for the evolution of main central bank functions in a global financial system over the recent decade. The assessment includes experiences gained during the global financial crisis, the recent COVID-19 pandemic crisis, and their impact on the conduct of central banks' operations. **Chapter 8** debates on the New Global Financial System, which is dominated by issues relating to the influence of modern technologies. One of the financial innovations that are spreading about the globe is digital currencies. In this technological race (where the power over the financial system is at stake) also central banks want to take part – by issuing CBDCs. The aim of **Chapter 9** is to investigate decentralized finance concept (DeFi) from different perspectives including legal one. It also gives a broad literature review of the definitions and scientific approaches to the concept of DeFi. **Chapter 10** focuses on increasing dissemination of private cryptocurrencies which forced central banks worldwide to foster their projects for own development of CBDCs. Some central banks of small economies just use national digital currencies, like Bahamas or Cambodia, others test pilot projects for future introduction, like China. **Chapter 11** refers mostly to the opportunities, challenges and dilemmas related to the CBDC in the context of differences in motives and needs (as well as risks) in advanced and emerging economies; thus the necessity for tailored design in the field of CBDC. The topic is discussed through the prism of the first international experiences in the field of CBDC and finally recommendations, including those regarding international coordination, are made. **Chapter 12** highlights the usefulness of CBDC in managing state welfare-oriented policy and the future challenges the commercial banks may also face when central bank-controlled digital currency would arrive.

We hope that this book will help the professionals and academic researchers to better understand The New Global Financial System with its important component–digital currency CBDC.

Ranjan Aneja and Robert Dygas

Editors biographies

Ranjan Aneja, Ph.D., is a professor of economics, Central University of Haryana, India. He completed his master's degree in economics from Kurukshetra University, India, and Ph.D. from Guru Jambheshwar University of Science and Technology, Hisar, India. He has 16 years of teaching and research experience. His areas of interest are economic modelling and policy analysis and macroeconomic stability. He has published several research papers in premium journals. He serves as a reviewer to multiple journals of international repute indexed in Scopus and Web of Science and listed in ABDC. He is also serving in editorial board of several journals such as *Journal of Public Affairs, Wiley, SN Business & Economics, Springer-Nature* and *Cognet Economics and Finance, Taylor & Francis*.

Robert Dygas, Ph.D., is an assistant professor in SGH Warsaw School of Economics at East Asian Economic Studies Department of the World Economy Research Institute. He completed his master studies at the Warsaw School of Economics, majoring in finance and banking, and at the University of Aarhus in Denmark, majoring in management. He received his Ph.D. degree in economics from the Warsaw School of Economics in 2003 (dissertation: "Strategic Management in the Mobile Telephony Industry in Poland in 1995–2001"). In 2011, he was awarded the executive master of business administration degree by the Warsaw University of Technology, Business School. He has 23 years of professional experience in multinational corporations in IT, telecommunications and public sectors. In 2015–2020, he worked also as the external expert for evaluation of Horizon 2020-ECI-FTI proposals (Research Executive Agency EASME under the power delegated by the European Commission).

1 Literature review regarding digital currencies and cryptocurrencies in the New Global Financial System

Ranjan Aneja and Robert Dygas

General literature review (2013–2021)

The introduction of various digital currencies backed by blockchain technologies is rapidly changing financial and industrial markets and decentralizing interactions between consumers, firms and policymakers across the world (Carbo-Valverde, 2018). There are various initiatives that seek to further promote innovative blockchain and cryptocurrency activities by practitioners, academicians, policymakers and industry leaders to ensure convenient and effective financial transactions. Some authors described companies across the world that used cryptocurrencies and other digital currencies for a host of investment, operational and transactional purposes (Raskin & Yermack, 2018). History reveals that human beings began using metal pieces as a medium for exchange of goods and services, the concept of money has begun evolving from then. First, it was metal to paper; then paper became plastic; then plastic became an application. Now, it seems that the human kind has been acquainted with new version of the money evolution, that is, cryptocurrency (Farras & Salmeron, 2018). In the traditional electronic payment, financial institutions used to charge higher service charges for the mediating services and it is completely based on trust-based model for all transactions (Dallyn, 2017). Some authors also indicated the regulation aspect as very important one. The state played a vital role in providing the much-needed currency backstop. The state, acting through central banks, can issue new money and regulate all other financial organizations that create intermediate money in practically all jurisdictions (Perkins, 2020). However, partially as a result of the global financial crisis of 2008 and partly as a result of technical advancements, a movement has emerged to decentralize money by separating the government from the issuance of money, with the goal of better handling financial crises. As a result, cryptocurrencies have emerged, with decentralization as their primary feature. The online trade increased the use of new technologies, and thus increased the demand for new electronic payment methods. This began especially in the mid-1990s with the information revolution, the decline in computer prices and the networking of the same (Reyna et al., 2018). Realizing the rapid emergence of digital currencies into the day-to-day life activities, central banks across the world began concentrating on research and development of central bank digital currencies (CBDCs) that can

DOI: 10.4324/9781003310365-1

be easily accessible to ordinary people. As per a survey conducted during late 2020, approximately 86 per cent of central banks worldwide were working on developing their own digital currencies (Auer et al., 2021; Boar & Wehrli, 2021). This can be considered as a natural progression of various central banks from issuing physical currencies. Most banks consider developing their own digital currencies as a way to ensure competition and smoothen the access to open markets. This will help them to get rid of the increased competition raised by big techs that have encroached into the digital payment systems. Among the cryptocurrencies, according to researchers, the Bitcoin have emerged as the most accepted cryptocurrency across the world (Ron & Shamir, 2013; Manimuthu et al., 2019). It is based on open-source technology that works as an independent payment mechanism in the peer-to-peer setup. As like other cryptocurrencies, Bitcoins can be handled easily and ensure privacy which attracts the public. In spite of all these peculiarities, users of these digital currencies face vulnerabilities associated with cybersecurity. Some authors discussed the role of Bitcoin and highlights problems and issues witnessed by Bitcoin users (Manimuthu et al., 2019). For some researchers, Bitcoin has a wider level of global acceptance as it enables secure payments and ensure faster than the traditional alternatives (Walch, 2015). The central banks in these countries claim that cryptocurrencies could pave way for financial misconduct and lead to economic instability as it can pump money for illegal activities. According to a report published by Law Library of Congress, around 42 nations across the world have curtailed cryptocurrency trade implicitly (LLC, 2021). Though the first digital currency was introduced in 2008, cryptocurrencies have begun to receive massive response during the post periods of the Great Recession and European sovereign debt crisis. This circumstance paved way for the demand for cryptocurrencies as the global economic situations were highly vulnerable (Candila, 2021). The value of cryptocurrencies has reached unprecedented levels and begun finding place in portfolios to ensure diversification and used for speculation purposes. Realizing the increased preference of portfolio managers and investors for cryptocurrency, many researchers began analysing the volatility and co-volatility between them (Chu et al., 2017; Catania et al., 2018; Caporale & Zekokh, 2019; Walther et al., 2019). There are many recent studies that analysed the interdependencies of cryptocurrencies with other assets (Cebrian-Hermandez & Jimenez-Rodriguez, 2021). The most relevant positions of the literature overview regarding digital currencies and the cryptocurrencies in the context of design of the New Global Financial Systemare presented in Table 1.1. The main conclusion is that the design of the New Global Financial System is strongly linked to new financial order based on the implementation of the digital currencies and cryptocurrencies in the global economy with a help of econometric models and statistics techniques.

By analysing Table 1.1, it can be stated that the number of the researches regarding digital currencies, cryptocurrencies and the New Financial System started to increase from 2017. More recent studies used econometric models and statistics techniques to explain the digital money and the cryptocurrencies with

Table 1.1 The most relevant literature review regarding digital currency in the New Global Financial System (2013–2021)

Year	*Author*	*Title*	*Comments*
2021	Balvers, R., McDonald, B.	Designing a global digital currency. *Journal of International Money and Finance*, vol. 111. https://doi.org/10.1016/j.jimonfin.2020.102317	Price stability is a key for digital currency design
2021	Candila, V.	Multivariate analysis of cryptocurrencies. *Econometrics*, vol. 9, p. 28. https://doi.org/10.3390/economterics9030028	Conditional covariance matrix for a panel of cryptocurrencies using some specifications belonging to the dynamic conditional correlation (DCC) class of models.
2021	Ogachi, D., Mugambi, P., Bares, L., Zeman, Z.	Idiosyncrasies of money: 21st century. *Evolution of Money Economies*, vol. 9(1), p. 40. https://doi.org/10.3390/economies9010040	A multiple regression analysis was used to draw an econometric model, explaining the relationship between the independent and dependent variables. The following variables were used as independent variables: monetary aggregate (M1), harmonized index of consumer prices (HICP), Euro Interbank Offered Rate (EURIBOR), US dollar/euro and the USD value of Bitcoin.
2021	Kahler, M.	The Bretton Woods moment. *Global Governance in a World of Change*, pp. 77–108. https://doi.org/10.1017/9781108915199.003	The governance of cross-border exchange, in which private actors operating under informal rules play a central role.
2021	Yefremov, D.	Digital yuan on the foreground: Initial conclusions from the Chinese experiment. *Chinese Studies*, vol. 1, https://doi.org/10.51198/chinesest2021.01.165.	The launch of digital currencies by central banks must overcome the limitations, be centralized and guaranteed by the authorities.
2021	Umar, M., Rizvi, S., Naqvi, B.	Dance with the devil? The nexus of fourth industrial revolution, technological financial products and volatility spillovers in global financial system. *Technological Forecasting and Social Change*, vol. 163, https://doi.org/10.1016/j.techfore.2020.120450	In case of an initial shock in the crypto market, the spillover effect is felt by all the financial markets, while the reverse is not true.

(*Continued*)

Table 1.1 (Continued)

Year	*Author*	*Title*	*Comments*
2021	Okoli, T., & Tewari, D.	Does the adoption process of financial technology in Africa follow an inverted U-shaped hypothesis? An evaluation of rogers diffusion of innovation theory. *Asian Academy of Management Journal of Accounting and Finance*, vol. 17(1). https://doi.org/10.21315/aamjaf2021.17.1.10	The New Global Financial System evolves towards a technology-enabled financial solution-fintech.
2021	Pashtova, L., Oseev, V., Klemenov, D.	Financial instrument of the new economy or a pyramid scheme: The issues of cryptocurrency security. *Finance and Credit*, vol. 27(6). https://doi.org/10.24891/fc.27.6.1395	Cryptocurrency really has significant prospects to become a valuable financial tool in the world economy.
2021	Linis, B., Praicheux, S.	Digital and blockchain-based legal regimes: An eea case study based on innovative legislations – comparison of French and Liechtenstein Domestic. *Financial Law Review*, vol. 22 (2). https://doi.org/10.4467/22996834flr.21.009.13977	Proposal of Blockchain or distributed ledger technology (DLT) applications and services.
2020	Safiullin, M., Savelichev, M., Elshin, L., Moiseev, V.	Potential of cryptocurrency as global money of the sixth technological mode based on the global financial system, *International Journal of Financial Research*, vol. 11(6). https://doi.org/10.5430/ijfr.v11n6p296	Cryptocurrencies tokens, smart contracts and crypto exchanges offer new opportunities for effective investment in technologies of the sixth technological mode.
2020	Shavshukov, V., Zhuravleva, N.	Global economy: New risks and leadership problems. *International Journal of Financial Studies*, vol. 8(1). https://doi.org/10.3390/ijfs8010007	Recessionary processes, their depth and global nature are caused by a combination of world financial system crises and general civilization problems.
2020	Artner, A.	Can China lead the change of the world? *Third World Quarterly*, vol. 41(11). https://doi.org/10.1080/01436597.2020.1793664	China could play a positive role as a new superpower in constructing a world beyond capitalism, if it does not give up the socialist project, keeps market forces under control, maintains accumulation without dispossession, preserves its financial independence and makes alliances with other nations on the global (semi-periphery).

2020	Schellhorn, C.	Financial system stability, the timing of climate change action and the federal reserve. *Journal of Central Banking Theory and Practice*, vol. 9(3). https://doi.org/10.2478/jcbtp-2020-0035	Timely and effective climate action is a precondition for the stability of the global financial system and for long-term, inclusive prosperity.
2020	Read, O., Schäfer, S.	Libra project: Regulators act on global stablecoins. *Intereconomics*, vol. 55(6). https://doi.org/10.1007/s10272-020-0936-7	Overall, the Libra project has raised many questions on the regulatory front.
2020	Dikau, S., Robins, N., Täger, M.	Building a sustainable financial system: The state of practice and future priorities. *Revista de Estabilidad Financiera. Banco de España*, vol. 37. DOI: N/A	The role of the central banks in building a sustainable new global financial system is crucial.
2020	Lutsyshyn, O.	How Fintech changes the world financial order. *World of Finance*, vol. 2(63). https://doi.org/10.35774/sf2020.02.102	The necessity of forming a new neo-financial world order of "contactless economy", which will be based on completely new principles, has been proved.
2020	Wullweber, J.	The COVID-19 financial crisis, global financial instabilities and transformations in the financial system. *SSRN Electronic Journal*. https://doi.org/10.2139/ssrn.3688453	The COVID-19 crisis has once again demonstrated that financial markets in their current form do not act as a firewall to avert economic downturns.
2020	Kochergin, D.	Economic nature and classification of stablecoins. *Finance: Theory and Practice*, vol. 24(6), https://doi.org/10.26794/2587-5671-2020-24-6-140-160	Stablecoins are to be interpreted as a new hybrid type of digital financial assets.
2020	Sielska, A.	Changes in the international monetary system: Opportunities and risks for the US dollar, *Economic Annals, XXI*, vol. 183(5–6). https://doi.org/10.21003/EA.V183-01	Abandoning the dollar is possible, but it would require significant financial and institutional changes.
2020	Amendola, A., Braione, M., Candila, V., Storti, G.	A model confidence set approach to the combination of multivariate volatility forecasts. *International Journal of Forecasting*, vol. 36, pp. 873–891.https://doi.org/10.1016/j.ijforecast.2019.10.001	Model Confidence Set (MCS) was used in predicting conditional covariance matrices of financial portfolios.

(*Continued*)

Table 1.1 (Continued)

Year	*Author*	*Title*	*Comments*
2020	Viñuela, C., Sapena, J., Wandosell, G.	The future of money and the central bank digital currency dilemma. *Sustainability (Switzerland)*, vol. 12(22), pp. 1–21. https://doi.org/10.3390/su12229697	In most CBDC proposals, it is impossible to have both of the following at the same time: (1) low levels of risk of a cashless society, risk of currency substitution and risk of economic and financial bubbles risks; and (2) low levels of risk of structural bank disintermediation.
2019	Khiaonarong, T., Humphrey, D.	Cash use across countries and the demand for central bank digital currency. *Journal of Payments Strategy and Systems*, vol. 13(1). https://doi.org/10.5089/9781484399606.001	Demand for digital currency will thus be weak in countries where the adoption of cash substitutes (e.g. cards, electronic money and mobile phone payments) has suppressed demand for cash.
2019	Khudyakova, L.S.	Launching a sustainable financial system in the European Union. *World Economy and International Relations*, vol. 63(7). https://doi.org/10.20542/0131-2227-2019-63-7-16-22	The approval of the Action Plan is an evidence of EU's ambition to keep its leading position in implementation of sustainable development goals within the framework of the UN Agenda 2030.
2019	Atıcı, G.	Bitcoin and blockchain: A threat or opportunity for the financial system. *European Journal of Economics and Business Studies*, vol. 4(3). https://doi.org/10.2478/ejes-2018-0063	The number of Bitcoins has been growing since 2009 and has reached almost 17 million as of September 2018.
2019	Belay, H.	Global financial regulation in the "new international economic order": The unfulfilled promise of equitable economic governance. *Journal of Financial Regulation and Compliance*, vol. 27(1). https://doi.org/10.1108/JFRC-10-2017-0086	The New Global Financial System after Bretton Wood is expected.
2019	Dimitropoulos, G.	Global currencies and domestic regulation: Embedding through enabling? *SSRN Electronic Journal*. https://doi.org/10.2139/ssrn.3397521	The cryptocurrencies can be seen as currency and technology.
2019	Vovchenko, N., Andreeva, O., Orobinsky, A., & Sichev, R.	Risk control in modelling financial management systems of large corporations in the digital economy. *International Journal of Economics and Business Administration*, vol. 7. Scopus:2-s2.0-85069639905	The research results may be implemented into financial management systems of large industrial corporations.

2019	Bataev, A., Plotnikova, E., Gladkova, S.	*Multiparametic forecast model with variable cryptocurrency capitalization assessment framework*. SPBPU IDE'19: Proceedings of the 2019 International SPBPU Scientific Conference on Innovations in Digital Economy October 2019 Article No. 4, pp. 1–8. https://doi.org/10.1145/3372177.3373090	A multi-parameter predictive econometric model that defines the main parameters affecting capitalization of cryptocurrencies was used
2018	Azarenkova, G., Shkodina, I., Samorodov, B., Babenko, M., & Onishchenko, I.	The influence of financial technologies on the global financial system stability. *Investment Management and Financial Innovations*, vol. 15(4). https://doi.org/10.21511/imfi.15(4).2018.19	The lack of institutional support for new financial technologies is the most important catalyst for the financial industry destabilization and the formation of financial bubbles in various market segments.
2018	Reznikova, N., & Ivashchenko, O.	Sovereign wealth funds in the system of global financial imbalances: An analysis of benefits and threads from the perspective of global financial stability. *Actual Problems of International Relations*, vol. 136. https://doi.org/10.17721/apmv.2018.136.0.60-66	SWF is, in fact, an effective actor in the economic policy implementation.
2018	Töpfer, L.	Inside global financial networks: The state, lead firms and the rise of fintech. *Dialogues in Human Geography*, vol. 8(3). https://doi.org/10.1177/2043820618797779	In case of China's integration to the New Global Financial System, the state remains central to our understanding of competitive hierarchies and firm behaviour in financial networks.
2018	Kuzubov, A., Shashlo, N., & Rodionov, A.	Cryptocurrency market: Prerequisites of formation, economic features, prospect directions of development. *Espacios*, vol. 39(50). Scopus:2-s2.0-85058559327	The influence of cryptocurrencies on the New Global Financial System is very high.
2018	Korniyenko, Y., Patnam, M., del Rio-Chanon, R., Porter, M.	Evolution of the global financial network and contagion: A new approach. *IMF Working Papers*, vol. 18(113). https://doi.org/10.5089/9781484353240.001	A novel multilayer network framework is applied to link debt and equity exposures across countries.

(*Continued*)

Table 1.1 (Continued)

Year	*Author*	*Title*	*Comments*
2018	Carbo-Valverde, S., Cuadros-Solas, P., Rodriguez-Fernandez, F	How do bank customers go digital? *A Machine Learning Approach.* http://doi.org/10.2139/ssrn.3195286	The machine learning technique based on random forest models is shown to outperform the forecasting accuracy of parametric econometric models. The results show that the adoption of digital banking services starts with information-based services (e.g. checking account balance), and it is then followed by transactional services (e.g. online or mobile money transfer).
2017	Knaack, P.	An unlikely champion of global finance: Why is China exceeding international banking standards? *Journal of Current Chinese Affairs*, vol. 46(2). https://doi.org/10.1177/186810261704600203	The power of reputation is for China a main driver to voluntarily subjecting itself to tougher regulatory standards than the rest of the world.
2016	Porfir'ev B.N.	Green trends in the global financial system. *World Economy and International Relations*, vol. 60(9). https://doi.org/10.20542/0131-2227-2016-60-9-5-16	The development of green should be highly interconnected with implementation of the Sustainable Development Goals.
2015	Hayes, A.	*What factors give cryptocurrencies their value: an empirical analysis*. Working Paper 06/2014 Department of Economics The New School for Social Research. http://dx.doi.org/10.2139/ssrn.2579445	The regression model used to determine likely source(s) of the cryptocurrencies have on the market and the commodity forms of money.
2014	Bohr, J., Bashir, M.	*Who uses Bitcoin? An exploration of the Bitcoin community*. Conference: 2014 Twelfth Annual Conference on Privacy, Security and Trust (PST). https://doi.org/10.1109/PST.2014.6890928	Application of a descriptive statistics for explanation of Bitcoin use.
2013	Kristoufek, L.	BitCoin meets Google trends and Wikipedia: Quantifying the relationship between phenomena of the Internet era. *Scientific Reports*, vol. 3(1), p. 3415. https://doi.org/10.1038/srep03415	A bivariate Vecto-Auto Regression (VAR) model for the weekly log-returns of Bitcoin prices and Google Trends and Wikipedia data.

Source: Based on own research with the use of Mendeley tool (Mendeley.com).

application of the financial technologies. The most relevant positions according to the authors of this chapter which have big impact on the design and implementation of the New Global Financial Systemare presented in Table 1.1. The idea of a design and implementation of the New Global Financial System seemed to be mature enough from the perspective of the researchers after the global recent economic problems related to pandemic COVID-19. A few authors like Muhammad Umar, Abbas Rizvi Syed Kumail and Bushra Naqvi (2021) talked about different shocks in the global financial system and its relation to Industrial Revolution 4.0, the other authors like Miles Kahler (2021) focused on the Global Governance in financial world, or Ronald Balvers and Bill McDonald (2021) analysed the design of digital money and price stability as a key for digital currency design. There is a significant change in the most recent researches with comparison to these older one presented in Table 1.1. The analysis from the period 2013–2016 mainly focused on very specific tools of the New Global Financial System such as digital currency applications or cryptocurrencies usage in chosen countries with support of econometric models and statistics techniques. From a couple of years, a new trend like holistic analysis with application of financial technologies (fintech) in global finance can be observed. Some of the authors like Annamaria Artner (2020), based on China example, stressed the importance of the government as the regulator in introducing a digital currency and some other researchers even raised the problem of the New Financial Order, which impacts a design of the future of the global financial system. Although the concept of cryptocurrencies developed much in the recent years, a much deeper understanding of the functionality of these novel versions of currency is needed. One of the challenging issues associated with the proliferation of digital currency usage is the approach and attitude of traditional banking institutions. Banking institutions set face against the new developments as emergence of digital currencies could wipe them out from the business. Many central banks across the world have banned cryptocurrencies during past years. Emerging economies such as China, India and Bangladesh continue to have a hot-and-cold relationship with cryptocurrencies explicitly. In China, money is being used as an instrument not just of economic policy, but potentially even social policy. That would be dangerous for the credibility of central bank money and for central banks themselves. A digital yuan (e-CNY) was introduced in China in 2022 with expiry date, which means that either it is spent or it will vanish in the certain timeframe. That forces the users to spend it which boosts the internal consumption. This unconventional monetary policy is known as a *Gesell currency*: expiring money which gives a Chinese government a control on the velocity of money in the system (Blanc, 2006). Some of the authors perceived China's actions regarding introduction of e-CNY as the attempt to upend the global financial order as e-CNY would be one of the most aggressive consolidations of economic power fully managed by the Chinese Communist Party and depriving of 1.3 billion Chinese to use a physical cash (cashless society). What is more interesting the usage of e-CNY is analysed by the mobile applications based on artificial intelligence models and can be a part of the Social Credit Score System (Huang, 2020).

Literature overview of the IMF's documents regarding money and payments in the new global financial system

One of the influential and decisive organisation regarding creation of New Global Financial System is the International Monetary Fund (IMF). The concept of CBDC and digital currency was discussed in one of the recent IMF research and analysis documents. The new instant payment system is scheduled by Federal Reserve of the United States on 2023. The main challenge is that there are still 7 million US citizens who do not have the bank accounts and also cross-border payments require a lot improvements in infrastructure, improving a speed of transactions and lower the fees for the bank transfers (as of the second quarter of 2021, the average cost of sending a remittance of 200 USD from the United States to other countries was 5.41 percent of the notional value of the transaction) (IMF, 2022a). The macro financial effects of digital money were discussed also in recent IMF's papers. The main aspect is the influence on the global monetary system stability, legal frameworks and regulation. Besides that, the set-up of the New Global Financial System and introduction of digital currency are linked also to digital transformation of the global economy and development of e-commerce platforms on the large scale. The main conclusion of this chapter is that CBDCs do not qualitatively change the economic forces that lead to the international use of currencies but quantitatively could reinforce the incentives behind currency substitution and currency internationalization (IMF, 2020). As the main forces of change for digital currency and the New Global Financial System, IMF indicated the following: a technological and payment infrastructure change, stability of currency value, efficiency of the payments, cross-border use, deployment of artificial intelligence and analysis of big data, consumer behaviour and expectations, COVID-19 pandemic effects on e-commerce transactions (IMF, 2021a). IMF partners organizations to implement the New Global Financial System namely with Bank of International Settlements Innovation HuB, the Committee on Payments and Market Infrastructures (CPMI), the Financial Stability Board (FSB) and The World Bank. The main goal of this close cooperation is to strengthen IMF's policy guidance for New Global Financial System implementation. According to IMF papers, the adoption of the digital currency and the New Global Financial System has a very high impact on structural policies, central banking and international cooperation. The framework of IMF's functions such as surveillance on each country level and capacity development related to digital money was also presented (IMF, 2021a). IMF in its Comprehensive Surveillance Review (CSR) recognizes that digital technology will have a major impact on future economic outcomes and shape the international monetary system (the New Financial Global System). As the digital money will gain a prominence, IMF explores further potential benefits and risk as well together with its international partners which is critical for The New Global Financial System adoption (IMF, 2021b). IMF published also Financial Sector Assessment Program Review (FSAP) which specified methods and tools for risks and benefits evaluations. FSAPs are usually conducted jointly with the World Bank in emerging markets and developing economies and by the Fund alone in advanced economies. FSAPs provide valuable analysis and policy recommendations for surveillance and capacity development (IMF, 2021c). Since the 2014 Review (IMF, 2014), financial stability assessments have put greater emphasis on macroprudential frameworks and policies, nonbank financial institutions (NBFIs) and analysis of interconnectedness. FSAP's key role in the Fund's efforts towards building more resilient and sustainable financial systems and expected the New Global Financial System. During each financial crisis, IMF plays a key role in stabilization of the global financial system. During last financial crisis started in 2008 in 2010, IMF's loans to low-income countries reached 175 billion USD (IMF, 2010). As the reaction on the global economy crisis caused by COVID-19 to secure and stabilize financial system, IMF prepared the Work Program which concentrates on three policy priorities: (1) to vaccinate the world, (2) calibrate bilateral and multilateral policies to support the recovery and reduce scarring and divergences and (3) accelerate the transformation of the global economy to make it greener, more digital and inclusive. These three polices are strongly related to IMF as the organization which maintains global financial safety (IMF, 2021d).

Ending time of COVID-19 seems to be a good time for biggest economies such as the US, China, India, Japan, Russia and international organizations like IMF and UN to think about changes in the global financial system. One of the facts that stimulate such activity to design the New Global Financial system is the opportunity to manage a global debt, especially government debt held by the central banks which reached 25 tn USD. The New Global Financial System should link existing currencies to digital currency or electronic Special Drawing Rights (eSDRs), the international assets created by IMF. Another proof for introducing the global system is the fact that major class of assets grew on average annually in period 1997–2018 faster than nominal GDP. The new system should allow the countries to base their economy development on production, trade and innovation rather than on debt creation which in long run will bring the problems to a global economy. That is why in the literature, the global financial reset is more often noticed as the way forward to design and implement the New Global Financial System (Watling, 2021). Implementation of such system may threaten the US dollar as in the history each period had its dominant currency moving from the gold through British pound (GBP) and then to US dollar. The New Global Financial System in opinion of some authors is going to be based on the cryptocurrencies (stablecoins such as USDC or Tether) which will be pegged on US dollar. The nice feature of such cryptocurrencies is that they are easy to trade and stable. Recently VISA and PayPal Holding have allowed payments with stablecoins on their platforms. Interesting enough is the fact that majority of use of such stablecoinsis in less developed countries than developed ones and decentralized finance concept (DeFi) gets more attention there as well (Bianco, 2021; Harvey et al., 2020). Of course, there is also a dispute by IMF as well if the framework of the New Global Financial System should be based on DeFi, stablecoins or eSDRs. The big issue is the global regulations and planned standards which has to be accepted by the economies and central banks (IMF, 2021e).

In the New Global Financial System, DeFi and cryptoasset technologies have potential as a tool for faster and cheaper cross-border payments but also create a stability problem. The IMF has discussed many critical issues relating to regulatory frameworks with respect to cryptoassets and digital money (IMF, 2020, 2021a). The non-stablecoins are also of high interest among the investors due to the fact that return on investment of non-stablecoins are higher comparing with other class of assets such as local currency bonds and also their low correlation with other type of assets, even though that volatility of non-stablecoins are high. The volatility example can be presented on Bitcoin, which lost its value from 63,503 USD on 17th April 2021 to 29,807 USD on the 20th of July 2021[1]. That is why IMF has a challenge to decide what sort of assets should be included in the framework of the New Global Financial System. The stablecoins are highly usable for settlement of spot and derivatives trades on exchanges. Additionally, a relative price stability of stablecoins protects users from moving their funds outside the crypto ecosystem. From the other hand, Bitcoin even though highly volatile is still a dominant cryptoasset, while DeFi allows user to trade cryptoassets without an intermediary and credit platforms that match borrowers and lenders without the need for a credit risk evaluation of the customer. DeFi is also a main driver for stablecoin payments, but mainly among the institutional players so it is not public and it is more used in developed economies then emerging markets (Chainalysis, 2021a). As the matter of fact, the use of cryptoassets payments and settlements is still limited but the growing exposure of the big global payment companies such as PayPal for integration with crypto system especially stablecoins can be observed on the financial market. As this market is growing also, a concern of cybersecurity is also related to hacking of customers' accounts and funds. This is another big issue which IMF together with the regulator needs to make the entire New Global Financial System stable and secure from the perspective of the transactions and legal aspects. The implementation of the required regulations set by the Financial Action Task Force (FATF) is still not enough (FATF, 2021). The implementation of the New Global Financial System which IMF works on depends much on the fact that existing global payment system is not efficient. Besides that in literature, there are "pull" and "push" factors indicated. One of the important push factors is unsound domestic macro polices and important pull factor is a relative cost of transaction and speed (IMF, 2021e).

Literature overview regarding a digital euro zone introduction by European Central Bank – review of available documents

The literature regarding a digital euro zone requires ordering to better understand the entire concept. A natural way of transforming euro zone to digital one is a process recommended by European Central Bank in its report from 2020 where Eurosystem framework was presented (ECB, 2020a, 2021a). The concept of Eurosystem is new and it is still under development. Basically Eurosystem consists of European Central Bank and national banks of countries that implemented euro.

A recent regulation of European Parliament EU 2021/694 sets a Single Digital Market where digital euro plays a key role (EU, 2021). The global impact of digital euro was also discussed by Fabio Panetta, the member of the Executive Board of the European Central Bank (ECB), who argued that digital euro can affect monetary and financial stability on three fronts: first, financial intermediation and capital allocation in normal times; second, financial stability in times of crisis; and third, the functioning of the international financial system (Panetta, 2021). As there is a global economy slowdown caused by the pandemic of COVID-19 especially the role of digital euro during crisis time is getting more important. During crisis time, a digital euro can accelerate a "digital run" from the commercial banks to the central banks. This risk is hardly controlled, that is why it may have a significant impact on Eurosystem. Other authors investigated how a digital euro can help the central bank with performing its functions and support a functionality of Eurosystem. Main conclusion was that a digital euro inevitably entail direct effects on the most essential functions of the Eurosystem (monetary policy, financial stability, payment system security and efficiency). Besides that there is a shift from commercial bank to digital euro holdings which might increase the cost of funding for banks and might result in higher interest rates on bank loans, potentially reducing the volume of bank credit to the economy (Urbinati et al., 2021). The authors also presented possible architecture of digital euro which was based on two models namely centralized account and token based. As it is now, a digital euro has not yet been implemented so the models are only theoretical. There was also a Digital Euro Experiment (Tiered Model) made by the Eurosystem's High-Level Task Force on Central Bank Digital Currency in September 2020. The experiment on a tiered approach brought together several central banks from the Eurosystem, namely Banque de France, Banca d'Italia, Banco de España, Banque centrale du Luxembourg, Banque Nationale de Belgique, the European Central Bank, Lietuvos Bankas and Oesterreichische National bank. The main conclusion from this experiment was that the combining centralized systems and distributed ledger technologies (DLTs) were feasible from a technical point of view, as experiments successfully combined diverse technological components and allowed to support the issuance of both retail CBDC and CBDC for interbank settlement (wholesale digital euro). It also allowed a wholesale use cases, such as the settlement of securities, cross-border and cross-currency payments (Banque de France, 2021).

There is a still question among the different authors whether Eurosystem can issue a digital euro from the legal perspective (Grünewald et al., 2021; Mooij, 2021) and if introducing of digital currency in general can help to optimize allocation of resources and inclusive community-building (Vitari, 2016). From the other perspective, ECB published report in 2020 mentioned at the beginning in which it concluded that it was confident of overcoming any challenges to implement digital euro. ECB tries to stay ahead of the rapidly changing world of digital currencies and payments but many central banks are afraid that eurozone could lose control of its money supply and that can impact an implementation of digital euro (Arnold, 2020). Moreover, IMF made also a contribution to the CBDC literature by suggesting a structured framework to organize discussions on whether or not to issue CBDC, with an operational focus and a project management perspective (Kiff et al., 2020). According to Denis Beau, First Deputy Governor of Banque de France, digital transformation in Europe and the development of the use of new settlement assets such as cryptoassets are likely to profoundly alter euro payments ecosystem but they also carry risks for the smooth functioning of Eurosystem namely in efficiency and its stability (Beau, 2021). Banque de France was involved in investigation phase of introduction of a ritual digital euro by Eurosystem in July 2021. This project was supported by Markets in Crypto-Assets (MiCA) regulation and the Digital Operational Resilience Act (DORA), presented in September 2020. In the opinion of some authors, DORA comes with several improvements for smaller banks, but proportionality should be discussed further in the ongoing negotiations (Wuermeling, 2021).

To make a digital euro a success, the aforementioned regulations needed to be coordinated at the international level with such organizations such as G7, G20, IMF especially on cryptoassets and the improvement of cross-border payments. As it can be seen from above, the introduction of a digital euro is only possible with the involvement of the international political and financial institutions. There are also other conditions indicated in the literature to introduce smoothly a digital euro otherwise introducing a digital euro could lead to bank disintermediation, threatening financial stability and monetary policy transmission through the bank lending channel. The first condition is that central bank would require proper mechanisms to manage the volume of digital euros in circulation, the second one is maintaining a bank deposit cost-equivalent funding source. These conditions are based on the Dutkowski and VanHoose framework model which proposed some tools such as leveraging the current central bank real-time gross settlement (RTGS) systemby setting up hard limits or seep accounts or using the overall rate of return of a digital euro for CBDC inclusive of charges and fees. In the opinion of the authors, overall rate of return on digital euro for a CBDC should never exceed the lower between zero (the physical cash nominal rate of return) and the key policy rate (the theoretical risk-free rate). The authors also proposed other instruments like bank reserve requirement which could act as the link between commercial bank deposit and a digital euro of CBDC by imposing rate differential on the two asset types (Fagatelli, 2021; Dutkowsky & Van Hoose, 2018, 2020). One of the important thoughts from Dutkowski and Van Haas model is that the design of the digital euro and the measures accompanying its introduction are key elements to define the final impact on banks' business and lending activities. According to ECB, implementing digital euro can bring some benefit to commercial banks such as contribution of a digital euro user's feed to revenue of the commercial bank or lower the level of excess reserves and their associated costs under a negative interest rate policy. That would be possible if same banks were allowed to act as agents or service providers on behalf of the central bank, offering dedicated access to CBDC and related administrative services to their clients (ECB, 2020a). That also means that commercial banks will be transferred to digital banks which are inline with a financial digitalization trend in the banking and finance sector. As the fact, the existing available literature is not describing how Eurosystem should be constructed and implemented in details. That is why the initiative from the commercial banks side is very important to stimulate introduction of a digital euro by CBDC (Van Hee & Wijngaard, 2021). Quite well perspective on the reasoning for introduction of a digital euro was presented by Atlantic Council organisation in its papers. The authors drew attention to geopolitical meaning of implementation of a digital euro which can be a tool in a global power play. In their opinion, it is not clear in which way a digital euro will evolve and keeping a digital euro only as the currency it is not enough. The banks should watch out the process as a digital euro might have a strong impact on the structural availability and cyclical volatility of deposit funding. Entire process of implementing a digital euro according also to ECB will not be completed before 2025 (Strauss-Kahn, 2021; Brosens, 2021). Other authors focused more on monetary policy problems created by the introduction of a digital euro by CBDC. In this area, it is stated that a digital euro can have impact on the strategy of monetary policy but its international impact is still not clear (Beniak, 2019). There are several pilot projects run by different countries regarding own digital currency. In case of Eurosystem, it is expected that a digital euro will be rather complementary to the existing currency then just substitute euro. Besides that, introducing a digital euro in eurozone requires common understanding and willingness for that from all 19 euro zone members, where Germany plays a key role in Eurosystem policy. If common standpoint is not reached by the all eurozone members, a temporary hybrid solution (bridging blockchain technology with euro) proposed by Germany could be applied (Kothawale, 2021). From the public consultation survey conducted by the Eurosystem, Monetary Authority of the Eurozone, it was evident that the first users of the euro give indisputable amount of importance to privacy, security and usability of the prospective CBDC (ECB, 2021b). The result of the analysis of earlier reviewed literature is that implementation of digital euro in Eurosystem is not clear regarding the time and its framework. Additionally, all existing eurozone member countries should cooperate and accept a common policy. That is a challenge as each of the eurozone member countries analyses the consequences and benefits from its point of view taking into consideration specific aspects of the economy development in each of these countries. There is also a dispute by some authors if Eurosystem from legal standpoint (mainly based on Article 128(1) TFEU and Article 16 ESCB B Statute on the basis of Treaty interpretation) can issue a digital euro. Both sources give the Eurosystem a right to issue a digital euro from one side and also put the limitation of that from the other side. Another aspect related to issuing is that "Issuing" essentially refers to the appearance as a liability on the central bank's balance sheet and does not per se imply that the euro must necessarily be expressed in tangible banknotes. It could be explained with the historical aspects of e-money development when during signing the Maastricht Treaty, the concept of digital euro was in the nutshell and in the minds of the dedicated working groups in ECB (Grünewald et al., 2021). It can be stated that legal regulations concerning digital euro follows the fintech development as the new functionalities are widely accepted and learnt by the public. In some moment of time due to not clear process of implementation of digital euro, 28 companies driven by Facebook (currently Meta) proposed a creation a new crypto currency Libra as the potential competition to a digital euro. The goal of these companies was to create a stable currency based on secure and open source blockchain, backed by reserve of real assets and governed by the independent Libra association (Mayer, 2019). As of now, the Libra Project was not implemented, which confirms the rule that only government financial institution could be entitled to issue a digital money.

Conclusion

As it can be concluded from aforementioned literature review, the process of implementing of a digital money is still ongoing (e.g. 2025 was declared by ECB for digital euro) but quite complex with many challenges especially on the geopolitical aspects (consent among eurozone member states, cooperation framework with international organizations such as G7, G20 and IMF). Surprisingly enough there was the competitive initiative named Libra Project, but it can be treated rather as the individual vision of "the big business" especially Meta (formerly Facebook) how e-money should be introduced. What is also worth noting is that legal aspects of implementing digital euro are much driven by the development of fintech technology and internet use by the EU society. Even though formally Eurosystem had been defined it does not operate in real life. It means that the financial digitalization process is not over yet. It seems also that China played a pivotal role in that process by implementing its e-CNY in 2022. It is possible that this framework could be a used globally especially if Chinese yuan may replace the US dollar in the future (such case was already considered by Saudi Arabia regarding Chinese oil sales). Recently also Fed has officially announced to implement digital US dollar. It seems that prospect and global trend to implement digital money is clear but the challenges regarding the implementation of the New Global Financial System are not resolved yet.

Note

1 https://coinmarketcap.com/currencies/bitcoin/, accessed 21.02.2022.

2 Impact of COVID-19 on the payment methods and rise of digital money

Waldemar Milewicz

Introduction

In March 2020, when the measures needed to contain COVID-19 led to a near-standstill of large parts of the economy and global supply chains, the global financial system entered crisis mode (Wullweber et al., 2020). Concerted action by leading central banks on an unprecedented scale was necessary to save the financial system from collapse. In addition, the pandemic has contributed to the fact that financial settlements, hitherto largely in cash form, have been transformed into a non-cash form. In other words, electronic payments and card payments have become more important. Although the rise of cashless payments occurred before the pandemic, the world of financial settlements has experienced during the COVID-19 crisis a kind of digitalisation of payments. The pandemic in conjunction with the development of fintech companies has thus brought about an unprecedented surge in digitalisation, which has also affected payment transactions. Thus, the wave of innovations which were observed in the past years had increased once again (Balz, 2020). The COVID-19 pandemic and the measures imposed by governments to contain it appear to have had a considerable influence on consumer payment behaviour (Kotkowski & Polasik, 2021). In other words, the pandemic has contributed to changing the structure of customer payment methods on a global scale. Clients have started to use cards more often instead of paying in cash. The reasons for this switch were justified by medical research. There has been speculation about the possible link between handling physical money and COVID-19 infections (Auer et al., 2020a). Indeed, one of scientific studies suggested that COVID-19 persisted on inanimate surfaces such as metal, glass or plastic for up to nine days, but could be effectively killed by disinfecting the surface (Kampf et al., 2020). Another study suggested that the virus could survive on plastic and steel for up to three days after contamination and on cardboard or copper for one day (van Doremalen, 2020). This state of affairs has led to the situation that a significant fraction of the population reduced their transactional use of cash in response to the pandemic.

DOI: 10.4324/9781003310365-2

Literature review

At this point, it is worth referring to how individual researchers have addressed the impact of COVID-19 on the payment methods in their publications. Musyaffi, Sari and Respati conducted a study which focuses on digital payment users in Indonesia. This evaluation shows that performance expectancy, effort expectancy and personal innovativeness have a significant positive effect on behavioural intention to use digital banking. This research's findings indicate that the use of technological and personal mental factors impacts the adoption of digital payments, especially in the COVID-19 pandemic (Musyaffi et al., 2021).

In her paper, Büşra Ağanhas focused on analysing the digital payment system's response to the COVID-19 pandemic process by showing developments of debit and credit card payment amount from 2019 to 2020 and also has found a causality linked between GDP and credit card spending. The findings have shown that the Granger causality test runs one-way from gross domestic product (GDP) to credit card and no other second-way causality among them (Ağan, 2020).

Gu, Ślusarczyk, Hajizada, Kovalyova and Sakhbieva in their article assessed the purchasing behaviour of online consumers, which identifies the most influential factors in their purchasing behaviour and provides an opportunity to evaluate the dynamics of their activity during the study period, to identify key trends and determine changes in their behaviour. The research revealed what changes in online consumer buying behaviour are typical in the COVID-19 pandemic. The impact of consumer awareness and experience has increased. Online consumers have become more experienced, which has influenced the activity of their buying behaviour. This study proved the shifting influence of online consumer purchasing behaviour factors during the pandemic. The increasing importance of the speed of decision-making by consumers when purchasing goods and services online was determined (Gu et al., 2021).

Singhal and Gupta studied the concept of digital payment along with the impact of COVID-19 on digital payment services especially at root level that is in towns and villages of India. The conclusion of research paper shows that there is a high increase in use of digital payments services through various applications in Indian towns and villages which was not much high before the happening of world-wide pandemic COVID-19 (Singhal & Gupta, 2021).

Kulisz, Bojanowska and Toborek defined the current attitudes of Poles versus cashless transactions and their perception of the related risk of COVID-19 infection. The studied population (of Polish consumers) was less willing to pay with cash during the pandemic than beforehand. This is related with avoiding contact with cash, as well as easy documentation of transactions, increasing their transparency. During the pandemic, Polish consumers were more willing to shop at Polish online shops or retail services (e.g. Allegro) than foreign ones (e.g. AliExpress). However, the study shows that Polish customers are more cautious in their shopping decisions during the pandemic, being afraid to lose financial liquidity (Kulisz et al., 2021).

The change of payment methods in chosen economies and raise of a digital currency – an overview

In its study on the payment attitudes of consumers in the euro area (SPACE), the European Central Bank presented that about 40% of respondents in the euro area curtailed their use of cash and 38% of them declared that the main stimulus for their changed payment behaviour was the possibility of being infected through handling banknotes (ECB, 2020c). Surveys conducted, in turn, by the Federal Reserve System of San Francisco Bank (Kim et al., 2020) and the Bank of Canada (Chen et al., 2020) reached similar conclusions, noting further that some risk-averse merchants ceased to accept cash as a means of payment. Some surprising data has also emerged. Despite a decline in the level of general consumption in Switzerland, Italy and France, there was a rapid increase in the adoption of cashless payments in these countries.

At this point, however, it is worth assessing what the impact on payment methods has been from a global perspective. For this purpose, the statistics will be used. The total value of non-paper-based or digital credit transfers grew strongly in both advanced economies (AEs) and developing economies (EMDEs). These payments cover transfers initiated via a mobile banking application, online banking or an automated transfer. As a result, the growth in total credit transfer usage was strong and the share of non-cash payments[1] in total GDP sharply increased across the globe (Figures 2.1 and 2.2).

Globally, the number of non-cash transactions grew by 6% from 2019 to 2020. Accordingly, cash payments declined by 16% in 2020. Although the

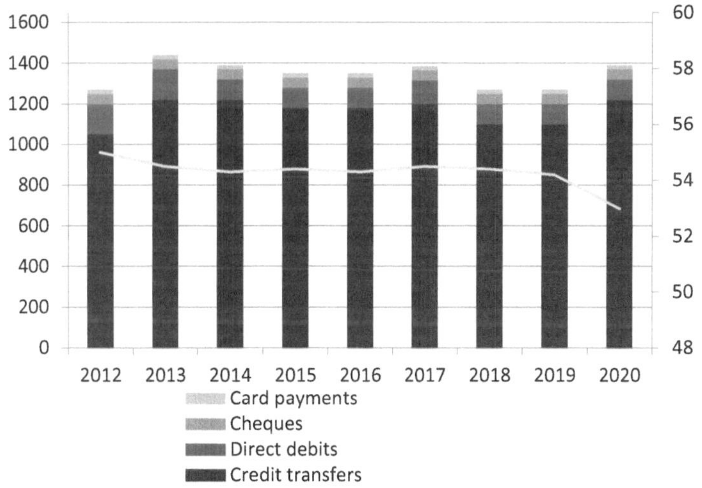

Figure 2.1 Credit transfer and contactless card usage in advanced economies, 2012–2020 (value – left-hand side, percentage of GDP – right-hand side)

Source: CPMI Red Book statistics; OECD main economic indicators and national account.

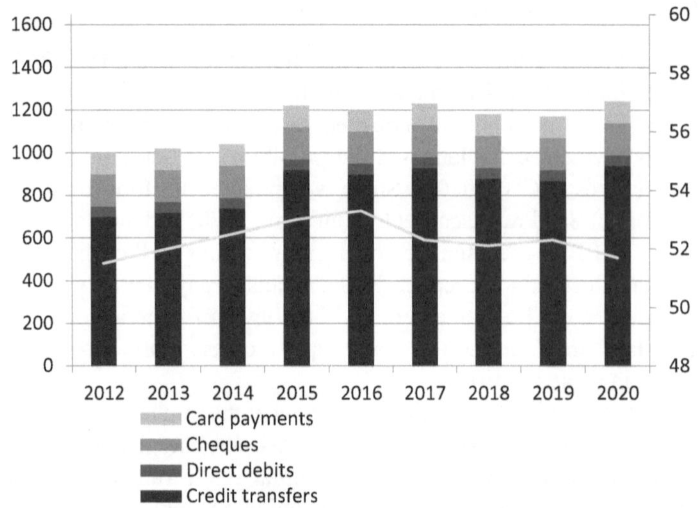

Figure 2.2 Credit transfer and contactless card usage in emerging market and developing economies, 2012–2020 (value – left-hand side, percentage of GDP – right-hand side)

Source: CPMI Red Book statistics; OECD main economic indicators and national accounts.

pandemic-driven temporary shuttering of many commercial venues was the primary trigger in this dramatic shift, other actions reinforced and accelerated behavioural changes already under way (e.g. countries like Argentina, Poland and Thailand increasing ATM withdrawal fees, and the continued downsizing of ATM networks in Europe) (Botta, 2021).

Both advanced and emerging market and developing economies have struggled with decline in the share of private consumption expenditure in GDP. This was accompanied by meaningful move away from cash payments. In addition to the decline in cash payments, the growth in the number of card payments lost momentum or even declined, which was presented on Figures 2.3 and 2.4.

The shift away from cash and cards towards digital credit transfers was driven by a combination of ongoing trends and COVID-19-related developments. The latter include the worldwide migration to working-from-home; temporary shutdowns of shops, hotels and restaurants; some merchants refusing cash payments (ECB, 2020a); the surge in e-commerce (Alfonso et al., 2021); the growth in digital person-to-person payments;[2] and the distribution of COVID-19 benefit payments by governments. Other data, in turn, indicate that the share of contactless payments in total card transactions increased in 2020 at its highest rate since 2015 (see Figure 2.5).

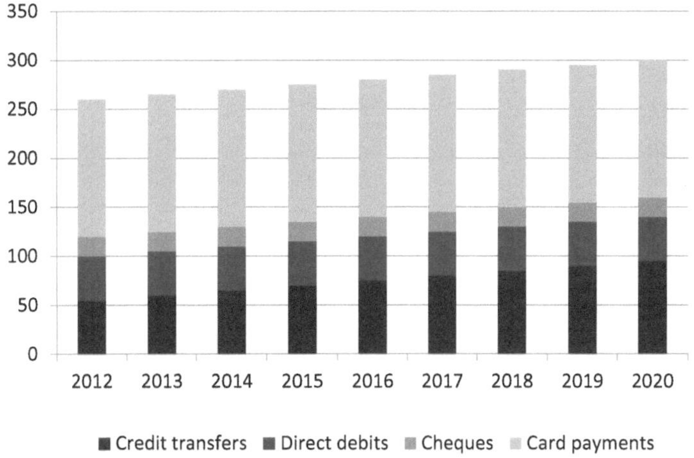

Figure 2.3 Credit transfer and contactless card usage in advanced economies, 2012–2020 (volume per 1,000 inhabitants)

Source: CPMI Red Book statistics; OECD main economic indicators and national accounts.

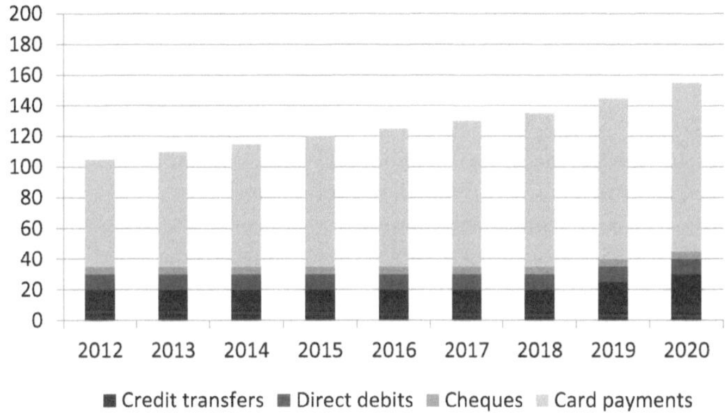

Figure 2.4 Credit transfer and contactless card usage in emerging market and developing economies, 2012–2020 (volume per 1,000 inhabitants)

Source: CPMI Red Book statistics; OECD main economic indicators and national accounts.

This may be explained by public fears of contagion and associated policy measures. For example, banks and card companies in many countries raised their value limits for contactless card payments[3] in response to the pandemic (NFCW, 2021). In most European countries, to reduce physical contact and reduce queues

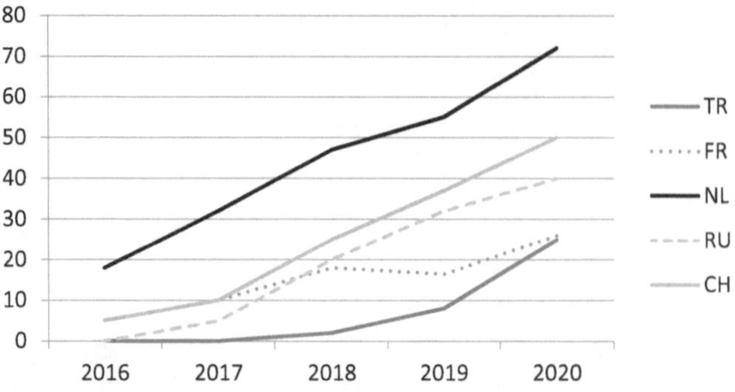

Figure 2.5 Volume of contactless card payments within all card payments, 2016–2020. TR – Turkey, FR – France, NL – Netherlands, RU – Russia, CH – Switzerland.

Source: CPMI Red Book statistics; OECD main economic indicators and national accounts.

at checkouts, the limit for contactless card payments was raised from USD 35 to USD 52 during COVID-19 period (Deutsche Bank Research, 2020).

The spread of the virus triggered action not only by card companies and commercial banks but also by central banks. Public concerns with regard to COVID-19 transmission have prompted "banks of banks" to respond to pandemic situation in three different ways. Several central banks (including the Bank of England, the Bundesbank, the Bank of Canada and the South African Reserve Bank) stated that the risks were low. Other central banks took more extensive precautionary measures. After the People's Bank of China (PBC), central banks in South Korea, Hungary and Kuwait also set about disinfecting and even destroying banknotes to contain the spread of the virus. Fearing the import of contaminated currency from Asia, the US Federal Reserve initiated quarantine measures for dollar banknotes from that region of the world. Several other governments and central banks (including those in India, Indonesia and Georgia) have explicitly endorsed cashless payments.

The aforementioned activities were adhoc measures. However, banks have also taken steps in this area in the longer term. Reservations about cash have contributed to the fact that central banks developed their own central bank digital currencies (CBDCs). Digital currency has become particularly desirable during an epidemic because of its efficiency, cost-effectiveness and convenience. Therefore central banks around the world have stepped up their initiatives for digital cash – 40% are experimenting with feasibility studies and 10% are already conducting pilot projects (Deutsche Bank Research, 2020). A recent survey finds that central banks representing a fifth of the world's population say they are likely to issue a CBDCs in the next few years (Boar et al., 2020; Boar & Wehrli, 2021). Several central banks are moving into more advanced stages of CBDC engagement, progressing from conceptual research towards practical experimentation.

Other central banks, meanwhile, are moving at a more measured pace with further research or consultation, while yet others have concluded that the risks currently outweigh the potential benefits. Central banks give a wide range of motivations for CBDC initiatives; for EMDE central banks, this includes promoting financial inclusion and payments efficiency (Auer et al., 2020).

Sweden, where cash in circulation accounts for only one per cent of GDP, announced in February 2020 that it had begun testing the e-krona and is expected to become the world's first cashless society by March 2023. The problem of rising of digital money with their forms and attributes was analysed by the authors from the International Monetary Fund (IMF). They perceived digital money rather as the opportunity and then a threat to the global economy. The main indicated benefit was a stability of e-money backed by the central banks in the long term. The central banks could ensure interoperability of payments and thus protect consumers from the growth of e-money monopolies offering payments among a large network of users (Tobias & Mancini-Griffoli, 2019). Sweden can be a positive example of introducing a digital currency. Indeed, the first publicly announced work on retail CBDCs was conducted by Sweden's Riksbank (SverigesRiksbank, 2017). In Sweden, cash use has been declining precipitously (see SverigesRiksbank, 2020) and the Riksbank has initiated a societal discussion on access to a central bank payments instrument for the general public. Over time, this "e-krona" project has been further developed (SverigesRiksbank, 2020). Another particularly advanced CBDC project at present is the electronic Chinese yuan (e-CNY) of the PBC. Since 2020, this CBDC has been piloted in several cities in China. Thee-CNY will be a cash-like liability of the PBC available to the general public – and to foreign visitors' of China – through account-based interfaces. Meanwhile, in October 2020, the Central Bank of the Bahamas issued the Sand Dollar, widely considered to be the first live retail CBDC. The Sand Dollar is issued through authorized financial institutions and allows accessibility to a digital wallet for residents via either a mobile phone application or a physical payment card. The Eastern Caribbean Central Bank (ECCB) launched its DCash in March 2021. DCash is distributed by licensed financial institutions and used for financial transactions between consumers and merchants, as well as in people-to-people (P2P) transactions.

Work on CBDCs has been under way at a number of central banks since at least the mid-2010s, accelerating into the 2020s. The stocktake in Auer et al. (2020) of all central bank publications shows that, as of mid-July 2021, at least 56 central banks had published retail or wholesale CBDC work. At least three countries (Ecuador, Ukraine and Uruguay) have completed a retail CBDC pilot. Eight retail CBDC pilots are ongoing, including in China, Korea and Sweden. Meanwhile, 40 central banks have published research on retail CBDCs, and 19 have announced research or development work on a wholesale CBDC (in some cases, in addition to work on retail CBDCs)(Auer et al., 2021).

Corona-related use of modern payment methods can be seen as a thoroughly positive development in the context of the generic trend towards promising methods of payment and implementing eMoney. The cash-only mentality at the checkout seems to have been broken. On the other hand, one should not now fall prey to the fallacy that all age groups will also follow this trend in the future. Especially for many older people who counted themselves among a risk group or switched out of consideration, the use of contactless payment might have served more as a "means to an end" than a permanent alternative (Jung, 2020).

The idea of creating a digital currency was not the only answer to the emergence of the pandemic. Another fact was that, in the aftermath of rapid spread of the coronavirus, citizens began to hoard food. Driven by a precautionary motive, they therefore created a situation in which the demand for cash increased significantly. Thus, paradoxically, despite the increasing importance of cashless means of payment during pandemic, the amount of cash in circulation worldwide has risen which was presented on Figure 2.6. Consistent with this trend, an increase in cash in circulation was observed in the euro zone. In March 2020, euro cash in circulation jumped by EUR 36 bn to EUR 1,344 bn. This was the highest monthly increase since the euro's inception with the exception of the financial crisis in October 2008 (+ EUR 44 bn). Year-on-year, in turn, the euro in circulation grew by 8%, the strongest growth since 2015 (Panetta, 2020a). It should therefore be concluded that the COVID-19 pandemic led to an exceptionally strong increase in the global demand for cash[4] (Heinonen, 2020). However, in many countries, retailers and the relevant lobby groups from the fintech and (credit) card industries pushed the use of electronic means of payment to the extreme.

During the pandemic crisis, in the wake of the insecurity, cash was "hoarded". However, it should also be noted that there was parallelly a decline in cash usage. The latter was reflected in the cash withdrawals data. Given the steep reduction of in-person purchases, ATM usage declined (after an initial wave of withdrawals by anxious consumers). For example, Germany and the US each saw spikes in cash withdrawals in the days leading up to lockdowns. The fear of contracting COVID-19 through high-traffic ATMs and, in some cases, the refusal

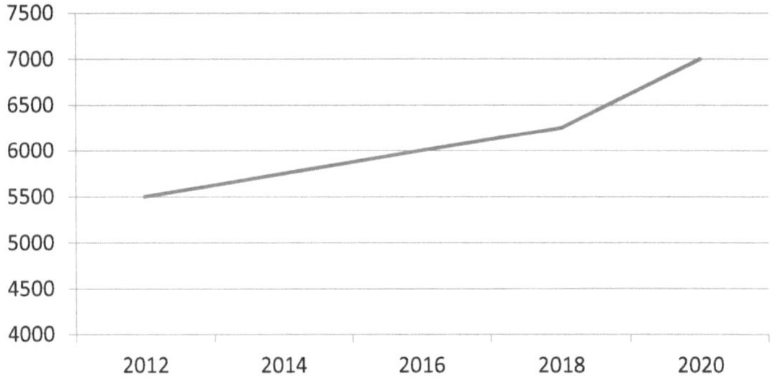

Figure 2.6 Cash in circulation worldwide, 2012–2020 in billion USD

Source: Based on (Rosl & Seitz, 2021), Institute for Monetary and Financial Stability, Goethe University Frankfurt, 2021. www.imfs-frankfurt.de/fileadmin/user_upload/IMFS_WP/IMFS_WP_150_web.pdf, accessed 04.04.2022.

of merchants to accept cash (often despite legal obligations) nudged consumers towards electronic payment options to complete purchases. ATM usage fell by 47% in April 2020 in India, while the United Kingdom experienced 46% declines per month on average from March to July 2020 (Botta, 2021). In general, the total number of cash withdrawals declined by 23%, exceeding the 10% decline in value (Committee on Payments and Market Infrastructures, 2021). This indicates that consumers withdrew cash less frequently, but when they did, they withdrew larger amounts (see Figures 2.7 and 2.8). The decline in withdrawals was due to fewer trips to commute and shop during the pandemic, and consumers refraining from using ATMs or visiting bank branches for fear of contracting the virus (Auer, 2021).

The rise in popularity of cashless methods of payment was not only the domain of the pandemic. In recent years, both debit and credit cards as well as direct debits have increased significantly. In 2019, card payments (with almost 50%) were the most widespread across Europe, followed by credit transfers and direct debits (each with almost 25%). Online payment services such as PayPal, on the other hand, have hardly played a role in most EU countries so far (European Central Bank, 2020). In the pandemic, the spread and use of cashless payment methods accelerated further – fuelled by fears that the virus could be spread via banknotes and coins. The increased use is visible in all age groups, but is particularly pronounced in the middle age groups (Mai, 2020).

This is particularly evident on the Asian continent, where penetration rate of digital payments is already very high. Given this, the impact of the virus on payment systems could be felt there sooner than in Europe and the US. At the end of 2018, around 73% of internet users in China used online payment services (up from 18 per cent in 2008).

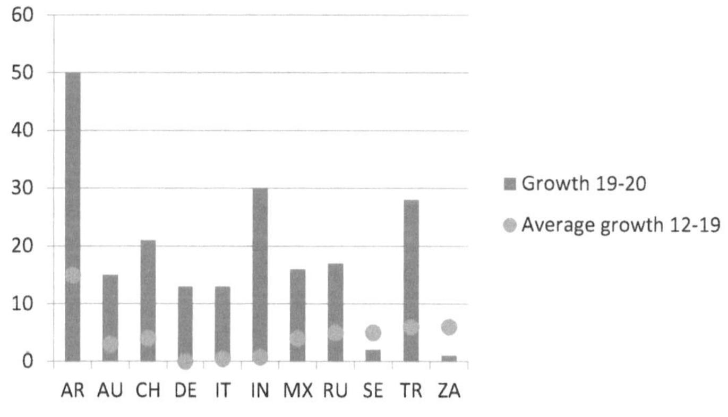

Figure 2.7 Value per withdrawal (per cent). AR – Argentina, AU – Australia, CH – Switzerland, DE – Germany, IT – Italy, IN – India, MX – Mexico, RU – Russia, SE – Sweden, TR – Turkey, ZA – Republic of South Africa.

Source: CPMI Red Book statistics, 2021.

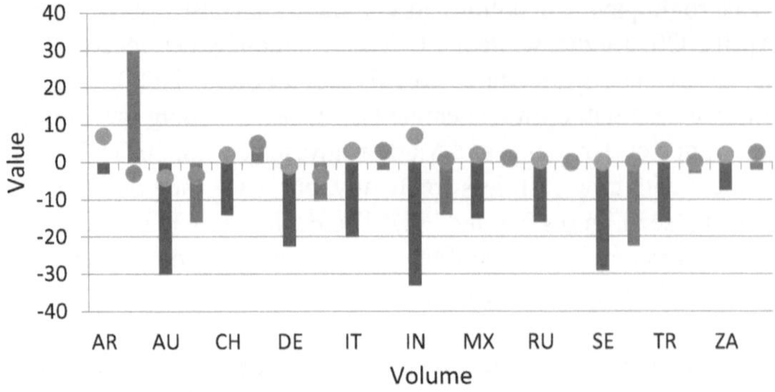

Figure 2.8 Developments of cash withdrawals (per capita, percentage of GDP). AR – Argentina, AU – Australia, CH – Switzerland, DE – Germany, IT – Italy, IN – India, MX – Mexico, RU – Russia, SE – Sweden, TR – Turkey, ZA – Republic of South Africa.

Source: CPMI Red Book statistics, 2021.

The reason for this is that the proportion of young people in China and Southeast Asian countries is significantly higher than that in Europe and the US – young people are more open to new technologies. Americans and Western Europeans are much more dependent on cash (Deutsche Bank Research, 2020).

Despite the attachment of European citizens to cash, the trend towards paying without notes and coins in the euro area has become stronger. In 2020, almost 102 billion payments (in 2019: 98 billion) were made without cash in the common currency zone. The total value of transactions rose by 8.7 per cent compared to 2019 to 167 trillion euros. Almost half (47 per cent) of the cashless transactions were card payments, with transfers (23 per cent) and direct debits (22 per cent) each accounting for almost a quarter. The rest were electronic payment methods such as Apple Pay or Google Pay, among others. Within the euro area, however, there are still large differences in the use of the main payment services. Portugal, for example, reportedly has the highest national percentage for card payments at around 70%. In the case of credit transfers, Slovakia had the highest percentage at around 38%, while in Germany, the share of direct debits is particularly high at a good 44% (Handelsblatt, 2021).

Conclusion

The COVID-19 pandemic in 2019–2020 caused a substantial change in the financial settlements globally especially in the change of the payments methods and rise of digital money. It was proved in this chapter based on the CPMI data for different developed and emerging markets globally. While the trends of declining cash and increasing card payments have so far been rather gradual, they have now experienced an abrupt level shift in favour of card payments in the course of COVID-19 (Schulz, 2021). This was driven in roughly equal parts by debit and credit cards. In parallel to this process, the use of ATMs has decreased. This qualitative change on the remittance market has been substantiated by scientific research, which has indicated that the virus persists longer on metal surfaces compared to plastic. Globally, this change in customer settlements was reflected in a 16% decline in cash transactions in 2020 compared to the previous year. Paradoxically, the decline in cash transactions led to an increase in cash in circulation globally. Indeed, consumers, with a precautionary motive in mind, did not just hoard food but also cash in response to the pandemic.

The risk of contamination by the virus found on coins and banknotes also prompted institutions such as central banks to take specific action. They undertook to disinfect cash and even destroy it. The more creative response of these banks to the pandemic, however, was the introduction of CBDC. However, digitalisation has also found its way into increased online payments, which have become more important especially in Asian countries due to the proportion of young people on the continent. The attachment to cash of citizens in Western Europe and North America has, in turn, translated into their lower level of use of mobile applications.

For the sake of accuracy, it should be noted at this point that the development towards a new type of payment behaviour has been empirically proven not only since the pandemic. The slow, but steady change in this area is continuously supported by empirical studies. Thus, high growth rates were recorded for modern payment methods even before the crisis. When it comes to the future, some forecasts predict that the pandemic will significantly increase the relevance and speed of mobile and contactless payment methods by 2025. In figures, cash is thus expected to account for only about one-third of sales in 2025, and modern solutions such as smartphone wallets and contactless payments will come to the fore. The last important conclusion is that adoption of digital currencies could be rapid and seemed to be the future of global financial settlement system backed and secured by the central banks.

Notes

1 Non-cash payments refer to payments made using a payment instrument other than cash, such as payment cards, credit transfers, direct debits and cheques. With the exception of payments made using a cheque or paper-based credit transfer, all non-cash payments are digital payments.
2 For example, in the US, person-to-person and mobile payments increased by 6% and 8%, respectively, during 2020 and the first months of 2021 (Akana, 2021).
3 Without having to authorize them with a PIN code.
4 In view of the move to non-cash settlement systems and the introduction of systems by central banks based on digital currencies, this seemingly surprising trend has found its justification in the parallel accumulation of cash by consumers at home.

3 It's a time to crypto for retail investors

Cryptocurrencies as an alternative asset class for optimising an all-equity portfolio

Smita Shukla, Shalini Talwar and Manish Talwar

Introduction

For any currency to be acceptable, it should be secure, recognisable in terms of a store of value, stable and easily transferable between two or more parties for settling transactions. In this context, Fiat is the traditionally accepted form of currency since it is issued by the sovereign government and holds legal tender. The comfort of using this currency is that banknotes and coins issued by the governments or the central banking entities across the world are rather difficult to counterfeit due to the use of sophisticated security features.

More recently, another form of currency, called cryptocurrency, has drawn the attention of regulators and investors alike. The key factor that makes cryptocurrencies attractive for transactions is that they are not issued by any central banking entity or government, making them theoretically immune to government interference or manipulation. Despite this, cryptocurrencies have not found widespread acceptance as a medium of exchange, remaining confined to limited transactions globally. However, they have emerged as an attractive investment avenue, particularly amongst retail investors. This has led to an exponential increase in the number of cryptocurrencies available for investment. Rather than proving to be a boon, the availability of many cryptos to choose from seems to have created confusion amongst investors, not to mention an increased risk of fraud and volatility.

An analysis of the responses collected through some one-on-one in-depth interviews with retail investors revealed that they were hesitant to invest in cryptos despite being aware of and interested in them due to the confusion created by the availability of many cryptos to choose from. The common theme that emerged from the interviews was that despite all the hype and visibility, there is no clarity about how to choose the right ones from the different cryptos available, what percentage of the portfolio should be devoted to cryptos, what are the valuation challenges, and what are the potential risks associated with investing in them.

DOI: 10.4324/9781003310365-3

Cryptocurrencies

Cryptocurrency is a digital medium of exchange which is secured by cryptography. Cryptography is a collection of sophisticated blockchain techniques used to secure transfer messages between sender and receiver so that only the intended receiver can decipher the message. Advanced techniques are used to scramble the message, which can be deciphered only through a secure key. The security standard in cryptocurrency is high, and digitally it can be used for transfer of value as well as medium of exchange.

Cryptocurrencies are programmatically generated and circulated by private companies and individuals. Most are decentralised networks based on blockchain technology, a distributed ledger enforced by a disparate network of computers (nodes) held by individuals. The process of adding new transactional details to the public ledger is called 'mining'. A natural question that arises here is why will these independent people, spread across the world, do mining (i.e., checking transactions, adding new blocks, maintaining the database with blockchain) and what is their incentive? The answer lies in the fact that the first person who comes up with proof of the genuineness of the transaction gets a new cryptocurrency in his/her account as a reward for mining.

Mining involves generating the hash (cryptographic encryption) of a block of a new transaction so that it is difficult to counterfeit, ensuring the entire blockchain's safety without needing a central system.

'Proof of work' and 'proof of stake' are the two major consensus mechanisms cryptocurrencies use for mining. Initial cryptocurrencies used proof of work consensus mechanism. Proof of work requires solving a complex mathematical puzzle. Since the reward for solving the puzzle first is a new mined unit of cryptocurrency, miners across the globe have started deploying more and more high-end and powerful computers and multiple parallel processing machines to solve it within seconds. This has resulted in thousands of powerful computers working 24×7 across the globe, consuming a huge amount of energy every day, raising multiple ethical and environmental concerns. For instance, estimates show that the mining of Bitcoin through proof of work uses 91 Terawatts-hours of energy every year, five times the entire electricity consumption of a country like Finland and seven times more than the energy used by Google in a year (Kim, 2021).

This problem has led to the introduction of alternative concepts to decide who gets the reward of mining apart from proof of work. These concepts do not use even a fraction of electricity used for Bitcoin mining through proof of work. A large number of the new cryptocurrencies are based on these alternatives. The most popular alternative concept is 'proof of stake' (Meunier, 2018). It requires the users to stake their cryptocurrency (e.g., Ethereum) to take the position of validator in the network. Unlike proof of work, these validators do not use high computational power as they are selected randomly and are not competing with each other. To explain further, they do not mine blocks; rather, they just create blocks when selected and validate the proposed blocks if they are not. Such validation is called attesting. Validators get rewarded for proposing new blocks as well as for attesting the ones they have checked.

Types of cryptocurrencies

Cryptocurrencies can be classified based on their utility into two types – coins and tokens. A *digital coin* is created on a blockchain. Acting like traditional money, it stores value and serves as a medium of exchange between parties transacting with each other. Such coins can be further divided into two types – Bitcoins and Altcoins. Bitcoinis the first mined cryptocurrency that caught the imagination of many and initiated the cycle. It is still the most popular cryptocurrency, with a 41% market share and market capitalisation of over USD 1.2 trillion in 2021. However, its market capitalisation has been quite volatile over the years, as seen in Figure 3.1.

All other coins except Bitcoin are considered 'Altcoin' or alternatives to Bitcoin. Most of the first altcoins were forked from Bitcoin while trying to improve upon the basic Bitcoin structure. Ethereum, XRP, Tether, Cardano, Polkadot, Solana and so on are all altcoins. Ethereum is considered the most popular altcoin, with the second-highest market cap after Bitcoin. It has a market share of around 19%. The market capitalisation of Ethereum is presented in Figure 3.2.

To give an idea about the market size and value of cryptocurrencies, Table 3.1 exhibits the top-ten cryptocurrencies by market capitalisation as of April 8, 2022.

Coming to *tokens*, all cryptocurrencies are actually tokens, but of late, all cryptocurrencies except Bitcoin and Ethereum are considered to be tokens. The widely accepted definition of tokens is 'tokens are digital assets that run on

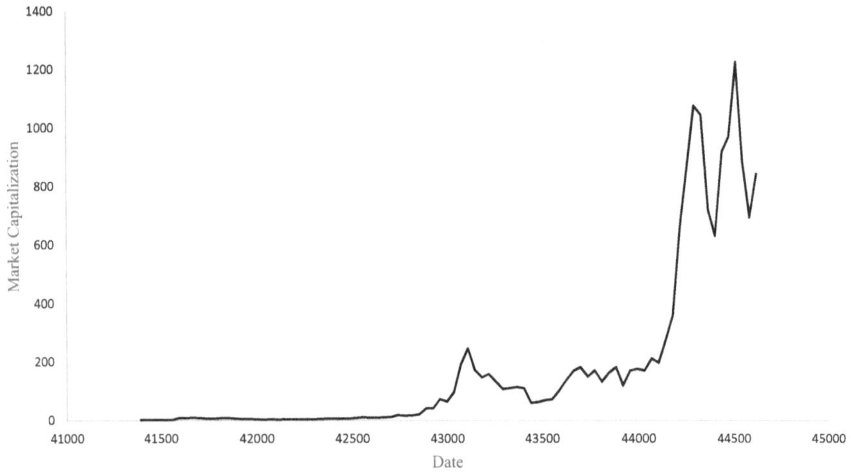

Figure 3.1 Bitcoin market capitalisation (2015–2022)

Data source: https://coinmarketcap.com/currencies/bitcoin/

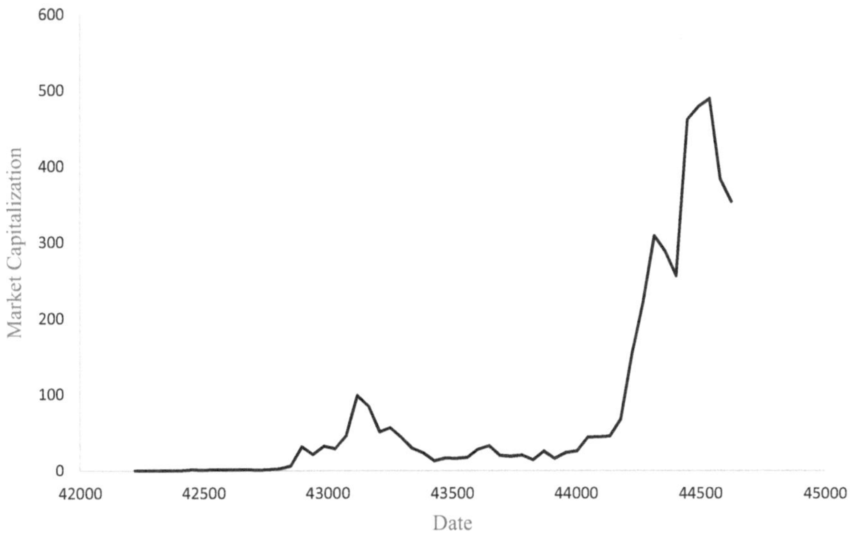

Figure 3.2 Ethereum market capitalisation (2016–2022)

Data source: https://coinmarketcap.com/currencies/thereum/

Table 3.1 The market capitalisation of cryptocurrencies

Coin	*Price*	*24-hour change*	*24-hour volume*	*Market capitalization*
Bitcoin (BTC)	$43,515.27	−0.83%	$24.12 B	$824.58 B
Ethereum (ETH)	$3,280.66	−0.41%	$16.91 B	$392.36 B
Tether (USDT)	$1.01	−0.02%	$60.07 B	$82.52 B
BNB (BNB)	$428.60	−1.29%	$2.04 B	$70.8 B
USD Coin (USDC)	$1.00	−0.01%	$3.59 B	$50.96 B
Solana (SOL)	$116.73	−1.06%	$2.28 B	$37.83 B
XRP (XRP)	$0.776	−1.49%	$1.45 B	$37.21 B
Cardano (ADA)	$1.08	−1.11%	$905.84 M	$36.27 B
Terra (LUNA)	$99.88	−6.22%	$2.66 B	$35.3 B
Avalanche (AVAX)	$87.75	2.17%	$1.38 B	$23.35 B

Source: Prepared by the authors based on data available on https://coinmarketcap.com/

B = billion; M = million.

top of other cryptocurrencies' blockchains. So, while Bitcoins have their blockchain, the assets like 'Chainlink' or 'AAVE' do not have their dedicated blockchain and run on the top of other cryptocurrency blockchains, such as Ethereum. Tokens can be of various types. Some of the main types of tokens are presented in Table 3.2.

Table 3.2 Types of tokens

Type	*Main feature*	*Examples*
Utility tokens	Used for providing access to platform or service where they reside.	Funfair, Basic Attention Token, Brickblock, Timicoin, Sirin Labs Token and Golem
Security tokens	Usage and issuance are governed by financial regulation. These can either be equity tokens similar to traditional stocks in form and operation or asset-backed tokens backed by real-world assets as underlying value.	Sia Funds, B cap (Blockchain Capital) and Science Blockchain
Payment tokens	Used to pay for goods and services within or outside their platforms.	Monero, Ethereum and Bitcoin
Exchange tokens	Issued by crypto exchanges to facilitate the buying and selling of other tokens.	Binance Coin or BNB token, Gemini USD, FTX Coin for FTX Exchange, Uni token, HT for Huobi exchange, Shushi etc.
Non-fungible tokens	These are digital ownership certificates of unique, non-replaceable items and one-of-kind assets on the blockchain.	Jack Dorsey's first tweet is available as NTF. Anyone can create it for any digital work, which can be bought or sold.
DeFi tokens or Decentralized finance tokens	They refer to financial applications that directly render financial and money control to the user. Users can use these for borrowing, lending, saving, investing, growing, buying insurance etc.	Solana, Chainlink, Uniswap, Polkadot, AAVE.
Stablecoins	Stable tokens are backed by real assets, like USD or euro, and remain fairly valued like any Fiat currency. They are used to buy other tokens or coins.	Whether USD coin etc.
Asset-backed tokens	Asset-backed tokens have underlying value based on a real-world asset such as other money and stock.	OilCoin, Petroleum coin, energy web token etc.
Privacy tokens	Used for privacy applications. These tokens have better privacy than other mainstream cryptocurrencies.	Zcash, Horizen, Verge, Beam etc.

Source: Prepared by the authors based on information available athttps://coinmarketcap.com/.

Investing in cryptocurrencies

Cryptocurrencies have attracted the attention of institutional and retail investors, having different profiles, as an asset class that can offer portfolio diversification benefits. The trading volume of cryptocurrencies has increased substantially in India over the past two to three years. At the same time, trading in equity has also seen an uptrend.

Further, the retail investment activity has seen a paradigm shift after the onset of the pandemic in March 2020. Recent reports indicate that the equity ownership of retail investors in India increased by 9 per cent in 2020 in about 1,500 top National Stock Exchange (NSE) listed companies (Gopkumar, 2022). The unprecedented increase in retail participation continued in 2021, with more than 4.5 million new retail accounts added in April-May 2021 (Gopkumar, 2022). Recent reports have also noted increased retail investment in cryptos in 2021, with Bitcoinbeing the highest traded crypto since 2020 (Das, 2021; Kaul, 2021).

Research on various aspects of retail investors' decision-making needs to gain momentum in the light of the increase in their investment activity (e.g. Seth et al., 2020). The retail investors are particularly vulnerable and may suffer high losses during the events that increase volatility (S. Talwar et al., 2021; Corbet et al., 2020a). There is need to focus on the investment activity of retail investors, particularly in the wake of the recent pandemic (e.g. M. Talwar et al., 2021; Baker et al., 2020).

The idea of a portfolio comprising cryptocurrencies is well-rooted in the extant literature. Trimborn (2015) created an optimal crypto portfolio comprising currencies included in the Cryptocurrency Index. The portfolio was optimised by minimising variance. Viewing the secondary cryptocurrency market as a distinct asset class, Liu (2018) examined the possibility of creating an efficient pure crypto portfolio. More recently, Čuljak et al. (2022) discussed sectoral cryptocurrency classification portfolio optimisation using six optimisation targets employing the basic premise of Modern Portfolio Theory (Markowitz, 1952). Another study focused on crypto portfolio optimisation, and suggested a passive approach of equally weighting each component, which offered the best reward-risk ratio and hence optimisation (Brauneis & Mestel, 2019). Giving credence to passive fund allocation, Platanakis et al. (2018) compared the performance of an optimised portfolio with a portfolio based on equal funds across each component; to show the latter was a better option. Focusing on more comprehensive portfolios, scholars have also created optimal portfolios by allocating funds across cryptocurrency as one of the asset classes along with traditional assets such as equity, index funds, gold, real estate market index and so on (e.g. Chuen et al., 2017; Petukhina et al., 2021; Trimborn et al., 2019).

Overall, the existing evidence underscores the relevance of constructing a portfolio with funds allocated optimally across equities and cryptocurrencies, supporting the authors' conceptualisation. The choice of these two asset classes is relevant based on the fact, as presented earlier, that the interest of retail investors is deepening in these two asset classes.

Constructing optimal portfolios: Methodology

The chapter examines if including cryptocurrencies in an all-equity portfolio can help improve the reward-risk ratio, thereby constructing efficient equity-crypto portfolios that retail investors can be offered based on their risk preference. For this, the authors have used the mathematical model of MPT, a seminal portfolio analysis and construction approach, which is perhaps the most used approach to portfolio diversification to date, popular among both theorists and practitioners (Talwar, 2016). Before creating and comparing all-equity portfolios and portfolios comprising both equity and cryptocurrencies, the authors used financial econometric tools to confirm the suitability of data for constructing the planned portfolios. The two methodological approaches are described here:

Modern portfolio theory

Modern portfolio theory (MPT) can be best described as a theory of investment that provides an approach to constructing portfolios that give a maximum return for a given level of risk, or a minimum risk for a given level of return, by optimising the proportion of funds allocated to constituent assets. The theory is based on the premise that while seeking to spread their investible surplus across multiple assets within an asset class or across different asset classes, investors should assess not only each asset's risk but also the interactive risk between each pair of assets being included in the portfolio. The interactive risk captures the extent of co-movement between asset pairs and is measured through correlation and covariance. MPT suggests that only the asset pairs with low positive correlation should be included in the portfolio. To explain further, the ideal choice is a perfect negative correlation (i.e. a correlation value of −1), but since perfectly negatively correlated assets are more of a theoretical possibility, in practice, any value of negative correlations is acceptable. Positive correlations are also acceptable, provided they are not close to or equal to +1, which implies a perfect positive correlation. The theory also provides a mathematical model for calculating portfolio risk and return. The model (Talwar, 2016) is presented further. The model quantifies portfolio risk and returns using – expected returns of individual assets constituting the portfolio, variance or standard deviation of individual assets constituting the portfolio, and interactive risk (correlation/covariance) of pairs of individual assets constituting the portfolio.

The theory calculates portfolio return (expected) as a weighted average of the expected returns of the constituent assets. Symbolically,

$$R_p = \sum_{i=1}^{N} (X_i)(R_i)$$

where: R_p = portfolio return (expected), X_i = portion of funds invested in asset I (weight), R_i = return (expected) of asset I, N = total number of assets in the portfolio.

The inclusion of interactive risk makes portfolio risk calculation more complicated than the return calculation. Due to the consideration of pair-wise asset risk, the portfolio risk cannot be a simple weighted average of individual asset risk as in the case of portfolio returns (expected).

Symbolically:

$$\sigma_p^2 = \sum_{i=1}^{N}\sum_{j=1}^{N} X_i X_j r_{i.j} \sigma_i \sigma_j$$

where: σ_p^2= portfolio variance (expected), $\sigma_{i,j}$ = standard deviation (expected) of individual assets (I, j), $X_{i,j}$= portion of funds invested in assets I, j (weight), $r_{i.j}$= coefficient of correlation between assets I and j, N = total number of assets in the portfolio.

The resulting portfolios, generated by varying the proportion of funds allocated to each constituent asset, represent the best risk-return combination. These portfolios, called the efficient or dominant portfolios, plot along an envelope curve called the "efficient frontier". To elaborate, the efficient frontier is the locus of all portfolios that offer returns (expected) higher than returns of any other portfolio for the same level of risk or vice versa (lower risk than any other portfolio offering the same level of return).

The key portfolios that the authors have generated are the minimum variance portfolio and optimal risky portfolio (a portfolio that has the highest Sharpe ratio among all the efficient portfolios). An optimal risky portfolio is a portfolio of all risky assets that would be preferred by all rational investors, whatever the level of their risk aversion or risk tolerance.

Mathematically, the Sharpe ratio is calculated as:

$$S_R = \left(R_p - r_f\right) / \sigma_p$$

where: R_p= portfolio return (expected), r_f = risk-free rate, σ_p= Portfolio standard deviation.

The analysis was conducted in MS Excel 2019, and portfolio optimisation was executed using Solver.

Financial econometrics

The authors used some financial econometrics tools to ascertain the statistical suitability of the data for constructing the proposed portfolio. Many recent studies have used these tests to ascertain the suitability of financial time series for further analysis (e.g. Talwar & Gupta-Bhattacharya, 2017; Talwar & Pansare, 2018). The data series were tested for the presence of unit root using two alternative tests – the Augmented Dickey-Fuller test (Dickey & Fuller, 1979) and Phillips and Perron (Phillips & Perron, 1988). Both tests propose to examine the null hypothesis of the presence of unit root. This step is important since financial time series often have unit roots, which make them non-stationary, and if such series is used for analysis, it can lead to spurious regression and results that are meaningless.

Achieving portfolio diversification by combining different assets is possible only if the financial time series representing these assets are not cointegrated in the long run. Therefore, the authors applied the Johansen cointegration test to confirm the absence of a long-run cointegrating relationship among the assets proposed to be used to construct the portfolios. Cointegration implies that in addition to the permanent changes that occur in individual variables with time, certain linear combinations of different individual variables may indicate along-run equilibrium relationship that binds them together. The test assumes an ordinary stochastic non-stationary process that underlies two processes X and Y. This test is interpreted through the outcome of two tests, the trace test and the maximum eigenvalue test. From the stationarity test to cointegration test, the entire analysis was conducted in EVIEWS 10.

Constructing optimal portfolios: Data

The data used for the study comprised two parts: equity-related data and cryptocurrency data. For the equity-related data, the authors considered BSE Sensex (S&P Bombay Stock Exchange Sensitive Index) as the benchmark and created an all-equity portfolio comprising stocks selected from the 30 Sensex constituents listed in Table 3.3. Sensex is an indicator of the movement in the Indian stock market and represents all key sectors in the economy. The reason behind the choice of stocks from Sensex for constructing portfolios under this study is that companies (i.e., stocks) comprising SENSEX are from different sectors and are larger representatives of the sector they belong to. These are well-researched and well-known companies with much relevant information available in the market about their prospects and expected stock price movement. Selected stocks also have a lot of liquidity, with buyers and sellers always available to transact in them.

The data for analysis comprised daily closing price data extracted for a period from June 1, 2020, to February 28, 2022, resulting in 439 data points. The risk-free rate is another relevant piece of information required for constructing the optimal risky portfolios. The same was extracted from the RBI website[1] (10-Year G-Sec Par Yield [FBIL] as of March 4, 2022). The rate was 6.82 per cent.

For cryptocurrency data, the authors used the daily price data for two cryptos, Ethereum and Bitcoin, since these are most traded and provide sufficient crypto exposure to retail investors without venturing into other less liquid and rather unknown cryptos. The data duration was matched with equity data (June 1, 2020, to February 28, 2022, resulting in 439 data points), with trading days considered being 252.

Constructing optimal portfolios: Results

Shortlisting of stocks for an all-equity portfolio: 'Adequate diversification', that is, the number of stocks to be included in a portfolio has always been debated. Following a well-rounded discussion in Talwar (2016), the authors have shortlisted 11 stocks for inclusion in the all-equity portfolio. All these stocks are a

Table 3.3 Constituents of BSE Sensex

Name	*Industry*	*Weight*
Bajaj Auto Ltd.	2/3 Wheelers	0.74%
HDFC Bank Ltd.	Banking	10.47%
ICICI Bank Ltd.	Banking	7.49%
Kotak Mahindra Bank Ltd.	Banking	4.45%
Axis Bank Ltd.	Banking	3.07%
State Bank of India	Banking	2.53%
IndusInd Bank Ltd	Banking	1.05%
Maruti Suzuki India Ltd.	Cars & Utility Vehicles	1.38%
Mahindra & Mahindra Ltd.	Cars & Utility Vehicles	1.11%
UltraTech Cement Ltd.	Cement & Cement Products	1.30%
ITC Ltd.	Cigarettes, Tobacco Products	3.12%
Larsen & Toubro Ltd.	Construction & Engineering	3.19%
POWERGRID	Electric Utilities	0.90%
NTPC Ltd.	Electric Utilities	0.88%
Bajaj Finance Ltd.	Finance (including NBFCs)	3.09%
Bajaj Finserv	Finance (including NBFCs)	1.67%
Nestle India Ltd.	FMCG	1.06%
Asian Paints Ltd.	Furniture, Furnishing, Paints	2.32%
Housing Development Finance Corporation Ltd.	Housing Finance	7.67%
Reliance Industries Ltd.	Integrated Oil & Gas	12.00%
Tata Steel Ltd.	Iron & Steel/Interm Products	1.51%
Infosys Ltd.	IT Consulting & Software	9.72%
Tata Consultancy Services Ltd.	IT Consulting & Software	5.99%
HCL Technologies Ltd.	IT Consulting & Software	2.20%
Tech Mahindra Ltd.	IT Consulting & Software	1.40%
Titan Company Ltd.	Other Apparels & Accessories	1.30%
Hindustan Unilever Ltd.	Personal Products	3.66%
Sun Pharmaceutical Industries Ltd.	Pharmaceuticals	1.24%
Dr. Reddy	Pharmaceuticals	0.87%
Bharti Airtel Ltd.	Telecom Services	2.61%

Source: Prepared by the authors based on information available athttps://tradebrains.in/sensex-30-companies-list/.

part of Sensex 30. For shortlisting, the authors were guided by two parameters: (i) belonging to a sector/industry for which most analysts are bullish and (ii) weightage within the sector/industry. As a result, following equity stocks were shortlisted: HDFC Bank (industry: Banks, weightage in Sensex:10.47%); Bajaj Finance (industry: Finance [including NBFCs], weightage in Sensex: 3.09%); Bharti Airtel (industry: Telecom Services, weightage in Sensex: 2.61%); Infosys (industry: IT Consulting & Software, weightage in Sensex: 9.72%); Larsen & Toubro Ltd. (industry: Construction & Engineering, weightage in Sensex: 3.19%); Mahindra & Mahindra (industry: Cars & Utility Vehicles, weightage in Sensex: 1.11%); Titan (industry: Other Apparels & Accessories, weightage in Sensex: 1.3%); Sun Pharma (industry: Pharmaceuticals, weightage in Sensex: 1.24%); Power Grid (industry: Electric Utilities, weightage in Sensex: 0.9%); Reliance (industry: Integrated Oil & Gas, weightage in Sensex: 12%) and TATA Steel (industry: Iron & Steel/ Interm.products, weightage in Sensex: 1.51%).

Data suitability for portfolio construction: The suitability of data for portfolio construction was ascertained in two ways: (i) correlations to confirm theoretical suitability from the perspective of MPT (as low correlations as possible), and (ii) stationarity and long-run co-movement from the perspective of statistical suitability.

All correlation values presented in Table 3.4 are less than +1. In fact, except for the Ethereum-Bitcoin pair, which has a correlation value of 0.75, other pairwise correlation values are quite low. This confirmed the theoretical suitability of the data for portfolio construction.

ADF and PP tests indicated that series were non-stationary at levels (i.e. closing price) but became stationary after first differencing (i.e. returns). After ascertaining the stationarity, long-run co-movement was checked using the Johansen cointegration test. The trace test and the maximum eigenvalue test statistics confirmed that the series were not cointegrated in the long run. This confirmed the statistical suitability of the data for constructing a portfolio.

Data description: The summary statistics (mean, standard error, standard deviation, sample variance, kurtosis, skewness, range, minimum and maximum) were generated to understand the nature of the data. The output for stocks is given in Table 3.5, and that for cryptocurrencies is given in Table 3.6.

All-equity portfolios: Applying the mathematical model proposed by MPT, the minimum variance portfolio was first generated by minimising portfolio standard deviation. After that, an optimal risky portfolio was generated by maximising the Sharpe Ratio. Multiple portfolios were generated between these two portfolios assuming different levels of returns and minimising the risk for them. The resultant portfolios with their respective risk-return profiles and constituents' weights are presented in Table 3.7. The locus of all these portfolios called the efficient or dominant portfolios (since they minimise risk for a given level of return or maximise return for a given level of risk), is the efficient frontier, illustrated in Figure 3.3.

Since an optimal risky portfolio is a portfolio of risky assets that all investors would prefer, the authors took forward this portfolio to construct optimal equity-crypto portfolios. The optimal risky portfolio has a portfolio expected return equal to 59.55 per cent, portfolio standard deviation equal to 1.26 per cent and Sharpe ratio equal to 41.89. It comprises five stocks – Bajaj Finance (12.84 per cent), Infosys (40.04 per cent), Titan (20.75 per cent), Power Grid (8.67 per cent) and Tata Steel (17.69 per cent).

To construct optimal risky equity-crypto portfolios, the authors used three combinations – (i) both cryptocurrencies (Ethereum and Bitcoin) combined with Bajaj Finance, Infosys, Titan, Power Grid and Tata Steel; (ii) Ethereum combined with Bajaj Finance, Infosys, Titan, Power Grid and Tata Steel; and (iii) Bitcoin combined with Bajaj Finance, Infosys, Titan, Power Grid and Tata Steel. The results of the analysis are presented in Table 3.8.

Table 3.4 Correlation matrix

	Ethereum	*Bitcoin*	*HDFC Bank*	*Bajaj Finance*	*Bharti Airtel*	*Infosys*	*Larsen & Toubro*	*Mahindra & Mahindra*	*Titan*	*Sun Pharma*	*Power Grid*	*Reliance*	*Tata Steel*
Ethereum	1.00												
Bitcoin	0.75	1.00											
HDFC Bank	0.03	0.00	1.00										
Bajaj Finance	0.05	0.02	0.52	1.00									
Bharti Airtel	0.15	0.11	0.28	0.37	1.00								
Infosys	0.05	0.07	0.21	0.18	0.16	1.00							
Larsen & Toubro	0.20	0.15	0.43	0.47	0.30	0.27	1.00						
Mahindra & Mahindra	0.05	0.08	0.36	0.40	0.28	0.25	0.46	1.00					
Titan	0.11	0.09	0.34	0.37	0.20	0.25	0.40	0.34	1.00				
Sun Pharma	0.12	0.11	0.18	0.22	0.31	0.25	0.29	0.32	0.24	1.00			
Power Grid	0.11	0.13	0.21	0.24	0.22	0.12	0.31	0.23	0.23	0.28	1.00		
Reliance	0.06	0.02	0.33	0.33	0.18	0.22	0.25	0.30	0.25	0.18	0.17	1.00	
Tata Steel	0.17	0.13	0.29	0.38	0.35	0.22	0.42	0.33	0.32	0.37	0.31	0.25	1.00

Source: Based on the authors' calculations.

Table 3.5 Summary statistics of selected stocks

Summary statistics	*HDFC Bank*	*Bajaj Finance*	*Bharti Airtel*	*Infosys*	*Larsen & Toubro*	*Mahindra & Mahindra*	*Titan*	*Sun Pharma*	*Power Grid*	*Reliance*	*Tata Steel*
Mean	0.085	0.269	0.048	0.212	0.162	0.127	0.225	0.141	0.157	0.102	0.320
Standard error	0.078	0.114	0.090	0.075	0.081	0.100	0.087	0.083	0.088	0.085	0.121
Standard deviation	1.632	2.393	1.894	1.565	1.686	2.083	1.817	1.729	1.848	1.773	2.539
Sample variance	2.664	5.728	3.586	2.449	2.841	4.340	3.301	2.988	3.414	3.143	6.448
Kurtosis	0.771	1.225	1.288	3.045	2.300	2.799	2.399	2.789	1.097	2.711	1.099
Skewness	0.137	0.276	0.134	0.699	0.547	0.540	0.473	0.429	0.533	-0.010	−0.099
Range	11.601	16.220	15.008	13.644	13.251	16.926	15.335	16.216	12.140	15.836	17.546
Minimum	−5.583	−7.705	−8.217	−4.447	−5.044	−6.716	−5.258	−6.601	−5.999	−9.012	−10.073
Maximum	6.018	8.516	6.791	9.197	8.206	10.210	10.077	9.615	6.141	6.824	7.473

Source: Based on the authors' calculations.

Table 3.6 Summary statistics of selected cryptocurrencies

Summary statistics	*Ethereum*	*Bitcoin*
Mean	0.563	0.330
Standard Error	0.292	0.215
Median	0.336	0.234
Standard Deviation	6.101	4.491
Sample Variance	37.225	20.165
Kurtosis	4.851	1.699
Skewness	−0.045	−0.081
Range	68.436	34.729
Minimum	−32.692	−15.547
Maximum	35.744	19.182

Source: Based on the authors' calculations.

Table 3.7 Efficient all-equity efficient portfolios constructed using the shortlisted stocks

Portfolio parameters	*MVP*	*Assumed return*	*Assumed return*	*Assumed return*	*Assumed return*	*ORP*	*Assumed return*	*Assumed return*
PR	36.51	40.00	45.00	50.00	55.00	59.55	65.00	70.00
PSTD	1.00	1.01	1.05	1.10	1.17	1.26	1.43	1.69
SR	29.63	32.82	36.45	39.30	41.21	41.89	40.71	37.42
Scrips	**Weights**							
HDFC Bank	14.04%	10.00%	5.64%	0.76%	0.00%	0.00%	0.00%	0.00%
Bajaj Finance	0.00%	0.00%	2.93%	6.51%	10.14%	12.84%	17.10%	21.35%
Bharti Airtel	10.00%	6.02%	1.96%	0.00%	0.00%	0.00%	0.00%	0.00%
Infosys	23.39%	27.68%	31.23%	34.46%	38.29%	40.04%	34.07%	21.21%
Larsen & Toubro	4.87%	6.31%	5.75%	4.44%	0.22%	0.00%	0.00%	0.00%
Mahindra & Mahindra	0.00%	0.00%	0.00%	0.00%	0.00%	0.00%	0.00%	0.00%
Titan	8.15%	12.08%	14.64%	16.94%	19.61%	20.75%	17.34%	8.80%
Sun Pharma	12.83%	12.44%	11.68%	10.07%	6.56%	0.00%	0.00%	0.00%
Power Grid	13.29%	14.16%	14.58%	14.52%	13.54%	8.67%	0.00%	0.00%
Reliance	13.43%	11.30%	9.13%	6.62%	1.10%	0.00%	0.00%	0.00%
Tata Steel	0.00%	0.00%	2.45%	5.69%	10.55%	17.69%	31.49%	48.64%

MVP = minimum variance portfolio; ORP = optimal risky portfolio; PR = portfolio expected return; PSTD = portfolio standard deviation; SR = Sharpe ratio

Source: Based on the authors' calculations.

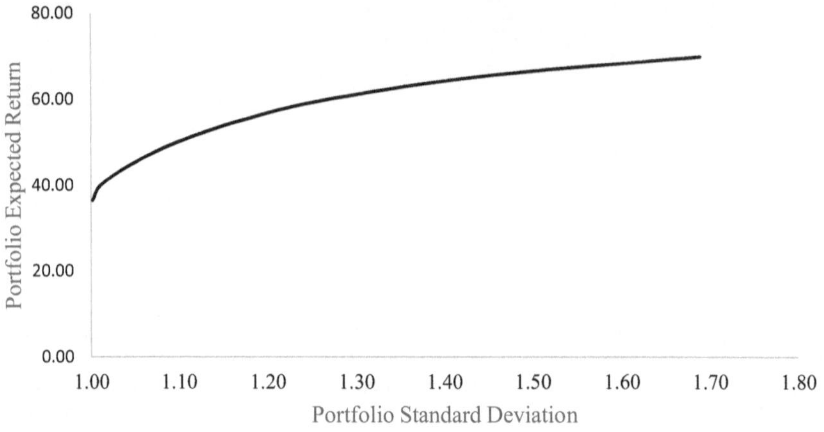

Figure 3.3 Efficient frontier comprising all-equity efficient portfolios constructed using the shortlisted stocks

Source: Based on the authors' calculations.

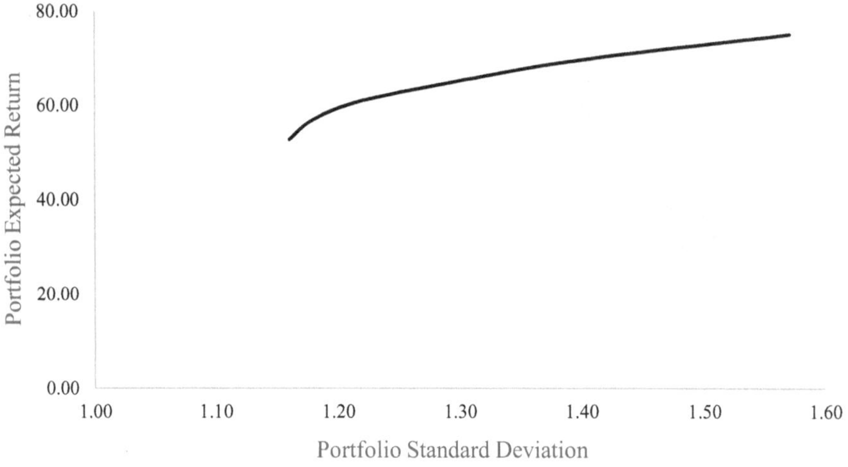

Figure 3.4 Efficient frontier comprising crypto-equity efficient portfolios constructed using the shortlisted stocks and Ethereum

Source: Based on the authors' calculations.

As explained in the case of all-equity portfolios, the authors also generated an efficient frontier comprising crypto-equity efficient portfolios constructed using the shortlisted stocks and Ethereum. The same is presented in Figure 3.4.

The results reveal that the optimal risky portfolio comprising Ethereum representing cryptocurrency and Bajaj Finance, Infosys, Titan, Power Grid and Tata

Table 3.8 Equity-crypto portfolios

Ethereum and Bitcoin	*MVP*	*EWP*	*ORP*	*Ethereum*	*MVP*	*EWP*	*ORP*	*Bitcoin*	*MVP*	*EWP*	*ORP*	*All-equity*	*MVP*	*EWP*	*ORP*
PR	52.63	74.74	66.01	PR	52.75	73.35	66.01	PR	52.73	63.54	61.61	PR	36.51	42.32	59.55
PSTD	1.15	1.82	1.32	PSTD	1.16	1.61	1.32	PSTD	1.15	1.41	1.26	PSTD	1.00	1.15	1.26
SR	39.74	37.28	44.96	SR	39.61	41.28	44.96	SR	39.83	40.15	43.50	SR	29.63	30.98	41.89
Weights Ethereum & Bitcoin	MVP	EWP	ORP	**Weights Ethereum**	MVP	EWP	ORP	**Weights** Bitcoin	MVP	EWP	ORP	**Weights All-equity**	MVP	EWP	ORP
Ethereum	0.00%	14.29%	8.00%	Ethereum	1.22%	16.67%	8.00%	Bitcoin	3.26%	16.67%	7.71%	HDFC Bank	14.04%	9.09%	0.00%
Bitcoin	3.27%	14.29%	0.00%	Bajaj Finance	7.14%	16.67%	13.40%	Bajaj Finance	7.36%	16.67%	13.40%	Bajaj Finance	0.00%	9.09%	12.84%
Bajaj Finance	7.46%	14.29%	13.40%	Infosys	42.40%	16.67%	38.78%	Infosys	41.60%	16.67%	37.72%	Bharti Airtel	10.00%	9.09%	0.00%
Infosys	41.65%	14.29%	38.78%	Titan	20.91%	16.67%	18.52%	Titan	20.55%	16.67%	19.02%	Infosys	23.39%	9.09%	40.04%
Titan	20.59%	14.29%	18.52%	Power Grid	27.21%	16.67%	6.84%	Power Grid	26.29%	16.67%	6.48%	Larsen & Toubro	4.87%	9.09%	0.00%
Power Grid	26.45%	14.29%	6.84%	Tata Steel	1.13%	16.67%	14.46%	Tata Steel	0.94%	16.67%	15.66%	Mahindra & Mahindra	0.00%	9.09%	0.00%
Tata Steel	0.57%	14.29%	14.46%									Titan	8.15%	9.09%	20.75%
												Sun Pharma	12.83%	9.09%	0.00%
												Power Grid	13.29%	9.09%	8.67%
												Reliance	13.43%	9.09%	0.00%
												Tata Steel	0.00%	9.09%	17.69%

MVP = minimum variance portfolio; EWP= equally weighted portfolio, ORP = optimal risky portfolio; PR = portfolio expected return; PSTD = portfolio standard deviation; SR = Sharpe ratio

Source: Based on the authors' calculations.

Steel representing equity has the best reward-risk ratio. It also offers a better reward-risk ratio as compared to an all-equity portfolio. Hence, the authors recommend this portfolio to retail investors interested in cryptocurrencies and equities. Further, they can achieve their desired risk level by following James Tobin's extension of MPT, that is, through risk-free borrowing and lending.

Note

1 www.rbi.org.in/Scripts/BS_NSDPDisplay.aspx?param=4

4 The impact of inequality and poverty on cryptocurrency use

Artur Tomeczek and Marta Tomeczek

Introduction

This research aims to establish the relationship between economic inequality and cryptocurrency use. Income and wealth inequalities are some of the most important aspects of modern economies, both developed and developing. As far as economics goes, many aspects of cryptocurrencies remain relatively unexplored. The chapter starts with the narrative literature review of relevant issues and then moves to empirical analysis. In this chapter, economic inequality in a quite different new aspect was considered.

Literature review

The possible impact of economic inequality on cryptocurrency use was explored. Since its inception, Bitcoin has been a revolutionary change in the monetary system. Its major feature is decentralization (Gupta & Shukla, 2019). These days, there are many other important cryptocurrencies, such as Litecoin, Dogecoin, Ether, XRM, and Dash (Będowska-Sójka et al., 2021). In 2018, there was an impressive amount of almost 2,000 different cryptocurrencies being traded (Aste, 2019). The discussion of the benefits of cryptocurrency use brings out some moral questions applicable to the normative approach, for example, privacy, censorship resistance, and financial inclusion (Bailey et al., 2021). Cybercrime is shown to have a destabilizing effect on the cryptocurrency market (Corbet et al., 2020b).

Other than conducting transactions, there are many reasons for buying cryptocurrencies, such as safeguarding against inflation (Blau et al., 2021; Rosales, 2021) or speculative investment (Baur et al., 2018; Grobys & Junttila, 2021). General motivations for Bitcoin investment can be classified into three categories (Mattke et al., 2021):

- Perception about Bitcoin (profit expectancy, ease of Bitcoin acquisition, support of Bitcoin ideology)
- Personal factors (investment skills, risk affinity)
- Regret sentiments (experienced inaction regret, anticipated inaction regret)

DOI: 10.4324/9781003310365-4

According to a survey conducted in Germany, cryptocurrency users are most likely to be young, well-educated, relatively wealthy, and male (Steinmetz et al., 2021). A survey of initial coin offering (ICO) investors also shows that they are predominantly well-educated educated males motivated by technological enthusiasm, financial gains, and ideology (Fisch et al., 2021).

Cryptocurrency forecasting is notoriously difficult due to their unpredictability. There are conditions for the creation of speculative bubbles in the cryptocurrency market, which increases the possibility of a sudden collapse in cryptocurrency prices (Fry, 2018). Cryptocurrencies as assets are characterized by very high volatility and large, abrupt price swings (Chaim & Laurini, 2019). This inherent volatility has led to many innovative approaches to cryptocurrency forecasting such as sentiment analysis (Kraaijeveld & De Smedt, 2020), machine learning (Chowdhury et al., 2020), and deep learning (Lahmiri & Bekiros, 2019; Livieris et al., 2020, 2021). Forecasting accuracy can be improved by the use of data obtained from Twitter (Kraaijeveld & De Smedt, 2020) or Google Trends (Nasir et al., 2019).

Income and wealth inequalities are some of the most important aspects of modern economies, both developed and developing. When it comes to the collection of reliable worldwide data, measurement, and spread of information about excessive economic inequality, Piketty (2015) provides one of the most important scientific contributions in the field of economic inequality. His works have contributed to the creation of a team of scientists named World Inequality Lab. Every year, the *World Inequality Report* is published. This global data source is unique in its completion and availability. The latest *World Inequality Report 2022* (Chancel et al., 2022) describes the income and wealth inequalities both in countries and all over the world. The methodology chosen by Chancel et al. (2022) makes it possible to quantify that half of the population with the lowest income/wealth consume globally less of the Earth's resources than the top 1% of the world's population (total CO_2 emissions: bottom 50% generate 12%, top 1% generate 17%).

Inequality is one of the most important problems of the market economy and social development. Mostly it is considered with poverty and the access to essential goods (food, drinking water, and energy), services (health and education), and opportunities (personal, social, and economic freedoms and rights). The issue of inequality has been the subject of many historical and modern-day debates. Influential authors have asked themselves how it is possible, that most of the benefits of economic growth are captured by the richest part of the population. The absolute income gap between the poorest and richest cannot disappear because of the same relatively measured growth (Atkinson & Brandolini, 2009).

Economic inequality was a lifetime subject of Atkinson's (Atkinson, 1970, 2015; Atkinson et al., 2011) scientific interest. His great contributions to the measurement of inequality include the Atkinson index. Atkinson (1970) points out the differences between the measures of inequality and the fact that the choice of the measure is extremely important. He also proposed many solutions for reducing the extensive inequality (Atkinson, 2015). Stiglitz (2013) puts special significance on the extremely high level of inequality in the United States. He finds that inequality has been on the rise since the implementation of Reaganomics and the deregulation of the financial sector in the late 1970s.

The issue of economic equality is commonly considered antagonistic to economic freedom. It became so controversial that it is relevant to apply for the issue both descriptive and prescriptive approaches (M. Tomeczek, 2017). Such an approach allows for characterization and measurement to be separate from norms and purposes. The descriptive approach is free from the normative view and controversies (Czarny, 2010). Although theoretically economic inequality can be seen as a force motivating greater individual efforts, many authors claim that unfettered inequality can be the cause of many severe problems in economies. For example, Kalecki (1942) shows that the issue of excessive inequalities can lead to a substantial reduction in global demand. Galbraith (2009) ascertains that the glaring inequality was one of the causes of the global crises. A commission chaired by Joseph E. Stiglitz (United Nations, 2009) similarly sees the growing inequality as one of the reasons for the 2008 financial crisis. Banerjee and Duflo (2003) find that the relationship between economic growth and inequality is nonlinear.

Economic inequality is closely related to one of the most important philosophic questions about justice itself. Social justice combines the philosophic concept of fairness and the economic dilemma of the income distribution. The validity of common social acceptance of the chosen way of distribution of goods is emphasized by Rawls (2013) with his famous "justice as fairness." Similarly, Sen (1979) has taken a keen interest and accomplished considerable academic work on the subject of justice. Equity – in some defined dimension – is for him the essential requirement of justice. He also provided the idea of basic capability equality (Sen, 1979).

The growing interest in this topic can be seen in a large number of empirical publications on the degree of economic inequality in individual economies. These include countries such as France (Jetten et al., 2020; Lefranc, 2018; Piketty, 2003), Germany (Alfani et al., 2022; Behringer et al., 2020; Biewen, 2000), Japan (Ohtake, 2008; A. F. Tomeczek, 2016; Yamada, 2012), Poland (Brzeziński, 2013; Panek, 2017; Szopa, 2005; Zwiech, 2016), and the United States (Heathcote et al., 2010; Rumberger, 2010; Saez & Zucman, 2016; Stiglitz, 2013).

Methodology

The method of empirical analysis used in this study is a linear regression model (ordinary least squares) based on cross-sectional data. The two working hypotheses were proposed. [H1] Income inequality has a statistically significant impact on cryptocurrency use. [H2] Wealth inequality has a statistically significant impact on cryptocurrency use.

Table 4.1 Variables

Variable	*Type*	*Definition*	*Source*	*Transformation*
CRYPTO	Dependent	The value of Global Crypto Adoption Index 2021	2021 Geography of Cryptocurrency Report	ln(x+1)
GDP	Regressor	Nominal value of gross domestic product, 2020 (billion USD)	World Economic Outlook	ln(x)
GDPPC	Regressor	Nominal value of gross domestic product per capita, 2020 (USD)	World Economic Outlook	ln(x)
CPI	Regressor	Average value of consumer price index, 2011–2020 (%)	World Economic Outlook	ln(x+1)
DEBT	Regressor	General government gross debt, 2020 (% of GDP)	World Economic Outlook	ln(x+1)
INCOME	Regressor	Top 1% share of the pre-tax national income, 2020 (%)	World Inequality Database	ln(x)
WEALTH	Regressor	Top 1% share of net personal wealth for adults, 2020 (%)	World Inequality Database	ln(x)

Source: Own preparation.

The data for the model is taken from the Global Crypto Adoption Index published in the *2021 Geography of Cryptocurrency Report* (Chainalysis, 2021), the World Economic Outlook (IMF, 2022c), and the World Inequality Database (WID, 2022). Table 4.1 shows the variables included in both linear regression models. The variables of interest are INCOME and WEALTH, representing both types of economic inequality. There should not be simultaneous causality between the dependent variable and regressors representing economic inequality since cryptocurrencies are a relatively new phenomenon.

There are 157 countries included in the 2021 Global Crypto Adoption Index(Chainalysis, 2021c). Economies with the highest value of this indicator are Vietnam, India, Pakistan, Ukraine, Kenya, Nigeria, Venezuela, the United States, Togo, and Argentina. Due to data availability, the main model (Model_1) includes 143 countries. The alternative model (Model_2) excludes two potential outliers: Vietnam (due to a very high Crypto Adoption Index) and Venezuela (due to a very high inflation rate).

Results

The results of the models are shown in Tables 4.2 and 4.3 Coefficients in Model_1 and Model_2 have relatively similar results for the variables of interest. Both models are statistically significant based on the calculated F-statistic and p-value.

Table 4.2 Summary: Model_1

```
## Residuals:
##     Min      1Q  Median     3Q     Max
## -1.4825 -0.3943 0.0592  0.3715  2.2392
##
## Coefficients:
##             EstimateStd. Error t  value Pr(>|t|)
## (Intercept) 3.87752     0.95236  4.072    7.89e-05 ***
## INCOME     -0.43136     0.24703  -1.746   0.0830.
## WEALTH      0.10798     0.30109  0.359    0.7204
## GDP         0.37031     0.03149  11.760   < 2e-16 ***
## GDPPC      -0.39439     0.05187  -7.603   4.25e-12 ***
## CPI         0.11024     0.06198  1.779    0.0775.
## DEBT        0.05249     0.08212  0.639    0.5238
## ---
## Signif. codes:  0 '***' 0.001 '**' 0.01 '*' 0.05 '.' 0.1 ' ' 1
##
## Residual standard error: 0.6046 on 136 degrees of freedom
## Multiple R-squared: 0.5522, Adjusted R-squared: 0.5324
## F-statistic: 27.95 on 6 and 136 DF, p-value: < 2.2e-16
```

Source: Own preparation.

Table 4.3 Summary: Model_2

```
## Residuals:
##      Min        1Q    Median       3Q      Max
## -1.41501  -0.39866   0.07349  0.38936  1.47069
##
## Coefficients:
##             EstimateStd. Error t  value  Pr(>|t|)
## (Intercept) 3.81690     0.92326  4.134   6.25e-05 ***
## INCOME     -0.44717     0.23513  -1.902   0.0594.
## WEALTH      0.20080     0.28617  0.702    0.4841
## GDP         0.36278     0.03017  12.024  < 2e-16 ***
## GDPPC      -0.40086     0.05144  -7.793  1.61e-12 ***
## CPI         0.03168     0.08259  0.384    0.7019
## DEBT        0.04674     0.07884  0.593    0.5543
## ---
## Signif. codes: 0 '***' 0.001 '**' 0.01 '*' 0.05 '.' 0.1 ' ' 1
##
## Residual standard error: 0.5729 on 134 degrees of freedom
## Multiple R-squared: 0.5559, Adjusted R-squared: 0.536
## F-statistic: 27.96 on 6 and 134 DF, p-value: < 2.2e-16
```

Source: Own preparation.

Table 4.4 Multicollinearity test

VIF	*INCOME*	*WEALTH*	*GDP*	*GDPPC*	*CPI*	*DEBT*
Model_1	2.474626	2.160117	1.351666	1.896699	1.406918	1.039493
Model_2	2.485527	2.170508	1.375946	2.0573	1.570531	1.015154

Source: Own preparation.

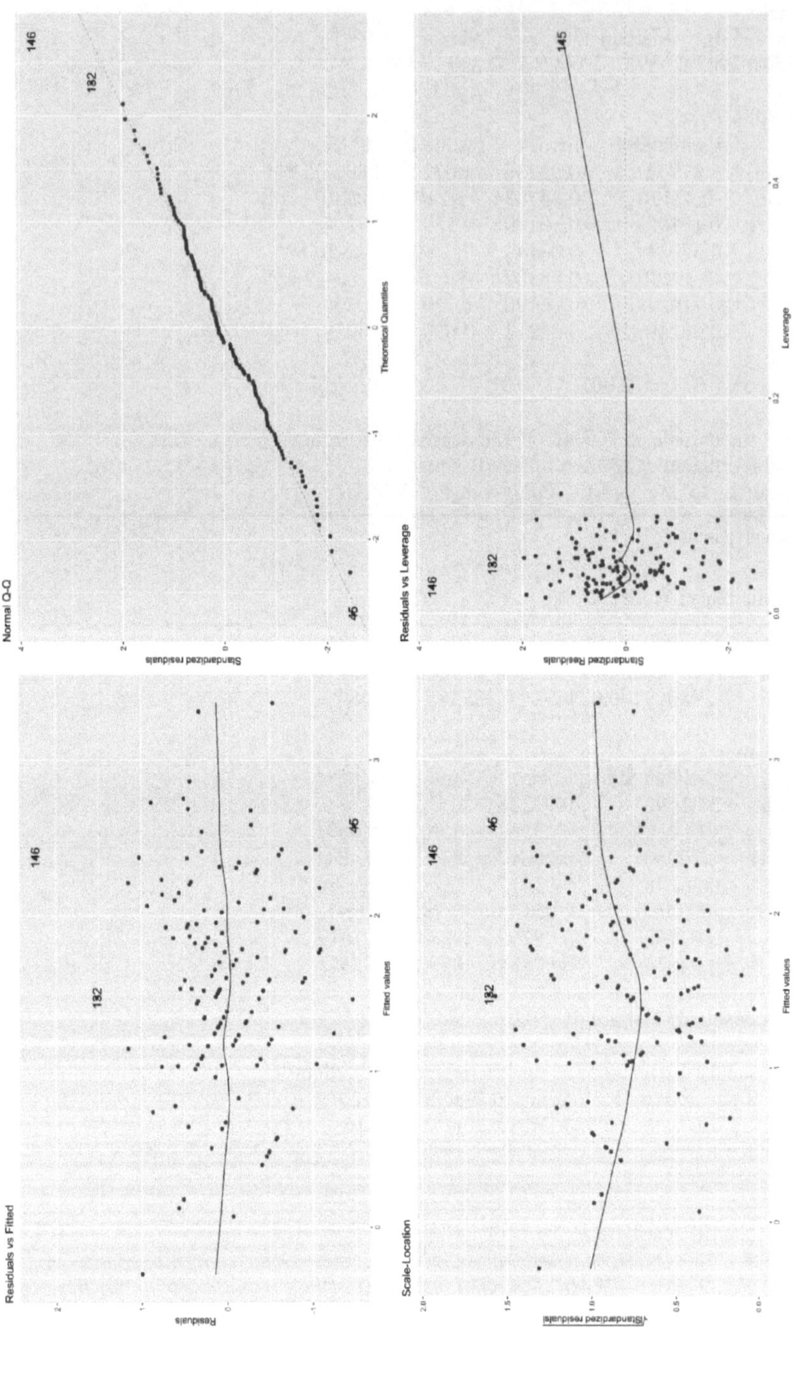

Figure 4.1 Residual diagnostics: Model_1

Source: Own preparation.

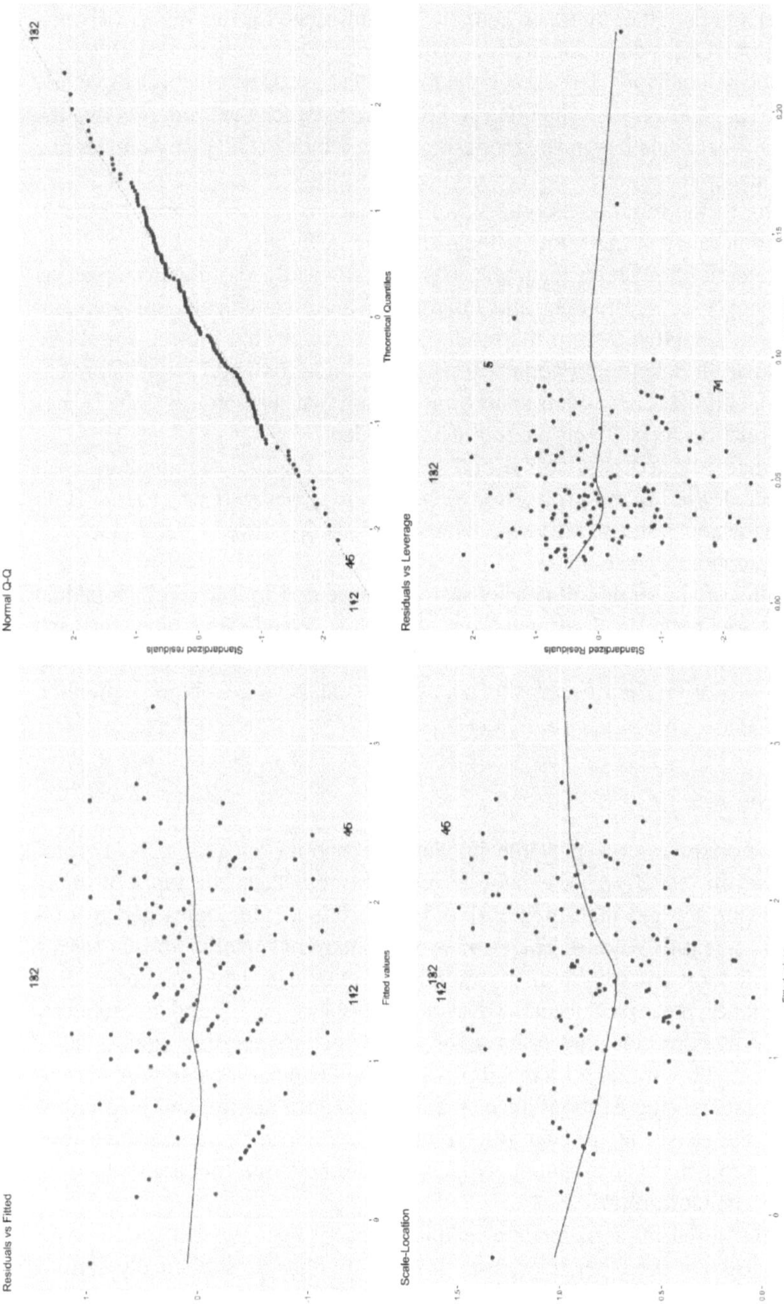

Figure 4.2 Residual diagnostics: Model_2

Source: Own preparation.

Somewhat surprisingly, the INCOME variable has a negative coefficient (−0.43136 in Model_1 and −0.44717 in Model_2). It is statistically significant at a 10% level. On the other hand, no statistical significance for the WEALTH variable was found. Gross domestic product (GDP) and GDP per capita (GDPPC) are statistically significant at a 0.1% level: the former has a positive relationship while the latter has a negative one. The biggest difference between the models is that the exclusion of Venezuela has pushed Consumer Price Index (CPI) way outside the 10% significance level.

According to the models, a country is more likely to have a high cryptocurrency adoption rate if it has a low value of income inequality and is a large, relatively poor economy. Wealth inequality has no statistically significant impact on cryptocurrency use. Public debt and inflation also are statistically insignificant (if Venezuela is excluded from the model). The safeguarding motive should be more prevalent in developing countries where the inflation and risk of depreciation are much higher. The models somewhat confirm that suspicion as GDPPC has a negative relationship with cryptocurrency adoption.

H1 is tentatively accepted so the null hypothesis at a 10% significance level can be rejected. For H2, no ground to reject the null hypothesis was found. Both models fail to show a statistically significant relationship between wealth inequality and cryptocurrency use.

The results of the multicollinearity test are presented in Table 4.2. Residual diagnostics are shown in Figures 4.1 and 4.2. They include four plots for each model: Residuals vs Fitted (linear relationship), Normal Q-Q (normal distribution), Scale-Location (homoscedasticity), and Residuals vs Leverage (influential observations).

Conclusion

This research explores the possible impact of economic inequality on cryptocurrency use. In recent years, economic inequality has been the topic of many descriptive (impact and measurement) and prescriptive (ideologies and recommendations) scientific studies. The proxies of economic inequality chosen for the analysis are income and wealth distribution in societies. Since their inception, Bitcoin and other cryptocurrencies have disrupted the status quo of modern monetary systems. Cryptocurrencies are often associated with safeguarding against inflation, speculative investment, financial privacy, and financial inclusion. Additionally, psychological (regret about missing a financial opportunity) and ideological (support of the cause) factors can play a significant role for potential investors. Despite the growing mainstream appeal, cryptocurrency investors are still a relatively homogeneous group.

According to the models, income inequality has a negative impact on cryptocurrency use. On the other hand, wealth inequality has no statistically significant relationship with cryptocurrency use. Additionally, a country is more likely to have a high cryptocurrency adoption rate if it is a large and relatively poor economy. The linear regression analysis is based on the data from the *2021 Geography of Cryptocurrency Report*, the World Economic Outlook, and the World Inequality Database. The safeguarding motive should be more prevalent in developing countries where the inflation and risk of depreciation are much higher. Our models somewhat confirm that suspicion as GDPPC has a negative relationship with cryptocurrency adoption.

5 The price and promise of cryptocurrencies

Meelis Kitsing

Introduction

The emergence of cryptocurrencies has led to considerable debates over their nature and purpose (Garcia-Corral et al., 2022). Advocates insist that they will increasingly start substituting traditional currencies. Sceptics dismiss such claims by arguing that cryptocurrencies can be seen as speculative investment products which lack characteristics of real money (Eichengreen, 2022).

However, it cannot be ignored that cryptocurrencies were worth almost two trillion US dollars in April 2022, which is about 15 percent of global foreign exchange reserves (Greene, 2022). By comparison, Microsoft, one of the largest digital platforms in the world, had market capitalization of slightly higher than two trillion US dollars in April 2022, while Meta Platforms (formerly Facebook) had market capitalization 3.5 times lower than that.

The ecosystem of cryptocurrencies is characterized by oligopolistic competition where a couple of players such as Bitcoin, Tether and Ethereum dominate while overall market participants come in different shapes and sizes.

This chapter will focus specifically on cryptocurrencies which is seen as a subset of broader category digital currencies. Obviously, such distinctions can often be blurred and are subject to conceptual stretching. However, even this inadequate self-imposed constraint leaves the discussion of digital currencies such as central bank digital currency to other chapters in this volume.

Considerable amount of research has been tackling cryptocurrencies from various angles (Garcia-Corral et al., 2022). This chapter starts by taking a perspective of governance of complex semi-public goods. Money as medium of exchange can be seen as a complex semi-public good. The chapter will explore whether cryptocurrencies have elements of complex semi-public goods, that is promise to become a substantial medium of exchange or is it just investment product which is more likely to be a private good.

This is followed by placing costs and benefits of cryptocurrencies into a wider context on exchange rate debates – particularly integrating questions over the volatility of cryptocurrencies with that of different perspectives in economics concerning exchange rates. Broadly, one school of thought has seen exchange rate as a price. As price controls are inefficient way to regulate the markets, then prices of

DOI: 10.4324/9781003310365-5

currencies should be allowed to fluctuate as well. They emphasize the economic costs of fixed exchange rates (Friedman & Mundell, 2001).

However, another school of thought sees the exchange rate as a promise where constant fluctuations represent a default on the commitment. It points out that exchange rate uncertainty imposes a cost for economic transactions similarly as tariffs and other taxes (Friedman & Mundell, 2001).

These conceptually different approaches will be extended to exploring the merits of different cryptocurrencies in the second part of the chapter. Most cryptocurrencies rely on the benefits of price adjustments in the markets while some such as so-called stablecoins have recognized uncertainty stemming from volatility of cryptocurrency valuations as the main obstacle for becoming substitutes for traditional currencies. The conclusion offers key take-aways from governance of complex semi-public goods for future trajectories of cryptocurrencies.

Currencies as complex semi-public goods

This chapter takes explicitly a public goods perspective by linking broader debates on governance of monetary systems with that governance of various cryptocurrencies. Monetary system can be seen as a public good because it is an essential backbone of modern economies (Felber, 2017; Montani, 2011). Particularly, monetary system can be seen as a public good because both benefits such as stability and costs such as volatility of currencies are exclusive, that is, positive and negative externalities are not internalized by providers of currency. If the monetary system is managed well, then all users of currency may benefit from its trust and stability. However, such view has been rejected by White (1999) because monetary holdings of private individuals are not equally accessible to everybody. In the case of typical public goods, consumption choices of individuals are non-rivalry (White, 1999).

However, public goods perspective on money does not imply that there are no distributional impacts, that is, some benefit more than others from monetary holdings and from monetary stability. The basic political economy suggests that there are always distributional impacts associated with public goods (Broz & Frieden, 2001). Usually, economists suggest that consumption of air as an example of public good and assume that air consumption by some individuals and firms does not affect consumption choices of other individuals. However, air in countryside may be fresher than in city or some parts of city may have fresher air than others because of smaller number of polluters.

Most importantly, well-governed monetary system has important elements mimicking public goods. It may be also a global public good such as the US dollar which remained the primary reserve currency while the relative economic might of United States has declined. To understand complexities involved in defining the nature of goods, it is worth reminding the typology of goods developed by Ostrom and Ostrom (1977).

They suggest that there are four types of goods. First, private goods where exclusion is easy and "subtractability" or rivalry is high. Second, public goods where exclusion is difficult and subtractability is easy. Third, common-pool resources where exclusion is difficult and subtractability is high. Fourth, toll or club goods with easy exclusion and low subtractability (Ostrom & Ostrom, 1977).

These four categories of goods suggest that the choice is not binary between public and private goods. There are grey areas between different types of goods as difficult or easy exclusion and high or low rivalry can be conceptualized differently. Most importantly, goods can be seen on spectrum where they evolve over time. Money used to be more similar to private good but has evolved over time to acquire elements of public good. Money is a semi-public good.

Semi-public goods

The conventional wisdom assumes that public goods are provided and governed by public sector organizations. For instance, European Central Bank is responsible for governance of the eurozone. At the same time, the governance of US Federal Reserve system can be seen as semi-public, not purely public, because of complex interactions between private and public sector actors.

Even more importantly, public goods can be provided also by private means as Coase (1974) has demonstrated. Conventional wisdom in economics often assumed that lighthouse is a classic example of so-called pure public good. Lighthouses are usually owned by the public sector and provide services that benefit everybody at sea who needs to follow signals. In other words, their services are exclusive and not rivalry. However, Coase (1974) showed on the basis of historical evidence that lighthouses have often been privately owned and operated. In other words, provision of public goods by private entities is a historical fact.

Another historical example is the free banking in Scotland in the 18th and 19th centuries where private banks had right to emit their own currencies which served as essential part of monetary system. White (1999) see free banking primarily in terms of private organizations and market forces at work. However, most banks were allowed to issue their own notes only on the basis of unlimited liability while three largest banks were granted limited liability by Scottish Parliament (Carr et al., 1989). In other words, there are semi-public elements in the free banking system. Similarly, the Bank of England, a central bank of UK, started as a private organization in 1694 but its charter had to be approved by the Parliament (Goodman, 2009). This should not surprise economic historians and political economists because 17–18th centuries were heydays of mercantilism in Britain where state and commercial interests were strongly intertwined.

In the digital realm, open-source software can be seen as a semi-public good which offer insights into nexus of digitalization and money as in the case of cryptocurrencies. Open-source software development is about process which is primarily carried out by private individuals and organizations (Schweik & English, 2012).

Anybody can freely use open-source software and its source code is also public. However, it does not mean that everybody can freely modify its source code because the governance and rules do not make it simple (Schweik & Kitsing,

2010). Furthermore, the use of open-source software can be also complicated for ordinary users and may require specific expertise. Hence, open-source software can be seen as complex semi-public good.

Essentially, cryptocurrencies have also elements of complex semi-public goods and similarities with open-source software are obvious. First, cryptocurrencies are primarily provided by private organizations. Second, the use of cryptocurrencies requires specific skills which is also the case with open-source software. Third, development of cryptocurrencies takes place through different organizational forms – ranging from social movements to for-profit platforms – which is a key characteristic to open-source software movement. Fourth, users are often developers and vice versa. Obviously, cryptocurrencies itself are not exclusive and non-rivalry. However, the cost and benefits of cryptocurrency system are not limited to its ultimate users. Mining of Bitcoin may bring about negative externalities for consumption of energy while digitalization of monetary system through cryptocurrencies may reduce transaction costs increasing overall efficiency.

Exchange rates

The key mechanism for governance of monetary system is through exchange rates by allowing either decentralized market mechanism or centralized authority to set the course. The debates between advocates of flexible interest rates and fixed interest rates has a long history in economics (Obstfeld & Rogoff, 1995). Essentially, it is a debate about the governance of monetary system where various alternatives between fixed and flexible arrangement represent trade-offs (Broz & Frieden, 2001). These trade-offs are well-summarized by a debate between two Nobel economics prize laureates Milton Friedman and Robert Mundell in 2001.

Obviously, the choice between fixed and flexible exchange rates is not binary because there are many grey areas between completely fixed and flexible interest rates which is emphasized by both Friedman and Mundell (Friedman & Mundell, 2001). There are different systems of fixed exchange rates such as "dollarization" where country adopts currency of other country in its daily use. For instance, Montenegro has adopted euro without joining the eurozone.

Another option is currency board where domestic currency in circulation is pegged to assets in foreign currency. For instance, Estonia operated a monetary system mimicking currency board from 1992 to 2011 before joining the eurozone. Initially, exchange rate of Estonian kroon was fixed to German mark which was later replaced by the euro. And then there are fixed exchange rate regimes such as in Denmark where Danish krona is fixed to euro. This is followed by variety of semi-pegged and semi-floating monetary regimes such as managed float where central banks may intervene in monetary system dependent on specific conditions (IMF, 2004).

Both Mundell and Friedman are sceptics of grey area of pegged rates. "The reasons why a pegged exchange rate is a ticking bomb are well known," argues Friedman (Friedman & Mundell, 2001). Mundell concurs: "I have never nor ever would advocate a general system of 'pegged' rates. Pegged rate systems always break down" (Friedman & Mundell, 2001).

In a nutshell, the case can be made for freely floating exchange rates or for fixed exchange rates if users of monetary system are willing to live with the consequences. As Meltzer argues: "You can't make much of a case for anything in between" (quoted in Deardorff, 2016).

However, the consequences are seen differently by advocates of fixed and floating exchange rates. Friedman highlights benefits of more flexible monetary arrangement, particularly for larger countries. Friedman argues:

> A country that enters into a hard-fixed rate bears an economic cost. The cost is discarding a means – a flexible exchange rate – of adjusting to external forces that impinge on it differently than on the other country or countries whose currency it shares.
>
> (Friedman & Mundell, 2001)

Mundell points out that he and Friedman share many basic assumptions and goals but they do differ in emphasizing the benefits and costs of different exchange rate arrangements. Mundell argues:

> A world currency of some sort has existed for most of the past 2,500 years. Two thousand years ago, in the age of Caesar Augustus, it was the Roman aureus . . .. A hundred years ago it was the gold sovereign. Less than thirty years ago it was the 1944 gold dollar. The world has been without a universal currency for only a tiny fraction of its history.
>
> (Friedman & Mundell, 2001)

Stark differences in understanding consequences of fixed and flexible exchange rate arrangements reveal how the nature of exchange rates is seen by economists. Bradford De Long has summarized the debate succinctly:

> To Mr. Friedman, an exchange rate is a price; therefore, it is an infringement on human freedom to peg it. To Mr. Mundell, an exchange rate is a promise; to change it is to default on a commitment.
>
> (quoted in Deardorff, 2016)

The focus on exchange rate either as a price or promise points towards the impossible trinity of goals for any monetary system. Ideally, decision-makers have three goals which are mutually incompatible. The first goal is monetary independence which presumes exchange rate flexibility and capital controls. Fixing exchange rates would reduce independence while capital controls give decision-makers more autonomy (Deardorff, 2016; Broz & Frieden, 2001).

The second goal is exchange rate stability which presumes fixing exchange rates and or capital controls. Both help to reduce market volatility which endangers stability. The third goal is full financial integration which is undermined by both capital controls and high market volatility. Only two out of three goals can be achieved at the same time.

Those who see exchange rate as a price are more likely to prefer floating exchange rates and full financial integration at the expense of exchange rate stability. Those who see exchange rate as a promise are more likely to prefer fixed exchange rate and full financial integration at the expense of monetary policy autonomy. The latter can obviously also boosted through capital controls which are still in fashion at some countries.

The impossible trinity for cryptocurrencies

These insights from dynamics of impossible trinity are relevant for cryptocurrencies. Most attention has been paid to decentralized cryptocurrencies such as Bitcoin and Ethereum, which emphasize the importance of price (Garcia-Corral et al., 2022). Such cryptocurrencies are based on exchange rate flexibility and financial integration vis-a-vis other currencies. However, the consequence is high volatility of price of such cryptocurrency which obviously reduces stability and increases transaction costs for their use (Eichengreen, 2022).

However, there are also another type of cryptocurrencies called stablecoins such as Tether and USD coins which are pegged to US dollar (Eichengreen, 2022; Stacey, 2022). There are also stablecoins fixed to gold such as PAX and Tether Gold. These cryptocurrencies follow the insights of Mundell by promising exchange rate stability. As a result, they have to give up benefits and costs of floating exchange rate as long as their goal is to secure financial integration, that is, tradability with other currencies. Indeed, stablecoins facilitate exchange between different cryptoassets as well as a bridge between traditional financial system and decentralized blockchain-based systems. Price stability makes stablecoins safe haven particularly for times with high volatility in other cryptocurrency markets (Lepcha, 2022).

The nature of cryptocurrencies

The market capitalization of cryptocurrencies was almost 1.9 trillion US dollars on April 12, 2022 (Slickcharts, 2022). Ten largest cryptocurrencies represent almost 80 percent of this market capitalization. The largest market capitalization of 763 billion USD belongs to Bitcoin with market share of 41 percent (Table 5.1). The second is Ethereum with market capitalization of 363 billion US dollars and market share of 19.5 percent. Decentralized cryptocurrencies with flexible exchange rates dominate according to market capitalization while only two stablecoins are among the top ten – Tether with market capitalization of 83 billion US dollars and market share of 4.4 percent as well as USD coin with market capitalization 51 billion US dollars and market share of 2.7 percent.

Essentially, cryptocurrencies have certain elements complex semi-public goods as was argued earlier. In many ways, cryptocurrencies are similar to open-source software which requires sophisticated skills. Hence, it is not surprising that most people shun from the use of cryptocurrencies as they do from open-source

Table 5.1 Top-ten cryptocurrencies by market capitalization and exchange rate

Currency	*Market capitalization (billion USD)*	*Approximate Market share (%)*	*Exchange rate (flexible or fixed)*
Bitcoin	763	41	Flexible
Ethereum	363	19.5	Flexible
Tether	83	4.4	Fixed to USD
BNB	67	3.6	Flexible
USD Coin	51	2.7	Fixed to USD
XRP	34	1.8	Flexible
Solana	34	1.8	Flexible
Cardano	32	1.7	Flexible
Terra	30	1.6	Flexible
Avalanche	21	1.1	Flexible

Source: Author with data from Slickcharts (2022).

software. This has led sceptics of cryptocurrencies to conclude that they are not usable as money. Eichengreen points out:

> Most obviously, plain-vanilla cryptocurrencies lack the essential attributes of money, namely providing a stable store of value, accepted unit of account, and convenient means of payment. . . . This volatility makes it unattractive as a unit of account in which to price merchandise and set wages. It is inconvenient for payments, requiring the user to possess a degree of technological sophistication, a secure digital wallet, a reliably recalled password, and, not least, a counterparty prepared to accept it. Validating transactions through so-called Proof of Work, in which users of the distributed ledger solve arbitrary mathematical problems, is notoriously intensive in its consumption of energy and computational resources.
>
> (Eichengreen, 2022)

Eichengreen's summary on complexities, however, overstates the difficulties in using cryptocurrencies and understates benefits stemming from decentralization and digitalization. As with open-source software, dedicated individuals with appropriate skillset can still use cryptocurrencies as a medium of exchange.

Most importantly, cryptocurrencies have similarities with user-driven innovation present in open-source software development where developers are often also users of software. Similarly, Bitcoin miners are also users of Bitcoin. Furthermore, not all traditional monetary systems are also hallmarks of stability and currency convertibility. In such systems, cryptocurrencies can serve as substitutes for traditional money despite the complexities because concrete trade-offs over even more complex use of traditional currency. The use of US dollar or euro may not be easily available.

Stablecoins

The volatility of cryptocurrencies is tackled by stablecoins such as Tether and US Coin which have fixed their exchange rate to US dollar. This arrangement ensures exchange rate stability and convertibility which, in turn, should increase trust in stablecoins. Approximate market share of stablecoins was 8 percent in April 2022. This indicates that most users of prefer more volatile cryptocurrencies. Another more pessimistic interpretation might be that potential users are not confident how is credible commitment to fixed exchange rate. One of the sceptics Eichengreen points out:

> A stablecoin is only as stable as the collateral standing behind it. If an issuer holds a dollar's worth of US cash in reserve for every dollar coin it issues, then there should be no question about its ability to redeem that stablecoin at par on demand. But having to raise a dollar of capital from investors in order to issue a dollar's worth of stablecoin is expensive, unprofitable, and therefore nonviable.
>
> (Eichengreen, 2022)

However, the exchange rate fragility can be to certain extent present in any currency based on fixed exchange rate. Particularly, acute can it be in the fractional reserve banking of developing countries and emerging economies. Argentina used to have a currency board (strongest type of fixed exchange rate regimes) which in the end did not stop the country to go successive devaluations of its currency (Feldstein, 2002). At the same time, significantly smaller Estonia was able to maintain stability of currency board system for almost two decades before joining the eurozone (OECD, 2011). The commitment to exchange rate was hold in the turbulent times of financial crisis of 2008–2009 which saw Estonian's GDP to shrink 20 percent while currency traders in London questioned the credibility of exchange rate commitment. Whether the stablecoins will become Argentina or Estonia remains to be seen.

Most importantly, emerging elements of complex semi-public goods cannot be dismissed immediately. If the stablecoins provide currency stability instead of ad hoc volatility, then they are also more likely to increase trust and wider use – essential for becoming semi-public goods.

Fictional currencies

There is also third category of cryptocurrencies which are primarily usable within specific digital ecosystems and cannot be traded with outside players. For instance, Farm Ville, which was once the most popular game on Facebook, used Farm Cash for transactions within the game. As players, many of them under age, ran up significant debts Farmville's developer was heavily criticized and the game was closed down in 2021.

In a way, such systems are similar to the non-convertible currency of China where independence of monetary system is secured by exchange rate management and capital controls. In other words, such currencies have sacrificed full financial integration. Obviously, there is also market for converting Farm Cash into convertible currency but such markets are limited and cost of transactions is high – as it would be the case with converting Chinese currency into convertible currencies.

Secretive US company Lantern has developed cryptocurrency called Yinbi which can be used to compensate those who allow their computers to act as hubs within decentralized peer-to-peer network (Gilbert, 2022). The company offers VPN-like service, which is more effective than traditional VPN in accessing websites that authorities have decided to block. The Lantern app is widely used in Russia and China. Yinbi as a cryptocurrency for transactions within the Lantern ecosystem is increasingly relevant in Russia because the rouble has become non-convertible. Other examples of cryptocurrencies used within specific ecosystems can be found in video games such as Poke dollars in Pokemon, Simoleons in the Sims, Minecoins in Minecraft or Rings in the Sonic which can be called "fictional currencies" (Wilson, 2021).

In sum, such fictional currencies are not representatives of other cryptocurrencies with the exception – perhaps– of Yinbi and similar currencies. They are less likely to emerge into semi-public goods and more likely to stay private instruments for the use within particular private ecosystem.

Conclusion

Sceptics argue that decentralized cryptocurrencies like Bitcoin are too volatile to possess the essential attributes of medium of exchange. They are really meant for speculative investments. For sceptics, stablecoins with fixed exchange rates have fragile currency pegs that diminish their utility in transactions.

While admitting that many issues pose difficulties for cryptocurrencies to serve as a medium of exchange, this chapter highlighted emerging elements in cryptocurrencies which allow them to become semi-public goods used by a wider set of stakeholders. Indeed, harsh reality of cryptocurrencies should not be benchmarked against idealized world of traditional currencies. Many imperfections present in cryptocurrencies can be found also in traditional currency systems. Most currencies are semi-public goods with significant distributional impacts for their users.

Borrowing from the literature on the governance of complex semi-public goods, the chapter argued that many promising features are present in cryptocurrencies. As in the case of open-source software development, cryptocurrencies are often led by user-driven innovation. Although some entities dominate such as Bitcoin, diversity of different actors in all shapes and sizes combining elements of voluntary movement and profit-seeking entities bear also resemblance to open-source software development. This is quite different in the era of digitalization where a few centralized platforms dominate.

If cryptocurrencies emphasize such promising features rather than pure price, then they have prospects to develop into fully fledged medium of exchange which would be widely used. This requires a credible commitment to exchange rate stability which comes at the expense of autonomy. However, convertibility of cryptocurrencies requires dependence on traditional finance. It is a small price to pay for the promise.

6 The impact of money supply on the development of virtual currencies

Aneta Hryckiewicz and Piotr Filipiak

Introduction

In 2021, the total capitalization of Bitcoin, the most popular virtual currency, exceeded a trillion dollars, equivalent to more than 1 percent of global GDP (Morris, 2021; The World Bank, 2021). The virtual currency market has developed to such an extent in just twelve years. At the same time, since 2008, when Satoshi Nakamoto published an article entitled "Bitcoin: A Peer-to-Peer Electronic Cash System" (Nakamoto, 2008), a dramatic money supply in the global economy stemming from the rescue packages after the financial crisis of 2008 was noticed. Figure 6.1 shows the development of money supply in OECD countries measured by M3 and the annual average Bitcoin capitalization between the periods 2009 and 2022, when the first statistics for the virtual currency became available.

The potential correlation between Bitcoin capitalization and dramatic worldwide money supply raises the question of whether these two events could be interrelated. More specifically, the main interest is in the factors contributing to such dramatic development of the virtual currency market and thus its tremendous capitalization. One of the theories is that the loss of faith in the national governments and currencies, as a result of the financial crisis of 2008, has forced people to search for possibilities to invest their money outside the traditional financial sector (Carney, 2014). This behaviour has been further motived by the appearance of Satoshi Nakamoto's paper about Bitcoin, which has immediately gained the attraction of investors (Wolfson, 2015). At the same time, the governments were forced to implement the quantitative easing policy (QE) and reduce the interest rates to almost zero percentage to rescue the economies after the collapse of the global financial sector. This trend has brought a massive amount of cheap capital to the market, further incentivizing investors' interest in the virtual currency market.

The academic literature documents that "cheap" money increases investors' risk appetite and motivates them to search for potential investments outside the traditional financial sector. For example, Ridderstaat et al. (2017) document that an increase in money supply is positively correlated with the higher investment in Karaibes, such as in restaurants or hotels. However, Goetzmann et al. (2011) show that higher stock returns translate into higher demand for the art investment.

DOI: 10.4324/9781003310365-6

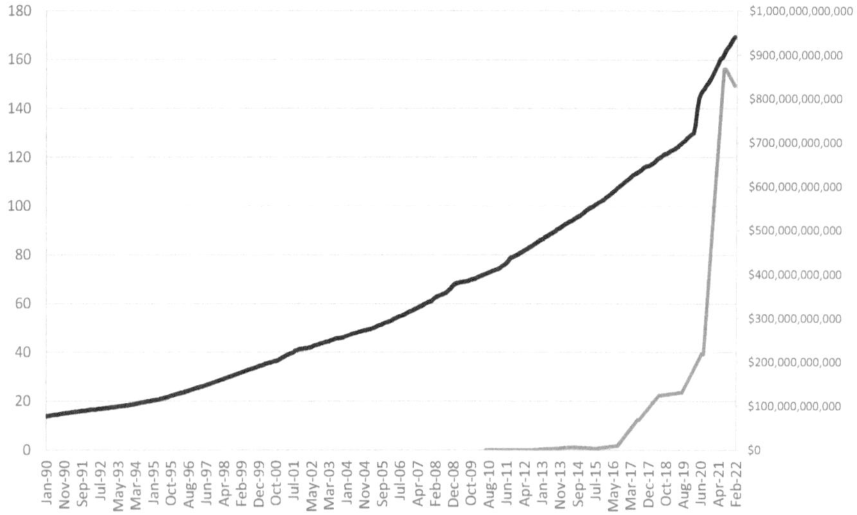

Figure 6.1 OECD M3 money supply (black; left axis; 2015 = 100), BTC market cap annual average (grey; right axis) (January 1990–February 2022)

Source: Own study based on Blockchain.com (2022) and OECD (2022b).

At the same time, if the investors' incentive was to make money outside the traditional financial sector, it should be expected that the virtual currency market to behave independently from the monetary policy decision and, thus, not be influenced by the money supply itself. For example, Corbet et al. (2017) claim that Bitcoin, due to its decentralized nature and independence from central institutions, should behave neutrally towards the monetary policy of individual countries and thus should not react to central bank announcements. However, the researchers find something opposite. The authors used Bitcoin to analyse how Bitcoin prices behave in the case of monetary policy announcements and the introduction of QE decisions from four central banks of the United States, the European Union, the United Kingdom and Japan. The authors examining the period between 2010 and 2016 document that all QE messages from the four central banks had a statistically significant positive impact on Bitcoin price volatility. Consequently, the authors concluded that since the central banks' decisions were reflected in the behaviour of Bitcoin, the virtual currency market, despite its decentralized nature, does not show independence from national monetary policies.

In this chapter, this topic was explored further. More specifically, there is an interest in whether the virtual currency market has been stimulated by the quantitative easing policy and dramatic money supply following the financial crisis of 2008. If so, this could provide an important message for the investors that the currencies do not behave independently from the national monetary policy and thus should be probably treated as another asset class.

The chapter is structured as follows. In the beginning, the development of the virtual currency was described and market and academic literature was analysed trying to examine the determinants of virtual currency development. Then the aspect of how the virtual currency market and different monetary policy regimes have translated into the attraction of this kind of investment. In the fourth section, the regression results documenting the effect of money supply in different countries on the transmission of the virtual currency market was presented. The final section concludes considerations and summarizes the results.

The development of the virtual currency market

The modern history of virtual currencies began with the publication of the article "Bitcoin: A Peer-to-Peer Electronic Cash System" by a person or a group of people hiding under the pseudonym Satoshi Nakamoto (Nakamoto, 2008). The article was published in 2008 on the cryptography discussion forum (Marr, 2017). The primary motivation for creating a virtual currency indicated by Satoshi Nakamoto was the desire to eliminate the so-called trusted third party from the payment transaction process, preventing double-spending. The proposed solution to the problem is a peer-to-peer network that stamps transactions with a timestamp, creating a blockchain that cannot be changed until the next transaction is performed. Satoshi pointed out that there is no equivalent of a value carrier on the Internet (cash, precious metals), which is passed from hand to hand, without the participation of a financial institution, as a provider of confidence in the transaction. A cash transaction is irreversible, while a transaction with electronic money and the use of a trusted provider is inherently reversible, as financial institutions cannot wholly withdraw from the issue of mediation between the parties to the transaction. The first Bitcoin block was created on January 3, 2009, by Satoshi Nakamoto. This block is called the "Genesis Block". In March 2010, the first exchange – bitcoinmarket.com, was created where the virtual currency could be traded, and investors could exchange US dollars for Bitcoins. Shortly afterwards, the largest and most popular stock exchange – Mt. Gox – was established.

A significant milestone in the history of the virtual currency market was the first purchase using Bitcoin. Laszlo Hanyecz, on May 22, 2010, ordered two pizzas and paid ten thousand Bitcoins for them. Figure 6.2 presents the subjective choice of the most critical events in the virtual currency market.

Bitcoin's popularity has also given rise to the development of other virtual currencies. At the end of 2021, more than 15,000 different virtual currencies were available on the market. The dynamics of the increase in the number of virtual currencies are presented in Figure 6.3.

Bitcoin was the first virtual currency, and it is still the most dominant virtual currency, reaching more than 40 percent dominance in terms of total capitalization at the beginning of 2022. Bitcoin held more than 80 percent dominance from its inception until March 2017, when there was a surge in interest in virtual currencies. In January 2018, its market share dropped to 39 percent due to some national restrictions; however, it then again increased its market share to 50 percent in August 2018, while coming back to its dominant 68 percent market

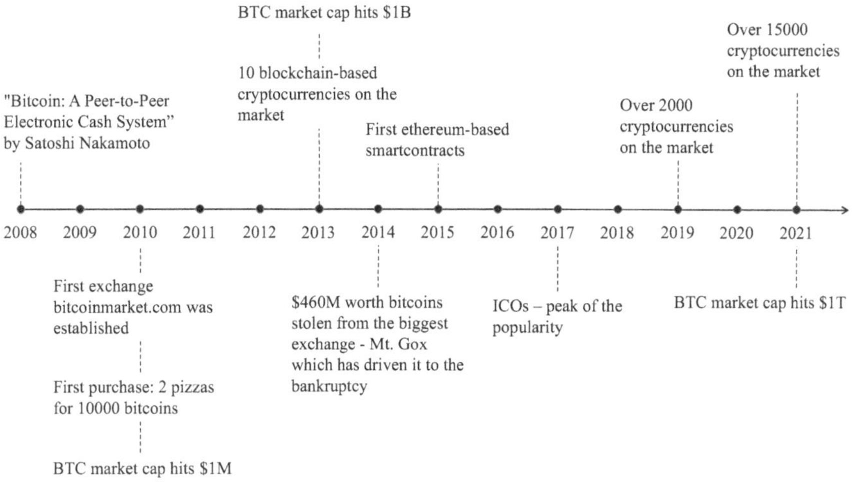

Figure 6.2 The most significant events in the virtual currency market development

Source: Own elaboration based on data from Coinmarketcap.com (2022).

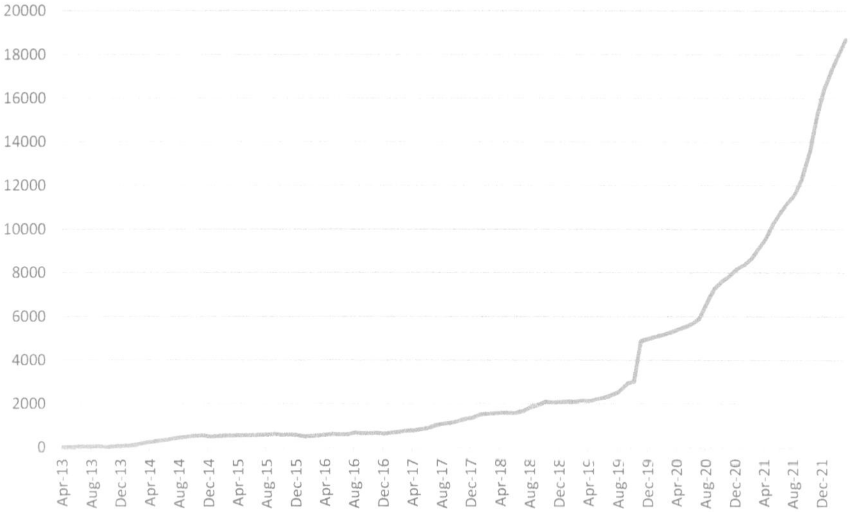

Figure 6.3 Number of virtual currencies in 2013–2022

Source: Own elaboration based on Coinmarketcap.com (2022).

share in August 2019 and then dropping to 40% level in April 2021. The second most popular virtual currency is Ethereum which has almost ten times lower capitalization than Bitcoin. Ethereum relies on blockchain technology and allows to send the virtual money "Ether" and settle different contracts using intelligent applications. The platform was created in 2013 on the initiative of Vitalik Buterin, a 20-one-year-old programmer from Russia ("Vitalik Buterin"), in order to enable the creation of decentralized applications. The third popular virtual currency is Ripple (XRP) which has almost sixteen times lower capitalization than Bitcoin. Figure 6.4 shows the market shares of different virtual currencies between 2013 and 2022.

According to the *reports of the "Global crypto assets benchmarking study"* (Hileman & Rauchs, 2017; Rauchs et al., 2019), the virtual currency economy is geographically diversified. In 2017, Asia-Pacific region accounted for 36 percent of virtual currency-related companies, Europe had 29 percent, and North America 27 percent. South America and Africa accounted for 6 percent and 2 percent, respectively. In 2018, Europe overtook the Asia-Pacific region, accounting for 43 percent of the global virtual currency market. Asia-Pacific accounted for 24 percent and North America for 17 percent. An increase in Africa was recently noticed – the Middle East (6 percent) and South America (9 percent). The global share of individual regions in the virtual currency business (measured by the ratio of number of companies operated on the virtual currency market to total companies) is shown in Table 6.1.

The countries with more than 20 cryptocurrency-established companies are the United States, China, Japan, India, Canada and the United Kingdom (Rauchs et al., 2019). Although the virtual currency's specificity requires only the internet, most companies have their operational centres in the same country where the headquarters are located. This fact is related to a more relaxed regulatory environment favourable to the virtual currency market (Rauchs et al., 2019).

Virtual currency and its pricing

In the international debate, the question of the phenomenon of virtual currencies has been highly discussed. However, this debate has mainly been unanswered. It is still unknown what factors have contributed to such a great interest and development of virtual currencies globally. An even bigger mystery is the extreme

Table 6.1 Participation in the global virtual currency industry

Region	*Participation in the global virtual currency industry*	
	2017	*2018*
Africa – Middle East	2%	6%
South America	6%	9%
North America	27%	17%
Asia-Pacific	36%	24%
Europe	29%	43%

Source: Own study based on Hileman & Rauchs (2017) and Rauchs et al. (2019).

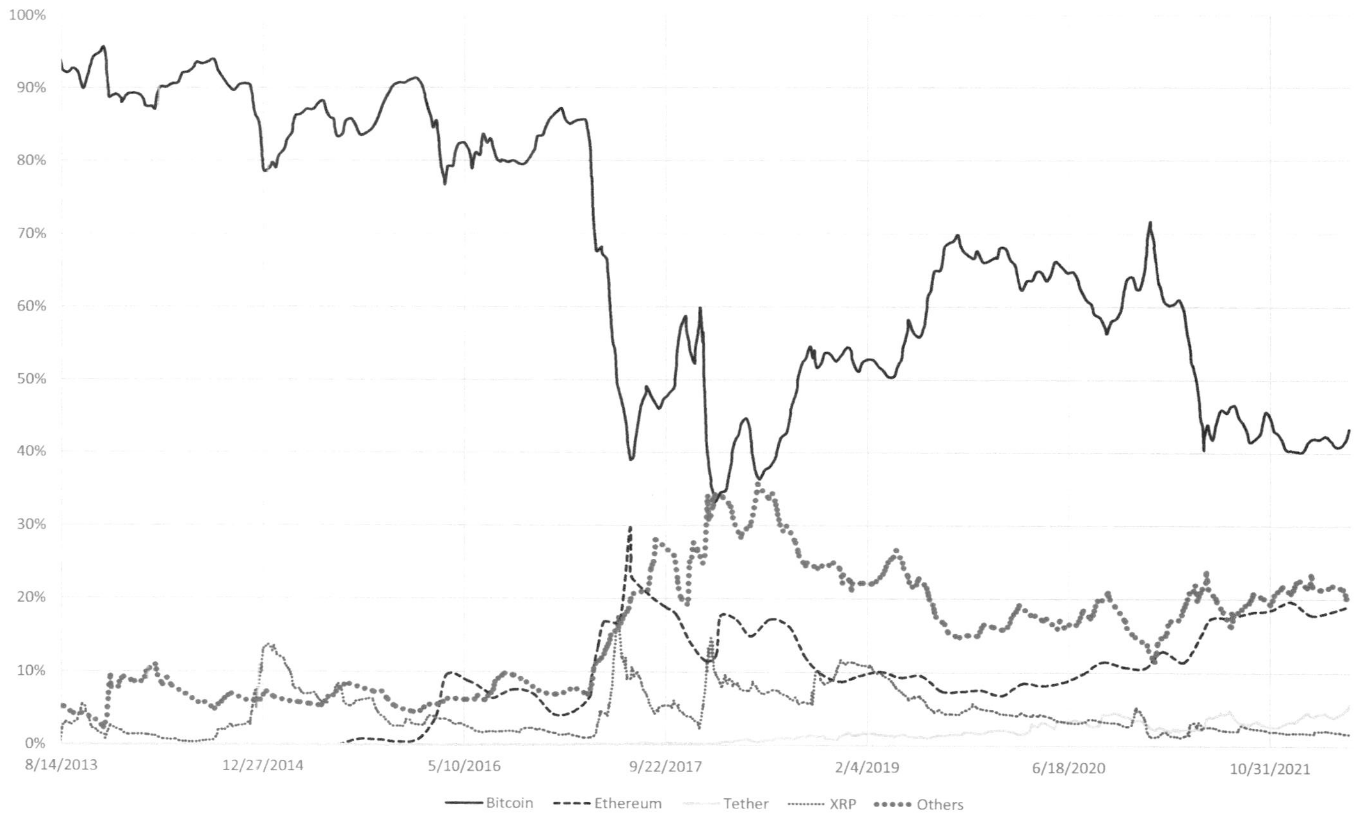

Figure 6.4 Capitalization of virtual currencies concerning total capitalization

Source: (Coinmarketcap.com, 2022).

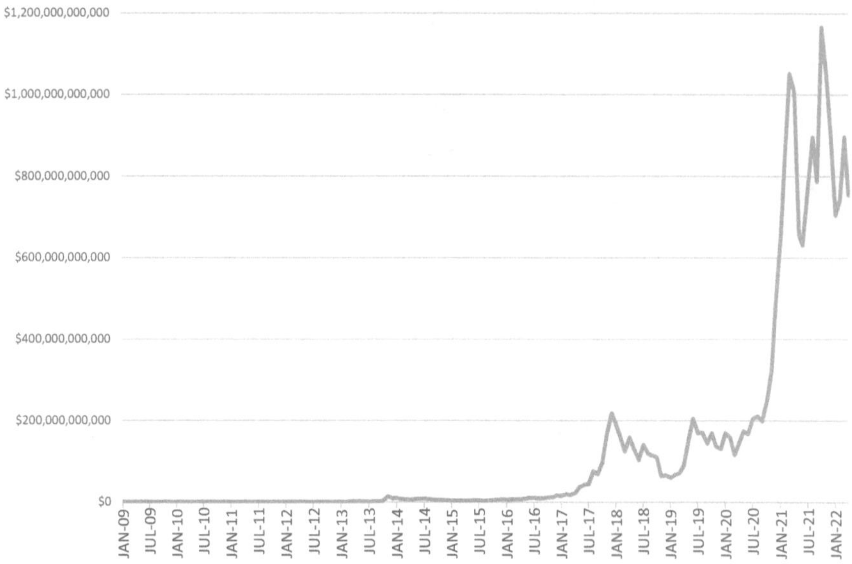

Figure 6.5 The total capitalization of Bitcoin expressed in USD between 2009 and May 2022

Source: Blockchain.com, 2022

valuation of some virtual currencies. Figure 6.5 shows a valuation of Bitcoin – the most popular virtual currency according to "Google trend" statistics was presented.

In the academic literature, several studies are trying to answer the question about the popularity of virtual currencies and thus the factors affecting their valuation. In general, there are two streams of literature. One stream argues that investors have treated virtual currency as an alternative non-financial asset, and thus its valuation is not related to any economic factors. Consequently, Hayes (2017), using a sample of 66 different virtual currencies, tests several different hypotheses: (a) the computing power involved in the extraction of virtual currency positively affects Bitcoin valuation; (b) the number of virtual currencies mined per minute is negatively correlated with the price of the currency; (c) the percentage of mined coins to the total number of coins increases the virtual currency price; (d) the maturity of a given virtual currency is positively correlated with its value. The research results indicate a high correlation between the valuation of virtual currencies with computing power, a negative correlation with the number of virtual currencies appearing on the market, and a positive correlation with the length of the virtual currency existence.

Interestingly, Cheah and Fry (2015) examine the potential bubble in the Bitcoin market. They ask whether the Bitcoin was dealing with a bubble and whether the currency's fundamental value can be estimated. The authors find that Bitcoin – treated as money – should allow payments to be made using it and store the value. However, Bitcoin has become a reflection of market sentiment, which caused unpredictable volatility of value. The authors also asked if it could link Bitcoin prices to people's interest as measured by the "Google trend" index. The authors examine daily closing prices for Bitcoin between 2010 and 2014. The authors document that Bitcoin's predicted fundamental value was not statistically different from zero over the long term. In addition, researchers prove that there was a speculative bubble in the Bitcoin market in 2013. Li and Wang (2017) claim that the difficulty of mining Bitcoin, and thus its limited supply, is positively correlated with the price of Bitcoin. In addition, the authors also test how the popularity of Bitcoin price measured by the "Google trend" index is correlated with the price of this currency. The researchers document that number of Bitcoins in circulation and volume traded has a statistically significant effect on Bitcoin price.

Another stream of the literature claims that the virtual currencies move with the economic factors, and consequently, they can be considered a separate financial asset class. Li and Wang (2017) also test the impact of economic factors on Bitcoin valuation. More specifically, using the US as a sample, they test how the price of Bitcoin reacts to factors such as changes in interest rates, gross domestic product (GDP) and inflation. The authors claim that Bitcoin, in the early stage of the market, was perceived as a "new phenomenon" and thus has been highly demanded on the market. Consequently, it was the object of speculation and did not follow any market fundamentals. In turn, in later period (since 2013), the authors observe that the change in interest rates in the United States and the number of transactions on the market have become more critical in Bitcoin pricing. Its valuation has followed some economic indicators. Interestingly, the authors also observe that the difficulty in mining Bitcoin had a statistically significant impact on the price of Bitcoin expressed in dollars in the early stage; however, this effect decreased later. The results of Li and Wang (2017) document that in the beginning, Bitcoin was treated as an alternative asset class, while since 2013 started to behave as a regular financial asset reacting to similar economic factors.

Bouoiyour and Selmi (2017) analyse the correlation between Bitcoin price and macroeconomic factors. The authors test how the Bitcoin price has reacted to the significant world events in 2016, such as: the vote on the UK's exit from the European Union, the election of Donald Trump as president of the United States or the economic slowdown in China. Interestingly, the authors notice three groups of factors influencing the Bitcoin price development. The first group includes such factors as: the volume of Bitcoin used for payments, Brexit and the slowdown in China. The second group factor was the uncertainty surrounding the election of Donald Trump as president of the United States.

The authors document that an increasing uncertainty has spurred the Bitcoin price increase, documenting that investors were treating the Bitcoin as gold and a "safe haven" against the global uncertainty. This also confirms the results of studies documenting that the Bitcoin's popularity has increased due to investors' runaway from the traditional monetary policy (Carney, 2014). Moreover, finally, the last group of factors influencing the Bitcoin price have been identified: velocity of circulation, interest in Bitcoin of Venezuelans and the price of gold.

Also, Sukmawati and Sikora (2018) examine the role of macroeconomic factors in determining Bitcoin price. The authors test the impact of the Dow Jones Industrial Average stock market index, demand and supply effects, and gold price. Interestingly, the document that Dow Jones Industrial Average is correlated with the price of Bitcoin – is both in the long and short term. Like other researchers, the authors document that the demand for Bitcoin is also significantly positively correlated with the Bitcoin price. Interestingly, the researchers also find that the supply factors affect the Bitcoin price, however, only in the short-term period but not in the long term. However, the value of gold has also been highly correlated with the price of Bitcoin –in both the short and long terms.

Caporale and Plastun (2019), interested in the phenomenon of Bitcoin price volatility, compare and test the volatility of different financial asset classes against four virtual currencies (Bitcoin, Litecoin, Ripple and Dash) volatility between May 2013 and December 2017. The authors argue that behavioural and economic factors highly drive the virtual currency price changes. The researchers found that the average daily price amplitude of the cryptocurrency market is ten times greater than the price amplitude of the forex market, more than seven times the amplitude of the stock market, and up to five times the amplitude of the commodity market.

Virtual currency market and money supply

Sample and methodology

The financial literature documents a significant role of macroeconomic policy on demand for different asset classes. While several studies examine the role of demand factors in virtual currency development, there are almost no studies explaining what has determined this demand. The academic literature documents that in the period of low interest rates investors tend to search for alternative asset class investment, as they can accept more risk, as compared to higher interest rate environment (Goetzmann et al., 2011; Ridderstaat et al., 2017). Therefore, it might be argued that QE and consequent low interest rate policy, which was experienced after the financial crisis of 2008, met the sensitive ground, and encouraged the investors to invest in the virtual currencies contributing to its significant development. Hereby, the money supply in countries the most active in the virtual currency market was presented.

The money supply in China and Russia increased about fivefold between 2008 and 2020, while in the United States and the Eurozone, it doubled at the same time. There were more than twofold increases in M2. M2 in China is growing linearly, and the figure does not show any significant shocks. However, money growth in Russia is characterized by strong seasonality. In addition, unlike in other countries, a temporary decline in the money supply can be observed, which took place in 2009. Concerning Asian countries, excluding China, the money supply increased significantly in Singapore and South Korea. Taiwan's money supply growth throughout the period is linear, and over 12 years, it grew by 76 percent. In turn, Japan experienced the smallest increase in the monetary base. Between 2008 and 2020, the base grew by only 40 percent, which is closer to Eurozone countries than to other Asian economies.

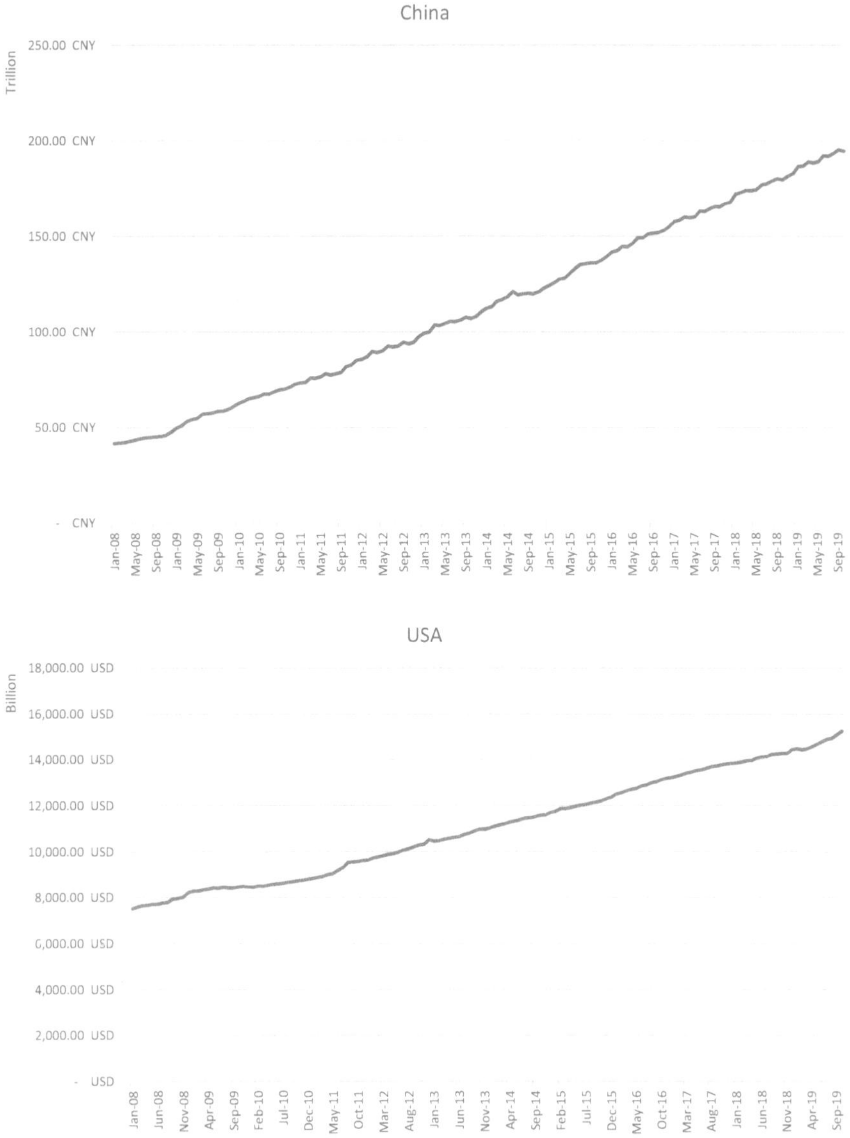

Figure 6.6 The money supply measured by M2 in China, the United States, Eurozone and Russia

Source: Bloomberg (2020).

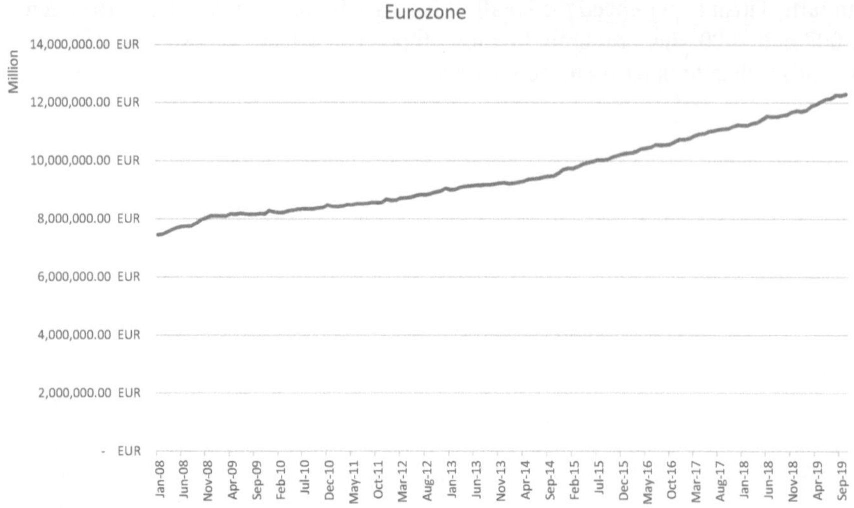

Figure 6.6 (Continued)

In order to test the hypotheses of whether the money supply has increased the demand for virtual currency, the sample of 16 countries was used that had the largest share in the global volume of Bitcoin conversion according to the Bloomberg Report produced by Russo et al. (2017). It includes the Eurozone region, Brazil, China, Denmark, Japan, Canada, South Korea, Mexico, Norway, Russia,

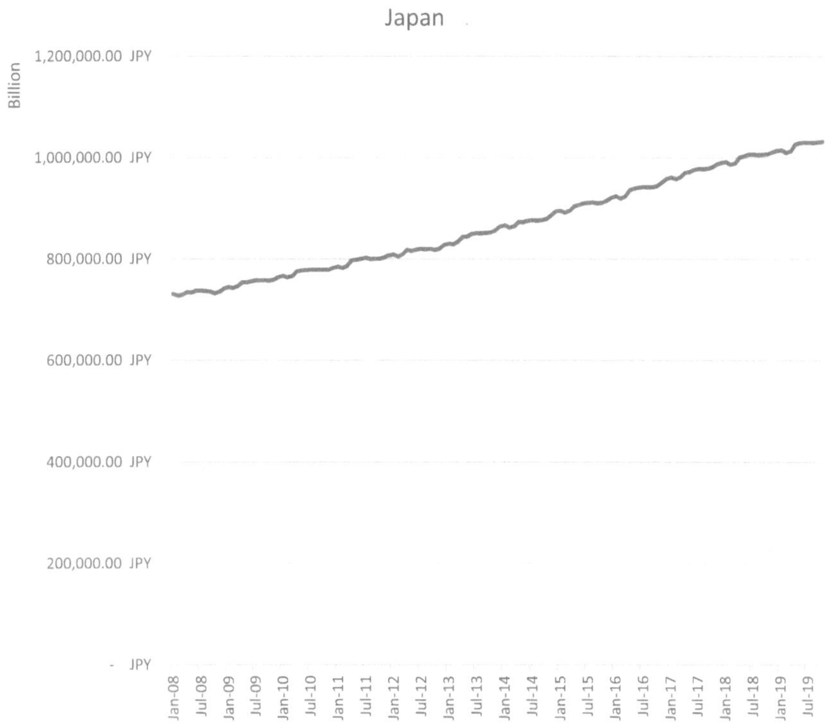

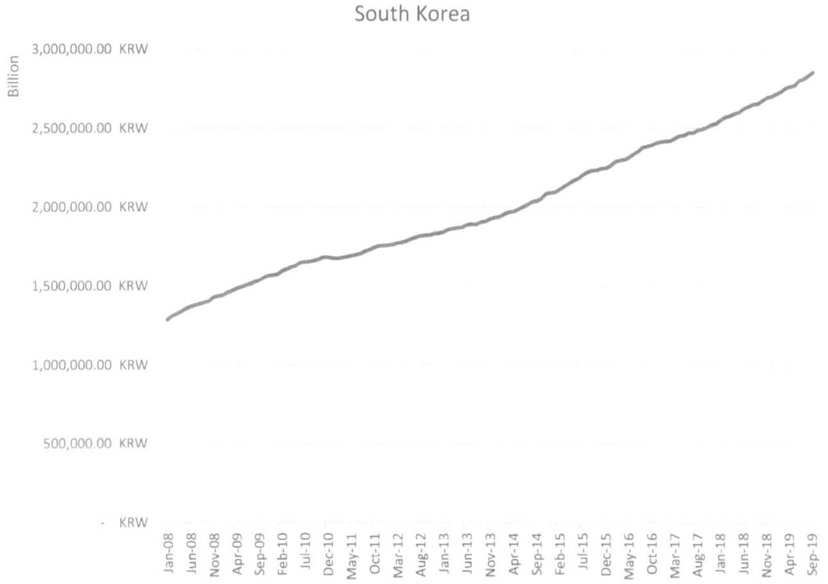

Figure 6.7 The money supply measured by M2 in Japan, South Korea, Singapore and Taiwan

Source: Bloomberg (2020).

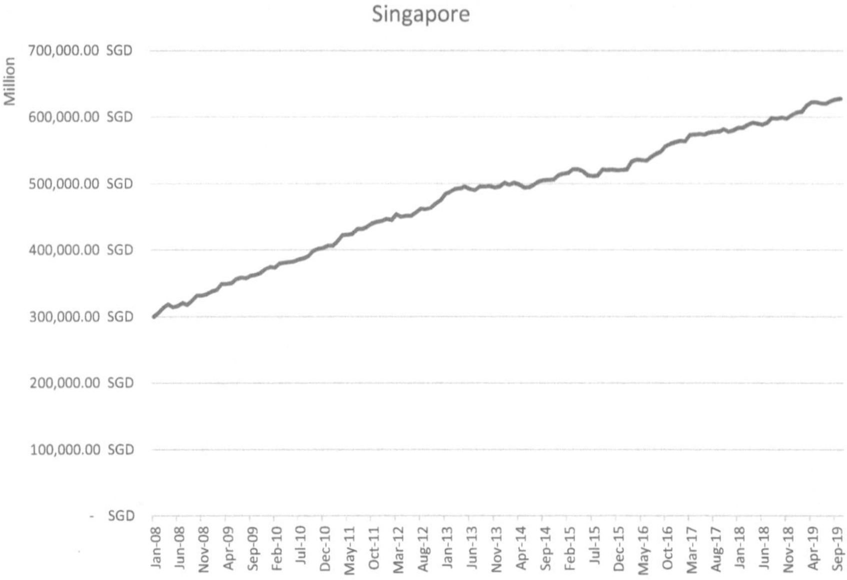

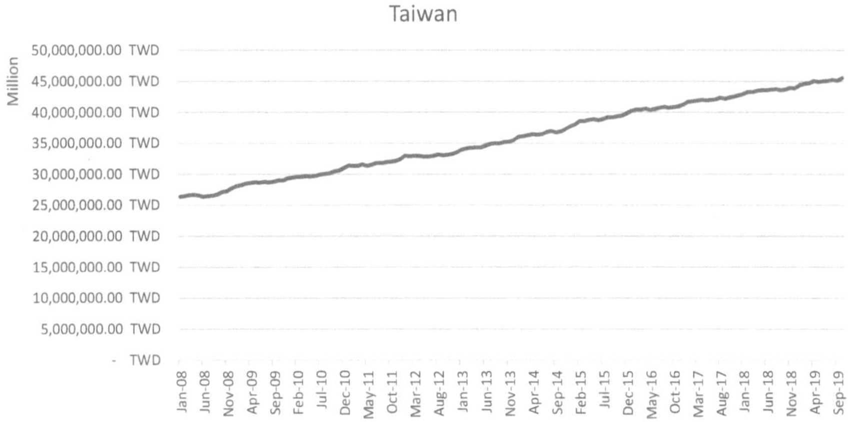

Figure 6.7 (Continued)

South Africa, Singapore, Switzerland, Sweden, Taiwan and the United States. As a measure of money supply, M2 was taken for each of sample countries between 2009 and 2019. The M2 indicator is widely used in the literature dealing with the impact of changes in the money supply on the behaviour of financial assets (Al-Kandari & Abul, 2019; Habibullah & Baharumshah, 1996; Salleh et al., 2007;

Table 6.2 Indicators for virtual currency market development

Indicator	*Period*
Bitcoin capitalization	08.2010–12.2019
Bitcoin price	08.2010–12.2019
"*Google trend*" index	12.2008–12.2019
Number of virtual currencies	12.2008–12.2019
Number of *blockchain* wallets	11.2011–12.2019
Number of confirmed transactions per day	01.2009–12.2019
USD/BTC exchange volume	02.2013–12.2019
Bitcoin supply	12.2008–12.2019

Source: Own elaboration.

Sirucek, 2014; Swanson, 1998). However, it needs to be stated that the definition of M2 might vary between sample countries. This will not significantly influence the results as there is not an interest in the changes between M2 across different countries but rather in the time-period differences within one country. As a set of measures explaining the virtual currency market development, the following indicators were used: market capitalization, Bitcoin price, number of wallets, number of daily transactions, the volume of exchange and Bitcoin supply (source: Blockchain.com, 2022; the number of virtual currencies (data was collected manually from historical CoinMarketCap snapshots); "Google trend" index; and M2 for money supply aggregates (source: Bloomberg, 2020). The monthly data between December 2008 and December 2019 was used; however, data panel is unbalanced as some virtual currency indicators are lacking due to late reporting at the beginning of the analysed period. For example, the USD/BTC exchange volume started to be reported in February 2013. The number of user wallets has been reported since November 2011, while the Bitcoin price and total capitalization have been accessible since August 2010. Apart from the aforementioned, the panel is complete and has no missing records. Table 6.2 presents the summary of the indicators used for the analysis.

The linear regression model was used to verify the hypothesis while using the virtual market indicators as dependent variables and the M2 of the sample countries as control variables. In addition, in the latter part of the analysis, other financial market indicators were included such as: S&P 500 index, Nikkei index, Shanghai Composite index, Hang Seng index, commodity index, and the yield for ten-year American bonds. The other stock and bond market indices were tested; however, they appeared in the regressions as statistically insignificant. These variables allow to test how the virtual currency market moves compared to other markets. According to recent academic studies, the virtual currency market sometimes co-moves with the traditional stock market, mainly the US one (Sovbetov, 2018), while other studies document that it behaves opposite to it (Klein et al., 2018). Therefore, additional control variables to proxy for the performance of other global markets were added to the analysis. The regression equation (1) takes the following form:

$$y_{it} = \beta_1 x_{i1} + \beta_2 x_{i2} + \ldots + \beta_n x_{in} + \alpha_i G_{it} + \epsilon \in_i \quad (1)$$

where:

y_{it} – i indicator of the virtual currency at time t.

x_{it} – monetary supply measured by M2 in a country i at time t appearing as the lag variable. The number of lags of M2 for each country has been selected using the Vector Autoregressive Model (VAR).

G_{it} – financial market variables of a country i at time t.

Regression results

The regression results are presented in Table 6.3.

The results present interesting conclusions. Firstly, they document a strong correlation between the money supply and the development of the virtual currency market. In 13 out of 16 sample countries, the increase in money supply has a direct and positive causal effect on the virtual currency indicators. However, four countries deserve special attention: Canada, Switzerland, Singapore and the United States. The M2 measures appear the most statistically significant in all these countries, with the highest number of lags driving the virtual currency market.

Table 6.3 Summary of the regression results

Variable	*Model 1 Bitcoin capitalization*	*Model 2 Bitcoin Price*	*Model 3 Google trend index*	*Model 4 Number of wallets*	*Model 5 Volume traded*	*Median*
	Lags					
d11_Canada_M2	7, 9, 10	9	0		10	9
d11_Switzerland_M2	3	4	0	0	3	3
d11_Singapore_M2	2	2		0	9	2
d11_China_M2		3	4	5		4
d11_USA_M2	2	2	4			2
d11_Korea_M2				5, 9		7
d11_RPA_M2				6	6	6
d11_Norway_M2				10		10
d11_Brasil_M2		9				9
d11_Mexico_M2					7	7
d11_Euro_M2			6			6
d11_Russia_M2			0			0
d11_Sweden_M2				0		0

Source: Own elaboration.

Interestingly, Canada is a leading country with five lags correlated with the virtual market indicators. At the same time, M2 of Switzerland, Singapore and the United States appear three times statistically and positively correlated with the virtual currency measures. All M2 measures from these countries are mainly correlated with the Bitcoin indicators and volume traded.

Moreover, it can be also noticed that virtual currency indicators react to changes in money supply with different delays across the countries. While significant delays was seen in Canada as of nine and ten months, these delays are much shorter in Switzerland, Singapore and China. However, in the United States, the transmission mechanism from M2 to the virtual currency market seems to be the lowest (two months). These differences in transmission period may result from several reasons. One of them might be related to an individual country's development of the financial system, the banking sector's competitiveness, the flexibility of the labour market and the structure of production or the openness of the economy. Another reason might be the different channels of monetary policy transmission prevailing in individual countries. While some countries dominate the interest rate channel or risk-taking channel, in other countries, it can be found a dominance of the credit channel (Kapuściński et al., 2018). The more developed the financial markets, the shorter the transmission period from monetary policy into the financial market (Kapuściński et al., 2018; Georgiadis, 2014; Mateju, 2013; Rusnák et al., 2011).

In contrast, more bank-based countries such as Switzerland or Canada, with prevailing credit channels, have more extended transmission periods. The academic literature proves that the former channels transmit the mechanisms faster than the credit channel. Therefore, a short transmission period in such countries as Singapore and the United States can be noticed, which have well-developed financial markets with a solid risk-taking channel.

In this research, it can be interesting how the performance of other markets has influenced the development of the virtual currency market. The same type of analysis was performed while including other financial market indicators to this extent. The regression results are presented in Table 6.4.

As a result in most cases, the financial market indicators appear statistically significant, however, affecting the virtual currency market with different lags. Interestingly, these lags give similar conclusions as in the case of monetary policy indicator – M2. The shortest transmission comes from S&P500, which coincides with the previous results showing that the United States transmits the monetary mechanisms with the highest speed. However, it is also worth noticing the impact of Shanghai stock market, which also appears with a relatively short transmission period. However, while the American stock market positively affects the virtual currency indicators, the Shanghai index has a negative effect. These results are in line with the existing studies. Sovbetov (2018) documents that the interest in Bitcoin increases during a good performance of the American stock market. However, Bouri et al. (2017) find a negative result for the Shanghai Index. The latter indicates that virtual currency can be used as a hedging instrument in the Asian

Table 6.4 Summary of the regression results using other financial asset classes

Financial market indicator	*Number of lags and the direction*	*Impact*
Nikkei Index	4 (3+ 1-)	Mainly positive
Shanghai Index	2 (2-)	Negative
10-year Bond Yield	3 (3-)	Negative
S&P500	1 (1+)	Positive
Hang Seng Index	3 (3+)	Positive
Commodity Index	2 (2-)	Negative

Source: Own elaboration.

Table 6.5 Summary of the regression results of M2 and different asset classes in the virtual currency market

Dependent variable (Y): dll_Google_trends	*(1)*	*(2)*
const	−0.43	−0.51
dll_Canada_M2	47.42	41.19
dll_China_M2_4	−7.18	
dll_Euro_M2_6	23.59	30.96
dll_Russia_M2	5.25	5.02
dll_Switzerland_M2	22.08	14.49
dll_USA_M2_4	30.93	28.69
dum201607	−1.08	−1.36
dll_SP500		4.28
dll_HangSeng_3		2.03
dll_Commodity		−0.91
dll_Bond Market		−1.36
Adjusted R^2	0.35	0.45

Source: Own elaboration.

market while not in the United States. It can be concluded that virtual currency indicators are negatively correlated with the commodity index and bond market indicators, indicating a good hedge against these instruments.

Not all financial market variables are statistically significant in all specifications. However, the money supply appears always to be statistically significant in all the regressions. It should also be noticed that the regression results vary depending on the indicators used for the virtual currency market. Table 6.5 presents the representative regression results using the "Google trend" index dependent variable.

Interestingly, in the presented regression results, it can be observed that while controlling for the other financial asset classes, two additional countries tend to be necessary for the virtual currency market. These are Europe and Russia. This might happen when other financial markets might appear as important channels of the monetary policy. This issue, however, does not change a primary consideration that the dramatic increase in M2 has significantly raised the interest in the investment in the virtual currency market, and this transmission has mainly come from Canada, China, the United States and Switzerland.

Conclusion

The development of the virtual currency market has raised much debate on the public and academic scene. The questions were related to the determinants of such a big attraction of virtual currency investment people. The academic literature is unclear why investors have massively invested in virtual currency. Some researchers explain this fact by the behavioural factors (Bouri, Gupta et al., 2018). Other studies try to explain the changes in this market by the economic factors (Corbet et al., 2017; Li & Wang, 2017; Bouoiyour & Selmi, 2017; Sukmawati& Sikora, 2018).

In this chapter, it was analysed whether the increase in the interest in the virtual currency market has been driven by the "cheap money" introduced by the governments over the globe after the financial crisis of 2008 and the behaviour of other financial markets. This cheap money might have also been considered with the lost faith in the traditional financial sector; however, this behavioural aspect is out of the scope of this analysis.

The results confirmed that quantitative easing and a low interest environment increased the attraction of the virtual currency market. In other words, the regression results documented that monetary policy affected the condition of the virtual currency market. This can be explained by the fact that investors tend to increase their investment in riskier alternative assets during low interest rates. In other words, the access to "cheap money" increases their risk appetite. However, the regression results also proved that this effect was not uniform across the countries. More specifically, the transmission mechanism from a more excellent money supply to virtual currency development materialized differently depending on the country's institutional development (and thus different regulatory environment). The shortest transmission can be observed in countries such as the United States and Singapore, which have the most developed financial markets. Other countries such as Canada, Switzerland and even China have more extended transmission mechanisms, as the credit channel is probably responsible for the transmission.

Interestingly, the performance of other markets also influenced the virtual currency market. This result was not surprising as the monetary policy strongly affected the movements of other markets. However, the regression results showed that the virtual currency market did not react consistently towards the performance of different asset classes. Additionally, the heterogeneity effects across the countries. While there is a positive correlation of virtual currency with S&P 500, the findings indicated a negative correlation with the Shanghai index, commodity market and American bond market.

The conclusion brings essential insights for policymakers about the potential consequences of the monetary policy, while for investors, they inform about the interdependence between the monetary policy and virtual currency performance suggesting the hedging strategies.

7 Post-pandemic challenges for global central banking

Łukasz Kurowski and Paweł Smaga

Introduction

Over the recent decades, many economic and financial trends have been reshaping the environment in which central banks operate (e.g. globalisation, financialisation and digitalisation). These trends created the need to gradually evolve central banks' mandates, which have to constantly adapt their polices to continue effectively fulfilling legally enshrined goals. Using critical review of literature and regulatory framework, the aim of this chapter is to assess the four main challenges and identify relevant policy actions for central banks. First, the chapter explores how inflation-targeting strategy worked in practice and whether it should be improved. Second, it attempts to find the missing link – that is, the desired policy mix between price and financial stability mandates. The third part discusses how central banks should tackle the emergence of cyber and climate risks. The final section concludes the chapter.

Inflation targeting strategy after the crisis

Inflation targeting (IT) gained much prominence in the end of XXI century, while other strategies (e.g. exchange-rate targeting, monetary targeting) were largely abandoned. The Reserve Bank of New Zealand was the first to introduce a strategy known as inflation targeting in 1989, and in the 1990s, IT spread to other advanced economies and later on to some emerging market economies, as well as transition countries (Niedźwiedzińska, 2018, 2022). An IT or quasi-IT strategy is now used by more than 40 economies and others are preparing to join the group of inflation targeters. In many cases, the adoption of an IT framework, especially in the initial years, was a decision taken in crisis circumstances or the final stage of a longer preparation process. To date no IT country has decided to change it for another strategy. The IT strategy includes acknowledging price stability as the primary goal of monetary policy, a public announcement of a numerical inflation target, formulating monetary policy on the basis of a very broad set of data, using a floating exchange rate regime, preparation of forecasts and applying high transparency and accountability standards, as well as independence to central bank policies (Mishkin, 2001, 2004).

DOI: 10.4324/9781003310365-7

Many researchers attempted to assess the effectives of IT, but with mixed outcomes. Sceptics prove that that inflation targeting itself has mixed effects on inflation and its variability, as those variables are determined to a larger extent by the credibility and transparency of monetary policy (Lin & Ye, 2007; Baxa et al., 2015). Another panel study elaborates that there is no significant difference in the impact on inflation in inflation targeters versus non-inflation targeters (Ardakani et al., 2018). Also there seems to be not positive effect of IT on growth (Rose, 2014). In contrast, others argue that the adoption of IT in addition to reducing inflation volatility can drive inflation down and is especially useful for countries that must enhance their monetary policy credibility (Ferreira de Mendonça & de Guimarães e Souza, 2012). Similarly, inflation targeters have been able to better anchor long-run inflation expectations in comparison with non-IT countries (Bean, 2009; Gürkaynak et al., 2010). Countries with an IT monetary regime weathered the global financial crisis much better and have systematically outperformed those with other regimes in terms of economic growth during the period 2007–2013 (Barnebeck et al., 2015). However, central bank responses to the COVID-19 pandemic didn't seem to depend on the adoption of an IT framework (Niedźwiedzińska, 2021).

The impact of IT strategy on financial stability remains ambiguous. On average, inflation targeters are financially more vulnerable than non-targeters. Contrary to their counterparts, most targeting central banks respond to financial imbalances with tighter policy, and are more financially unstable (Fouejieu, 2017). In contrast, others argue that national banking systems in an IT country (i) are more stable; (ii) possess sounder systemically important banks; and (iii) are less distressed than other banks during crisis periods (Fazio et al., 2015).

Global financial crisis (2007+) led to an intensive discussion on reforming IT, as it focuses too much on stabilising inflation, making monetary policy less effective (Polański, 2011; Andersson & Claussen, 2017). The criticism of IT can be summarised in three points:

- Inflation targeting policies do not take unemployment and production sufficiently into account, which contributed to unnecessarily passive and restrictive monetary policy during and after the global crisis.
- Inflation targeting policies take too little account of financial risks and imbalances.
- Inflation targeting cannot stimulate demand sufficiently when the interest rate is close to its lower bound, something that has been a problem in recent years.

Although central banks with IT that aimed for a low inflation rate have generally been successful at stabilising inflation in the past, such an approach is not as well-suited for a low interest rate environment (Williams, 2016). There simply may not be enough room for central banks to cut interest rates in response to an economic downturn when both natural rates and inflation are very low (zero lower bound problem). This is currently the case, for example, in the Eurozone and in the US. Monetary policy (reacting to cyclical recessions and a dampened inflation outlook over the recent decades) of central banks themselves had a significant impact on the creation of this phenomenon. Additionally, it is fuelled by structural reasons like demographic developments (ageing of society), lower productivity growth in a secular stagnation and a global savings glut (ESRB, 2016, 2021).

At least two solutions are possible (Williams, 2016). First, central banks can pursue a somewhat higher inflation target, as this would imply a higher average level of interest rates and thereby give monetary policy more room for manoeuvre. An alternative would be to replace the fixed inflation target with a more flexible average price-level (or even a nominal GDP target). Going further, a dual mandate (when central banks have two explicit and equal goals for monetary policy) should in theory help stabilise inflation and the real economy at the same time (i.e. flexible IT framework). Another solution would be to induce monetary policy to prevent the build-up of imbalances and risks on the financial markets (as explored in the next section in this chapter). However, many uncertainties arise concerning the measurement of "additional" goals for monetary policy, bringing less clarity and potentially more time-inconsistency. Alternative solutions to IT include regular reliance on unconventional policy tools and negative interest rates, thus profoundly changing the hitherto classic paradigm of monetary policy-making. Yet, any "upgrade" to the flexible IT framework should in principle lead to the central bank being able to stabilise inflation and the real economy more effectively. Even within the flexible IT framework itself, there are practical dilemmas (Vredin, 2015) concerning: a quantitative definition of the inflation target, gross domestic product (GDP), any additional variable that is taken into account; weights assigned to them in the Taylor rule; forecast horizon; interpretation of "interest rate smoothing"; and the long-run level of the nominal policy rate.

In mid-2020, the Fed took some first modest steps and adjusted its strategy for achieving inflation goal of 2 percent by noting that it "seeks to achieve inflation that averages 2 percent over time." Similarly, the European Central Bank (ECB) in mid-2021 reviewed its monetary strategy, among others by creating a roadmap foreseeing wider inclusion of housing costs in HICP; implementing the price stability objective as an unambiguous and *symmetric* target; increasing flexibility in medium-term orientation allowing for taking into account other factors (like employment or financial stability). The ECB also plans to further include climate change considerations in its monetary policy framework. Those changes can be thus considered as an evolution, not revolution, in the IT strategy of the Fed and the ECB, by maintaining the core principles of such strategy and correctly adjusting their approach to the current economic trends.

So far, the notable enhancement of the IT framework seems to be forward guidance (FG). The FG, although present before the GFC, has only been increasingly used by main central banks since then, as a key element of their monetary policy (Filardo & Hofmann, 2014). The objective of FG is to clarify (using communication tools) the intended policy rate path and increase transparency of monetary policy. Use of FG is expected to reduce uncertainty, and thereby impact expectations of the future path of short-term rates and on long-term bond yields, as well as reduce the volatility of expected future rates and possibly also risk premia.

FGenables provision of additional monetary stimulus, especially when the central bank is operating at the effective lower bound on interest rates. The potential usefulness of FG depends on it being seen as a credible and clearly communicated commitment. The key trade-off of FG policy includes the strength (clarity) of the commitment versus future policy flexibility. The collegial nature of monetary policy decision-making and the need to work-out decisions based on consensus may water down the clarity and credibility of FG.

Major central banks over time adopted and experimented with different approaches to FG. Still, the use of FG exposes central banks to different reputation and credibility risks if poorly communicated. When the FG guidance is binding, it might lead to undue delay in the speed of monetary policy adjustment, but also cause financial market distress when the guidance itself is (suddenly) changed. Empirically evidence on FG effectiveness for monetary policy remains mixed (Kool & Thornton, 2015; Smith & Becke, 2015; Swanson, 2021). Given the heightened uncertainty during the COVID-19 pandemic and the need to react flexibly, credible use of FG might become more difficult in the future.

The missing link between financial and price stability mandates

After the global financial crisis, the mandates of many central banks were changed by introducing (or strengthening) their responsibility for maintaining financial stability, apart from price stability. Although price stability usually remains as the overriding objective, there is a need to achieve both mandates (price and financial stability) at the same time. Thus, this necessitates coordination and seeking a successful policy mix.

Monetary and financial stability goals are materially intertwined. Both policies impact bank lending and funding conditions, the balance sheet structure of banks and their profitability, as well as their risk appetite (Beyer et al., 2017). On the one hand, restrictive monetary policy reduces credit supply, lowers debt-servicing capacity of borrowers and increases bank market funding costs. On the other hand, expansive monetary policy, that is, prolonged period of low interest rates, burdens bank interest income. In the medium term, it also fosters over-indebtedness of the non-financial sector (gradual increase in credit risk), as well as supports proliferation of *search for yield* behaviour on financial markets and induces higher leverage (e.g. Nicolò et al., 2010; Geršl et al., 2015; ESRB, 2016, 2021; Heider et al., 2019). The impact of interest rates on cyclical systemic risk also depends on the current stage of the financial cycle (e.g. measured as credit-to-GDP gap), which is distinct from and most often not synchronized with the business cycle. For instance, lowering interest rates (as motivated by low inflation concerns) in an upswing of a credit cycle procyclically fuels accumulation of a credit boom, provided Empirical evidence points that procyclicality of interest rate changes was in fact usually higher when financial cycle gaps were increasing (expansion phase of the credit cycle). On average, complementariness between both objectives is in major economies much more frequent than cases with conflicting objectives (Kurowski & Smaga, 2018; Smaga, 2021).

Central banks face a challenge – how to incorporate financial stability concerns into the process of monetary policy decision-making in order to minimise any negative side effects its monetary policy might have on the financial system. From a practical point of view, there are two complimentary approaches: "soft" and "hard" ways of coordinating monetary and financial stability policies.

"Soft" coordination, largely unexplored in the literature, focuses on raising degree to which systemic risk issues are discussed and analysed by monetary policymakers. This might be visible in the content of documents and the scope of discussion on monetary policy council meetings. Empirical exploration of "soft" approach, by verifying how often inflation reports refer to financial stability, suggests that on average only 2 per cent of inflation report contents cover financial stability-related words, thus there is little evidence that a "soft" policy mix is present in Central, Eastern and Southeastern Europe (CESEE) countries (Kurowski & Smaga, 2022). There was only a short-lived increase in focus on financial stability in central banks' publications and speeches during the global crisis (Siklos et al., 2018; Johnson et al., 2019). Moreover, in macroprudential strategies in EU countries, the approach towards a policy mix between monetary and macroprudential polices is almost non-existent, further pointing to the weak link between those policies in practice.

At the same time, there is much more research on a "hard" approach to the policy mix, for example, including various financial variables into the Taylor rule (often used by inflation targeters) like credit growth and credit-related data (e.g. Christiano et al., 2010; Verona et al., 2017), exchange rates (Belke & Polleit, 2007), asset prices (Botzen & Marey, 2010; Hoffmann, 2013) and even an index of overall financial conditions (Castro, 2011). Another "hard" way is to include financial stability variables in the transmission mechanisms and the objective/reaction function in macroeconomic models used by central banks for policy purposes. Most researchers find that the interest rate policies of main central banks indeed respond to financial variables (Friedrich et al., 2019). These studies aim to explore whether there are any differences in the impact of such "enhanced" monetary policies on the economy (compared to "classic" interest rates).

While there is little controversy behind benefits of adopting the "soft" policy mix, the debate on the efficiency of the "hard" approach remains open. Cyclical systemic risks should be taken into account to the extent that they influence the inflation and growth outlook. However, the practical implementation of this notion is not trivial. Systemic risks accumulate and are assessed within a medium- to long-term perspective, which often goes beyond the short-term inflation forecast horizon. The experiences of the GFC suggest a more active monetary response to accumulating risks in the financial system. Yet, this approach is hindered by the uncertainty in systemic risk identification and measurement – there is no desired "target level" of such risk, nor any easy assessment of current degree of risk accumulation. Furthermore, employing interest rates to – apart from inflation – also directly target financial imbalances might be ineffective and carry higher costs. If the monetary policy as a result becomes excessively restrictive, this ultimately would have a negative impact on inflation, its volatility and economic output (Raghavan & Dungey, 2015; Svensson, 2016; Ajello et al., 2019), while being able to stem the accumulation of systemic risks only to a limited extent (Badarau & Popescu, 2014). Moreover, monetary policy is too blunt (i.e. has to too wide-ranging effects) to selectively address pockets of vulnerabilities in the financial system (Suh, 2014). At the same time, other researchers also point to the potential positive effects of such policy in selected scenarios (Gambacorta & Signoretti, 2014; Ma & Zhang, 2016; Verona et al., 2017).

There are several practical solutions to the policy mix. Some central banks have so far explicitly stated that they descriptively include in their monetary policy strategies financial stability considerations (e.g. Bank of Korea, Central Bank of the Republic of Turkey, Norges Bank and the Riksbank), without giving further qualitative details. Additionally, an increase in importance of the financial stability mandate gave birth to the new macroprudential role for central banks. Ensuring financial stability remains within the merit of macroprudential policy, in which also the central banks very often play a dominant role. In this setup, monetary policy may continue to flexibly focus mostly on inflation and output concerns (also with a longer forecast horizon), while not being burdened by an additional explicit financial stability target. In this case, both monetary and macroprudential policy would complement each other (Bailliu et al., 2015). Nevertheless, this necessitates some degree of internal coordination within the central bank two functions, that is, to limit any negative side effects monetary policy might have on systemic risks (e.g. from low interest rates), without impeding the independence in the conduct of monetary policy. Sadly, the framework for coordination between both monetary and macro prudential policies is still missing and underdeveloped. The necessity of coordination becomes even more urgent in light of the COVID-19 crisis. In Q1 2020, both monetary and macro prudential policies were concurrently significantly eased to support the economic activity hit by the first pandemic shock. Yet those actions were coincidental, mostly driven by circumstances and not the result of a long-term and well-conceived coordination strategy.

Emergence of cyber and climate risks

Cyber risk

With financial systems becoming more digitalised and reliant on complex, interconnected and constantly evolving information and communication technologies, the probability and costs of attack cyber threats have increased in the recent years (Koop et al., 2017).[1] The COVID-19 pandemic (Aldasoro et al., 2021), along with the surge in remote work and accelerated take-up of digital financial services, as well as the proliferation of the cyber war in Russia and Ukraine in early 2022, has further aggravated cybersecurity risks.

Cyber risk (as a subtype of operational risk) is defined as the combination of the probability of cyber incidents occurring and their impact (FSB, 2018). A cyber event jeopardises the cyber security of an information system or the data the system processes (e.g. the confidentially, integrity and availability of the data). All institutions need to maintain cyber resilience, which is the ability to continue carrying out its mission by anticipating, adapting to and withstanding cyber threats, as well as rapidly recovering from cyber incidents. Cyber risk often stems from malicious intent and a successful cyberattack. Unlike most other "typical" sources of financial risks, it materialises quickly, can shut down a supervised entity immediately and spread to a system-wide contagion. Four broad origins of cyber risk include technical computer system failures, theft, hacktivists and terrorists, and state actors (Aldasoro et al., 2021). Cyber risk is a major threat to financial intuitions (e.g. banks), necessitating developing a prudential supervisory approach to strengthen cyber resilience in the financial system, which is a global public good. Due to the critical economic importance of provisions of financial services, the financial industry remains a prime target for cyber criminals and the disruption of those services by cyberattacks poses a risk to financial stability (Aldasoro et al., 2022). System-wide consequences are likely to materialise, especially when the cyberattack is targeted at critical market infrastructure. The cyber vulnerabilities are exacerbated by the growing role of fintech companies as providers of financial services, because of their excessive reliance on new technology (e.g. could computing) and de facto lack of regulatory oversight. A central bank, being responsible for financial stability, has to maintain financial system's resilience also to cyberattacks.

As for the preparedness phase, the first line of defence against cyber risk rests within financial institutions' own risk management, thus actions of supervisory authorities (among other central banks in its supervisory capacity) need to foster high-quality practices in this area (via regulations, guidances and standards). Additionally, there is a need to establish information gathering and disclosure standards on cyber incidents, to improve the quality of cyber risk identification. As measuring cyber risk remains a challenge, a starting point from the macroprudential perspective would be the development of a "cyber map" (Wilson et al., 2019) with systemically important nodes of the financial sector (e.g. payment systems, financial market infrastructures, financial institutions and third-party party service providers). Cyber risk exposure also arises from the common use of the same technologies (hardware and software). Cyber risk identification is challenging as there is no generally accepted framework to estimate and report the impact of cyber events. Quantitative economic analysis is hindered by the lack of useful and comparable data, which is usually confidential or available ex-post on a case-by-case basis.

Further, legal requirements on cyber risk for financial institutions have to be "technology neutral" to avoid gaps of non-compliant provision of financial services by non-banks. Such holistic framework has to be complemented by prudent, robust and risk-based supervisory actions, for example, including cyber risk as a fixed element of Supervisory Review and Evaluation Processes and reporting requirements (Crisanto & Prenio, 2017). The fluid and constantly evolving nature of cyber risk necessitates a principle-based approach rather than "check-box" compliance rules. Currently available preventive macroprudential tools may not prove effective in mitigation of risks from a cyber-incident. A macroprudential response to systemic cyber risk would comprise of its inclusion in the intermediate objectives, conceptualisation of an analytical framework and monitoring indicators, as well as the development, calibration and activation of systemic cyber risk-specific instruments that ensure a sufficient level of cyber resilience (ESRB, 2022). Cyber risk monitoring requires to be coupled with micro and macro cyber stress testing of the financial system, regular business continuity planning exercises and penetration tests of cyber defences. Any staffing gaps in this area have to be filled by experts commanding the mix of supervisory and IT skills.

A cyber event could most probably act as a trigger causing systemic consequences (ESRB, 2020). Central banks remain the main actors also in the crisis-management phase. In the very short term, a systemic cyberattack would likely cause a spike in market uncertainty, loss of confidence, lead to an operational outage to a liquidity contagion and disrupt the daily operation of financial institutions and the settlement of payments (Adelmann et al., 2020; Eisenbach et al., 2021). Further, financial institutions, being the victims of cyberattack (or of its second-round effects), face significant short- and medium-term consequences. These include a profitability hit,[2] higher operational expenses (necessary IT investments) and less measurable but potentially profound reputational costs (e.g. as a result of confidential data leakage), leading to loss of confidence, customer loyalty and as a result lower future revenue (Kopp et al., 2017). This would be magnified to a systemic scale if the "cyber-critical" financial institutions are affected, effectively becoming "too interconnected to fail", like central counterparties or messaging systems such as SWIFT.

However, the central bank itself, being the most critical node in the financial system, is the target of a cyberattack. Examples of such attacks to date included mainly data breaches, business disruptions and frauds (Bouveret, 2018). Cybersecurity-related risks for central banks should be addressed by operationalising sound internal risk management by establishing and strengthening an integrated risk management approach throughout the organisation, including a dedicated risk management unit, ongoing sensitising and training of board members and staff, clear reporting lines, regularly assessing cyber resilience and introducing risk management into strategic planning (Khan & Malaika, 2021).

As cyber risk is a global threat, this complicates the identification and attribution of cyber threats. Additionally, rising geopolitical tensions further increase the risk of disruption-motivated incidents. Therefore, international cooperation and information-sharing and reporting are essential. Sadly, the global response to the emergence of cyber risk has so far been slow and fragmented. International standards-setting bodies (e.g. BIS, FSB and the G7) have been promoting and publishing (more or less detailed) guidelines on cyber risk mitigation. However, the cyber-related legislation (e.g. on the EU level) is still in its infancy, hindering effective and prompt reaction of authorities to cyber incidents. At the same time, national-level jurisdictions in the EU only begin to update their regulatory requirements. The EU regulators are in the necessary process of streamlining currently complex and overlapping cyber risk regulation. Improving information-sharing and coordination on cyber risk between authorities in the EU is also the aim of the ESRB (ESRB/2021/17) necessitating the establishment of a pan-European systemic cyber incident coordination framework. This would allow for an effective Union-level coordinated response in the event of a cross-border major EU-wide cyber incident in the financial sector (ESRB, 2022). As for the ECB, in 2017, it introduced a strategy to improve the cyber resilience of the euro area financial sector, in particular strengthen financial market infrastructures, which is especially prone to interconnectedness risk (ECB, 2018). Moreover, the ECB in 2017 also established the Euro Cyber Resilience Board for pan-European Financial Infrastructures, among others to enhance intelligence sharing and exchanging best practices on cyber defence, enhance the regulatory dialogue with financial market infrastructures and overall contribute to cyber resilience of the financial sector. Further, the ECB in its supervisory capacity has already treated banks' IT and cyber risks as a priority for several years and conducted thematic reviews in this area. Central banks should actively participate in those international initiatives and continue to promote "cyber hygiene". However, a lot remains to be done in terms of analytical advances to measure and monitor cyber risk, which is the first step in adequately responding to it via regulatory framework.

Climate risk

Climate change has become another main challenge for central banks, which engage in monitoring and addressing climate risk as it impacts price stability and financial stability, achieving both of which are within central bank mandates.

There are two main channels through which climate change translates into financial risks – physical and transformation risk (Grippa et al., 2019). Physical risk is caused by the impact of the increasing frequency of extreme weather events (like droughts, floods, storms or whirlwinds), which increases the prices of consumer goods, causing inflationary pressure to surge abruptly (Heinen et al., 2019). Extreme weather events lead to infrastructure damage and losses of households and enterprises. This has negative consequences for the profitability of the insurance industry (Cremades et al., 2018). Entities affected by physical risk may, in turn, have problems with repayment of debt, exposing the banking sector to losses (Nieto, 2019). Transformation risk, in turn, results from the constant adaptation of the economic structure and processes to low-emission technologies, for example, to the target for reducing emissions of carbon dioxide and the related obligations of emitters to purchase emission allowances in the EU (Emission Trading System–ETS). Rising ETS prices make the exploitation of fossil fuels economically unprofitable, which reduces the value of mining companies. Also, the condition of households will likely deteriorate due to higher electricity bills – *green inflation* (Dunz et al., 2021; Frankovic, 2022). The scale of climate risk can reach systemic nature and trigger financial instability (Choudhury, 2021), necessitating central bank involvement even under the current mandate. However, incurring current costs of climate transition lessens the accumulation of physical risks in the future. Protracted reaction to climate risk only results in greater transformation and physical risks.

Within the monetary policy framework, central banks have at their disposal various types of instruments supporting climate risk mitigation. However, this requires a shift in the operating horizon – from short-term liquidity management to long-term sustainable development. One of the pro-ecological areas of central banks' monetary policy includes purchases of environment-friendly assets under quantitative easing programmes. Currently, beneficiaries of asset purchase programmes often include carbon-intensive sectors, which makes it difficult for the central bank to implement sustainability goals (Dafermos et al., 2020). Central banks may allocate part of their foreign reserves to environment-friendly assets (Boneva et al., 2021). However, this also requires a change in the approach to reserve management. To date, central banks have considered safety, liquidity and return when managing their reserves. Green central banking will require the implementation of another foreign reserve management target – environmental sustainability (BIS, 2019).

Out of 135 examined central banks, almost half have a mandate directly or through government policy to enhance sustainable economic development and only 15 banks out of the mentioned 70 have an explicit objective objectives related to sustainable economic growth (Dikau & Volz, 2021). Due to the fact that climate risk has recently become the focus of central banks' interest, the tools for its measurement are at an early stage of development. One of the most reliable methods used so far by a small group of central banks is climate stress testing, examining the resilience of the financial system to climate-related risks. Experiences in the application of this method are shared by Network for Greening the Financial System (NGFS), a group of central banks and supervisors that contribute to the development of climate risk management in the financial sector (NGFS, 2020).

Conclusion

This chapter elaborated the main challenges faced by central banks at the beginning of the XXI century. The rapid development of the financial system over the recent decades, its growth in size and complexity, broadens central banks' role beyond just maintaining price stability. New challenges and tasks force central banks to rethink and redesign their hitherto policy frameworks, and embrace new responsibilities to continue effectively performing a key stabilising role in the economy.

Disclaimer

The opinions expressed in this chapter are solely those of the authors and do not reflect those of the associated institution.

Notes

1 Global cyber losses have been estimated at $250 billion to $1 trillion (Koop et al., 2017).

2 Annual losses of financial institutions from cyberattacks could reach in an extreme scenario on average 9 per cent of banks net income, eroding bank profits and potentially threatening financial stability (Bouveret, 2018). Cyber losses can account for a significant share of total operational value-at-risk (Aldasoro et al., 2020).

8 Issue of central bank digital currencies – potential consequences for the shape of the financial system

Magdalena Kozińska

Introduction

The ubiquitous digitalization and implementation of the whole array of technological innovations are not the features of only commercial part of the financial system. Also public authorities are joining the race of innovation and digitalization. This results in the rising use of digital tools in their everyday tasks (e.g. when regulating [RegTech] and supervising [SupTech]). However, public authorities do not want to be only the recipients of the financial innovations who apply cutting-edge technologies in fulfilling their duties. More and more often, they try to enter the digitalized financial world with their own initiatives.

One of such initiatives are CBDC. So far, no common and binding definition of CBDCs has been worked out, but usually they are described as electronic form of central bank money (central bank liability) accessible to citizens (ECB, 2020a, p. 2; Board of Governors of the Federal Reserve System, 2022 p. 1). The reasons for CBDCs' implementation are divergent. The following economic arguments are cited most frequently by central banks:

- responsibility of central banks to provide the public with the constant access to the central bank money (especially digital one where the use of cash is declining) (SverigesRiksbank, 2018, pp. 2–8; Bindseil et al., 2021, p. 5),
- potential increase in the efficiency of national and international payment systems (SverigesRiksbank, 2018, p. 2).
- possibility to enhance financial inclusion (ECB, 2020a, p. 3; SverigesRiksbank, 2018, p. 8),
- potential to boost the monetary policy framework (SverigesRiksbank, 2017, pp. 27–29).

It should be noted here that many commentators question the economic premises for CBDCs' implementation (e.g. Waller, 2021, pp. 119–126). Even some central banks have reservations towards CBDCs, for example, U.S. Federal Reserve (which represents quite conservative and distanced approach towards CBDCs and started consultations quite late), Bank of England together with British Parliament

DOI: 10.4324/9781003310365-8

(House of Lords, 2022, p. 2) or National Bank of Poland (which preliminarily excluded the possibility to issue CBDC due to lack of real goals that might not be achieved without it) (National Bank of Poland, 2021, p. 4).

The crucial incentives for central banks to launch the analysis of CBDCs seemed to be however:

- increase in the popularity of cryptoassets (e.g. Bitcoin) as payment sources,
- emergence of stablecoins as potential new currencies and
- plans of some private companies to issue their own cryptoassets.[1]

The three facts listed earlier are definitely the most meaningful factors that persuaded central banks to extensively analyse the idea of issuing their own digital currencies, since they are directly connected with the scope of central banks' powers. The real incentive to introduce CBDCs might therefore be balancing private and public sphere of finance (Bolt et al., 2022, p. 7). However, central banks (and other public authorities) might be tempted to implement CBDCs not only due to the possibility to preserve their areas of influence in a new digitalized world. The reason might also be the fact that the CBDC might be structured in such a way that it functions not only as digital cash but also as new policy tool opening new opportunities to expand the dominance of central banks even if the economic premises for their implementation are weak. The desire of central banks to maintain their powerful position by upgrading the status of cash to the digital dimension is, however, not possible without costs – directly related to the development of the framework and infrastructure, as well as indirect connected with the consequences of CBDCs for the financial system.

Consequently, the decision whether or not to implement CBDCs should be contingent on thorough analysis of potential consequences for the financial system and the financial safety net. The aim of this chapter is to outline the potential consequences of CBDCs under two scenarios. Under scenario 1, the potential aftermath of CBDCs with the features analogous to cash are analysed. Under scenario 2, the likely outcome of the introduction of CBDCs with expanded (in comparison to cash) features are presented. This study delineates the general tendencies. It should be noted that all indicated consequences should be subject to meticulous, quantitative and qualitative analyses in all countries that consider CBDCs[2], which are too extensive to present them in one chapter.

The chapter is structured as follows. In the beginning, the notion of CBDCs is presented together with policy options regarding their design. Second part of the chapter is devoted to the analysis of the potential consequences of CBDCs for the financial system (banking sector and other sectors of financial system, central banks themselves and other financial safety net institutions) under two scenarios (with different features of CBDCs). Moreover, the study is concentrated on the elaboration of the CBDCs' impact mainly on the national financial system and safety net. The chapter ends with conclusions.

The idea of CBDCs

The idea of CBDCs is not entirely new. The very first attempts that might be associated with the emergence of CBDCs is the Dutch attempt to create Dukaton as a coin based on the distributed ledger technology (DLT). Meanwhile, other authorities actively engaged in the analysis, for example, Central Bank of Canada (project Jasper), Monetary Authority of Singapore (project Ubin) or Riksbank (project e-krona) (European Parliament, 2021, p. 2). The most advanced central banks are those in Bahamas, Eastern Caribbean or Nigeria that have already implemented the CBDCs. In 2022, also China launched pilot version of its digital yuan (Reuters, 2022).

CBDCs should be understood as digital payment instrument in the form of direct central bank liability denominated in the national unit of account (BIS et al., 2020, p. 3), not connected with credit risk of the issuer (similar to physical cash, but contrary to electronic payment instruments or financial instruments that are connected with are the liabilities of commercial entities that may always collapse) (Auer & Böhme, 2021, p. 6). It is not intended that CBDCs should entirely replace cash, but it cannot be ruled out that people start preferring CBDCs.

CBDCs can take various forms. The first criterion is whether it is issued only towards banks (or other registered and accepted by central bank institutions; so-called wholesale CBDCs[3]) or general public (so-called retail CBDCs). The next criteria defining CBDCs might be connected with their features, which should be compared with the features of cash, since CBDCs are officially develop to substitute cash. Consequently, for the next criteria, it can be distinguished through the following design options: anonymity, remuneration and expiry date.

Consequently, two possible CBDC options could be outlined:

1) cash-like CBDC: anonymous, not remunerated, without expiry date, and
2) CBDC with expanded features ("policy tool CBDC" or "expanded CBDC"): non-anonymous, remunerated and with predetermined expiry date.

The enumerated types of CBDC correspond with two scenarios of CBDCs' implementation that are analysed in the next part of the chapter. The enumerated types of CBDCs (cash-like and policy tool CBDC) might be technically delivered in the following ways:

a) form:
   - account-based (the holding of CBDC requires prior opening of an account) and
   - token-based (CBDC is hold as a token which requires the device able to store tokens, e.g., card or mobile app),

b) distribution:
   - one-tier system (CBDC is distributed directly by the central bank) and
   - two-tier system (CBDC is distributed by the central bank's agent).

Table 8.1 CBDCs' potential features compared to features of cash and bank sight deposit

Subject of claim	*Cash*	*CBDCs*	*Bank Deposit*
	Central bank	*Central bank*	*Commercial bank*
Guarantees	Full	Full	Partial (depending on the scope of the deposit insurance scheme)
Form	Coin or banknote	Token or account	Account
Anonymity	Yes	Might be (policy design option)	No
Remuneration	No	Possible (policy design option)	Yes (interest rates depending in the bank offer – might temporarily be equal to zero)
Expiry date	No	Possible (policy design option	Maturity (no maturity in case of sight deposits)
Distribution system	Through commercial banks	Directly by central bank or through commercial banks	Product delivered by commercial banks

Source: Own elaboration.

In every form and under every type of distribution, it is possible to technically implement each type of enumerated CBDCs: cash-like and policy tool CBDC (as evidenced by the functioning of Bitcoin (Bolt et al., 2022, p. 5). For example, it is possible to implement account-based, one-tier, cash-like CBDCs – through accounts at central bank that do not require prior identity verification (based on, e.g., logins), but such an option seems to be barely possible. Possible technical solutions are presented by, for example, Auer and Böhme (2021, pp. 9–13).

Assessment of the CBDCs consequences

Scenario 1: CBDCs with cash-like features

Cash-like CBDC assumes that it is anonymous, not remunerated and without expiry date. Such features results in the real supplement to the cash. The only difference is the way the cash is delivered – in the digital form (as entry on an account or as a token – both accessed through dedicated device or application) instead of coin or banknote.

Impact on the financial system

Cash-like CBDCs will probably not radically change the shape of the financial system. The tendency to convert physical cash into CBDC will depend on the people's susceptibility to financial innovations. Irrespective of the technical form of CBDC (account-based or token based), financial resources hold in the form of CBDC will be the next form of people's money in the electronic form. Nevertheless, it is unlikely that people will replace bank deposits or other form of capital allocation with CBDCs. Consequently, it is unlikely that the introduction of cash-like CBDCs will induce the rapid outflow of funds from financial institutions (mainly banks). The structure of financial institutions financing seems to retain stable, since cash-like CBDCs do not seem to be interesting investment opportunity acting as a competition towards available financial instruments. This, however, does not mean that the financial system does not change at all.

First and foremost, the increasing part of the operations in the financial systems will be conducted at the click of the button. That means that the flow of funds between institutions (and outside institutions – as a conversion to digital cash) might be accelerated having tremendous consequences at the time of crisis, especially systemic one (when there is general lack of confidence in the whole financial system and people prefer credit-risk-free instruments, e.g., cash). When people store their money as cash deposited on an account, it is necessary to go to the bank to switch it into physical cash (and benefit from risk-free mean of capital accumulation). With CBDCs, it will no longer be necessary, since access to both bank deposit and CBDCs might be remote. This may speed up the bank runs (panics) resulting in the more abrupt character of the liquidity crises. The relative ease in switching between different financial instruments and general openness to digital assets might lead to the increased interest in the new form of investments. Such a phenomenon combined with the low financial literacy might lead to the increased problem of financial scams. People may (especially at the initial phase) confuse CBDCs and their framework with fake one (prepared by swindlers in order to intercept the real money).

Second, although the sudden change in the structure of financing the institutions is barely probable, the CBDCs may dent the profitability of especially banks and other payment institutions, since they may allow to electronically settle debts without the necessity to use money transfer services. This means that part of the financial institutions' business (connected with money transfers and settlements) might erode. At the same time, new area of business (i.e., services connected with CBDCs) might arise what might be an opportunity to balance the lost sources in income. Here, however new players might enter the market enlarging the scope of shadow banking. Simultaneously, increased competition in the field of payment systems might favour further innovations (increasing the overall efficiency of payment infrastructure)[4] and be an opportunity to break the growing dominance of BigTech companies.

Third, the release of the next anonymous instrument of money storing and relocation (without the problem of physical presence of banknotes that take up a lot of place) might however spark the usage of CBDC to illegal purposes. Especially, the already acute problem of money laundering might sharpen, since cross-border use of CBDCs might be more convenient and cheaper (BIS, 2021, p. 76).

Impact on the central bank

The primary consequence for central bank is the necessity to create robust framework for CBDC's issuance and circulation, which is not tried and trusted so the risk of frequent technical glitches is high. The framework must be, however, robust to provide round-the-clock provision of services (otherwise people are cut off from the cash – not applicable in case of physical cash) and be immune to cyberattacks (that probably be more frequent). Any flaws in this respect are connected with reputational risks for central banks influencing its credibility in the field of monetary policy. At the same time, CBDC without remuneration will probably not offer considerable benefits in terms of expanding the monetary policy toolkit and increasing its efficiency.

The increased speed of money circulation, especially the ease to withdraw money from the failing bank should result in the enhancement of the central banks' lender of last resort function. In this respect, the expansion of monetary policy tools aimed at supplying the financial institutions with cash might be necessary. This may also provide an opportunity for central bank to general restructure of the monetary policy toolkit. There is also a need to meticulously explore the impact of CBDCs on monetary policy transmission, since it may alter the control of interest rates (Board of Governors of the Federal Reserve System, 2022 p. 18).

Impact on other financial safety net authorities

Increased sensitivity of financial institutions to the consequences of confidence loss should result in the more scrutiny in the financial institutions supervision. The monitoring of financial institutions' liquidity will definitely gain on importance. Also, the prudential framework for liquidity risk might need to be reinforced. Moreover, in face of the potential acceleration of money outflows, the supervisors should be able to identify the ailing institutions as early as possible to effectively prevent its unordinary and uncontrolled failure. In this regard, two potential consequences might occur. Firstly, the monitoring of financial institutions should rely on current data (not historical). Here, the application of innovations in the field of reporting as well as data science should be intensified. The SupTech might offer benefits. Secondly, where the prevention would fail, the expansion of resolution application might be necessary in order to secure viable and credible tools to resolve problematic institutions as early as possible (in the way that is least noticeable for their clients). Moreover, the increased risk of bank runs should also result in the enhancement of deposit guarantee and investor protection schemes. The increased dependency on electronic forms of money and payments, the robustness of their frameworks and increased risk of cyberattacks may result in the necessity to expand the financial safety net by enhancing especially cyber and Anti-Money Laundering (AML)-related supervision. Consequently, it seems that the role and the level of responsibility of financial safety net institutions will rise after the implementation of cash-like CBDCs.

Scenario 2: CBDCs with expanded features

Policy tool CBDC assumes that it is non-anonymous, remunerated and with expiry date. Such a compilation of features make it the most "extraordinary" form of CBDC that is discussed by the central banks. Probably, not all such features will be implemented by CBDCs, since – as evidenced later – they might have significant negative impact on the financial system. Nevertheless, each of distinguished features is analysed as a potential feature of CBDC; therefore, it is necessary to evaluate them all in order to enable the deliberate decisions.

Impact on the financial system

The expanded CBDCs will probably initiate more far-reaching changes in the financial sector. Remunerated CBDCs will probably incentivize broader group of entities (households and companies) to switch their deposits or other forms of capital allocation into CBDCs (the scale of such a phenomenon will depend on the level of CBDCs' profitability – the more lucrative CBDCs, the higher impact on the financial system). This may result in the following consequences:

- Significant change in the financing structure of financial institutions (especially banks) – the outflow of funds to CBDCs will result in the necessity to collect funds from other sources, for example, through issue of shares, bonds or securities – consequently the role of capital markets will probably increase; alternatively financial institutions (especially banks) may try to retain funds by bundling them with other products (ECB, 2021, p. 16) or by offering higher (than of CBDCs) interest rates.
- Changes in the profitability – similarly as for cash-like CBDCs, part of the settlement and money transfer business will be lost, partially to the benefit of the new market players specializing in the CBDCs' service (to the extent that the financial institutions themselves do not seize the opportunity to expand their offer); also, cheap source of funding (mass deposits of citizens) will be limited and the new sources of funding (as competing with CBDCs) will be more expensive.
- Higher cost of services of financial institutions (especially banks) – as a result of more expensive the funding, making the products less accessible for less wealthy people.

The disintermediation caused by the expanded CBDCs[5] might also undermine the banks' lending capacity – not only as the amount of funds at the banks' disposal might be lower, but also as a result of hindered capacity to evaluate clients' credit worthiness (when clients will not use bank deposits but CBDCs to pay for bills, banks will lose access to the information about people payment habits being their natural competitive advantage in the lending activity).

The predicted changes in the structure and the way of functioning of financial institutions might have further social consequences. The most important one is the possibility to sharpen the problem of financial exclusion (paradoxically denting the frequently cited goal of the CBDCs). Overpriced financial services and products will simply result in the narrower group of people that can afford them. Moreover, it might be necessary to own a device (e.g., card or app) to use CBDCs, what might undermine the CBDCs' aim of fighting the financial exclusion[6].

It should be noted that expanded CBDCs will also share a part of the problems that cash-like CBDCs might generate. This concerns mainly the consequences of the increased speed and ease of the money transfers. Consequently, the susceptibility to bank runs in the financial sector might increase. Also, due to the overall expansion of the electronic means of payment and capital accumulation, the sensitivity of the whole economy to financial scams might increase.

Impact on the central bank

The part of the consequences of the expanded CBDCs are the same as for cash-like CBDCs. This concerns mainly the responsibility to build efficient and robust framework for the issuance and circulation of CBDCs. Any imperfection or weaknesses in this field might result in the loss of confidence in the central bank, denting also the effectiveness of monetary policy. In case of expanded CBDCs, the additional issue that should be carefully addressed is the personal data governance. In this regard, central banks that will directly issue CBDCs will have to meet the requirements that currently payment systems storing customer data face. Due to the sensitivity of consumer data protection, any breach or leak of data from the system may result in the strong criticism of the central bank.

It should be noted however that expanded CBDCs have a great potential as a new monetary policy tool – mainly due to the possibility to adjust their remuneration and maturity. By setting the level of interest rates for CBDCs, central banks gain the next tool for affecting the level of real interest rates in the economy (contrary to cash, which is not remunerated and creates the limitation to the effectiveness of negative interest rates policy). Combining that with the possibility to implement the maturity of such CBDCs, digital currency of central banks might turn out to be a very effective tool in stimulating the economic growth. It would be no longer viable to hold cash if the value might disappear due to the expiry date – it is more beneficial to exchange such CBDCs for products. However, there is the risk that barter payments (exchange of goods) may gain on popularity (since goods do not have expiry dates and might be connected with lower storage costs than negative interest rate charged in the CBDC's holder).

Expanded CBDCs might also increase the efficiency of the quantitative easing (QE). Currently, any such form of economics' support is channelled through the financial system. Non-anonymous CBDCs give the opportunity to issue it directly to the beneficiary. The identification of any subsidies' receivers might also be facilitated, since thanks to the non-anonymity of CBDCs, it would be easy to control the amount of money hold by every citizen and company.

The issues mentioned earlier obviously show that there is also the risk of the over-dominance of central banks in the economy. Notably at the beginning of the switch from capital allocation instruments issued by financial institutions to CBDCs, the financial institutions (especially banks) will need to be supported by central banks liquidity. This might be the only way to prevent the systemic collapse of the financial system. The provision of liquidity is, however, conditioned by the appropriate collateral, which might be lacking in the situation of a "run" on the central bank liquidity[7]. In this way, the central bank might become the main entity providing financing for the economy. Also, the change of the structure of the financial system (as indicated earlier) might result in the necessity to redefine the tasks of the central banks. The currently overarching goal of financial stability might need to be reframed, since non-bank entities will gain on importance. This may result in the necessity to sharpen their oversight and analysis.

Moreover, due to the features of expanded CBDCs the level of central banks' power in the economy would be definitely higher. This however exposes them to the risk of being subject to political influences,[8] since appropriate actions and decisions of central banks might easily boost the economy without the support of the fiscal policy (disturbing the balance between monetary and fiscal policy within the policy mix). Under such circumstances, the consequences of the materialization of reputational risks are even higher.

Impact on other financial safety net authorities

It should be noted that expanded CBDCs might be treated by the consumers (householders and companies) as a form of capital allocation. At the same time, expanded CBDCs as central banks' liability are credit risk-free (central banks usually cannot collapse what is literally ensured within national legislation). Consequently, people's savings would be located in the form of credit-risk free instrument and, at the same time, the level of deposits in commercial banks – as indicated earlier – might decrease. Under such circumstances, the rationales for the functioning of deposit insurance schemes wane.

At the same time, the gravity of capital markets might increase, since financial institutions might be forced to collect funds on the markets in order to ensure the financing of its lending activity. Such funds might come from the general public (if offering better remuneration than expanded CBDCs). This means that the importance of retail investors on capital markets might increase. At the same time, the investor protection schemes are not as developed as deposit guarantee systems. Therefore, it might be necessary to put more emphasis on the expansion of this part of financial safety net.

Conclusion

The analysis of potential features of CBDCs clearly shows that their introduction will definitely impact the financial system and financial safety nets. The ultimate consequences of the implementation of the CBDCs will depend on their final form, which might be similar to cash-like CBDCs, policy tool CBDCs or be mixed.

Without establishing the features of CBDCs, any forecasts are extremely difficult to measure, since depending on the scenario, the results for particular market participants might be completely different (e.g. for deposit insurers). Moreover, the extent to which CBDCs will have an effect on the financial system and financial safety net system depends on the demand for CBDCs which is highly unknown.[9]

Nevertheless, when deciding on the final shape of CBDC, central bank should carefully consider all listed potential consequences (in every national economy the gravity of particular potential consequences might differ due to the national specificities, therefore each central bank should at least try to quantify the enumerated consequences in its jurisdiction). In designing the ultimate design of CBDCs, the superior objectives of the payment sphere should be followed: safety, integrity, efficiency and access (BIS, 2021, p. 70).

It should be noted that the study enumerates mainly national consequences of CBDCs (consequences for national financial system and financial safety net). However, the implementation of CBDCs will definitely change the world of international finances. In this regard also various options of mCBDCs (multi-CBDCs) should be analysed (BIS et al., 2021, pp. 4–19), since they have the capacity not only to foster international payments, but also to change the balance of forces in international economy, where especially pioneers might benefit (according to the rule of "first mover advantage").

The fundamental issue that should be answered by the central banks before the implementation of the CBDCs is however if CBDCs are really necessary, since most of the aims that are cited as the reasoning for their introduction might be accomplished with currently available solutions.

Notes

1 It seems that especially striking for central banks was the news that Facebook (currently Meta) starts works on the implementation of its own currency – Libra (later rebranded to Diem). As an internationally present network, it would have great potential to easily implement the currency used all over the world. Nevertheless, the project probably falls through.

2 In fact the listed, potential consequences might be subject of separate future papers. In this sense, the chapter might be treated as an elaboration of possible directions for further analysis of CBDCs.

3 In this publication, wholesale CBDC is not analysed. The study concentrates on

4 Similar assessments are provided by many public institutions, for example, BIS (2021, p. 66).

5 The preliminary studies suggest that the effect of disintermediation are not likely provided that bank possess market power in the deposit market (Chiu et al., 2019).

6 ECB directly states that due to the potential problem of sharpening financial exclusion with the introduction of CBDCs, the coins and banknotes should remain in circulation (ECB, 2020, p. 20).

7 Such a situation might force compel central banks to change (lower the requirements) for collateral exposing them to higher credit risk. Moreover, it may also have an impact on the markets for the assets (prices, yields, volatility, turnover) submitted as the collateral (if considerable share of the assets are pledged at the central bank).

8 First attempt to assess the level of political pressures connected with the issuance CBDCs is presented by the Niepelt (2018).

9 Both the central banks in their analysis and researchers presenting first estimates are widely divergent. For example, Norges Bank assumes demand of around 3% of Norwegian gross domestic product (GDP) (Norges Bank, 2021, p. 6).

9 The meaning of decentralised finance (DeFi)

Grzegorz Sobiecki, Krzysztof Piech and Aleksandra Kopeć

Introduction

Since the appearance of Bitcoin in 2009, and then Ethereum in 2015 with its first decentralised applications, various blockchain implementations have already rooted in financial markets. Moreover, it is dynamically developing: (1) creating new business models and applications of blockchain technology, (2) creating alternatives to financial services provided traditionally in a centralised manner and (3) extending the possibilities of providing traditional financial services. In this chapter, the authors focused on defining the concept of "decentralised finance" (DeFi), defining its scope, initial classification of services available under DeFi as well as the state and legal challenges resulting from the specificity of DeFi.

The meaning of decentralisation

Bitcoin and the blockchain technology on which it is built have brought a lot of new interests and discussions on the concept of decentralisation. One of its dimensions discussed in this chapter is the decentralisation of finance, which was tried to define in details. However, there are more aspects connected with this issue. In order to fully understand what decentralised finance is (and is not), it should be analysed at least in a glimpse how it is perceived not only in finance but also in other aspects.

Definitions of decentralisation

Decentralisation is usually defined as any act by which the central government formally cedes powers to actors and institutions at lower levels in a political-administrative and territorial hierarchy (Mawhood, 1983; Smith, 1985; Ribot, 2004, p. 7). It can also be viewed as the "transfer of authority and responsibility for public functions from the central government to subordinate or quasi-independent government organisations or the private sector" (Rondinelli, 1981) or "decentralisation is a process where central government transfers political, fiscal, and administrative powers to lower levels in an administrative and territorial hierarchy" (Duncan, 2007, p. 713). "Decentralisation is primarily a strategy for transferring

DOI: 10.4324/9781003310365-9

authority and responsibility from the central government to sub-national (regional and district) levels of government" (Ostrom, 1989; Stone, 1997)

Decentralisation may mean the process that has started from centralisation, and then some forces change the system and decentralise it. Hence, decentralisation is inevitably connected with its opposition. However, in blockchain technology, it is not necessarily spoken about decentralisation as a process where any central power gives it to other bodies. In most blockchain-based solutions, new inventions have been created without prior centralisation. For instance, the central banks did not give their powers to the people and companies; financial regulators usually do not empower non-governmental organisation (NGO) (but in Switzerland – Self-regulatory Organisation (SRO)), legislators did not set up the rules based on which "code is the law." These were the bottom-up inventions. Hence, the literal meaning of decentralisation as a transfer of power from an entity that first had it is not the right place in the case of blockchain technology applications.

Apart from the centralisation-decentralisation dichotomy, in network theory, very often "distribution" is added. And the following graphs by Baran (1962) are quoted:

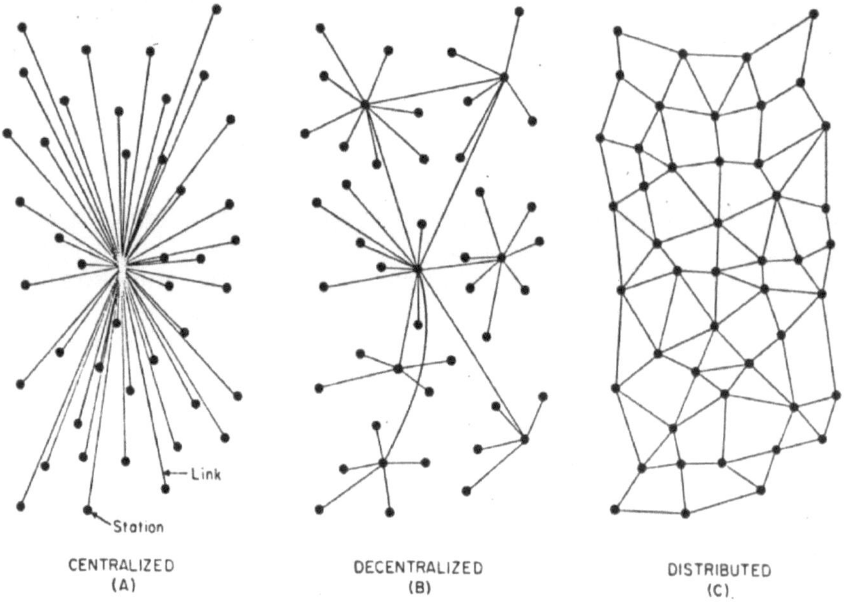

Figure 9.1 Types of networks

Source: Baran, 1962, p. 4.

As Baran wrote (1962, p. 3): "as destruction of a small number of nodes in a decentralized network can destroy communications, we shall turn to consider the properties, problems, and hopes of building communications networks that are as 'distributed' as possible." If the network is centralised, it is subject to the risks caused by its central servers, which becomes the "single point of failure" (SPoF). The security of communication, but in broader meaning also of management, finances and databases, requires identification and if possible – elimination of such SPoFs (through backups, redundant connections etc.). To secure blockchain technology applications, including DeFi, all possible SPoFs should be identified and eliminated, if possible.

Pros and cons of decentralisation and the blockchain trilemma

This, however, poses some drawbacks, which are widely discussed in the literature. The following obstacles hindering decentralisation are often listed: economies of scale (which intensify with centralisation), difficulties with coordination of decision-making process, too complex management of the system, poorer services if provided by small, decentralised units, the problems with satisfying some regulatory and legal requirements by smaller, undercapitalised units, higher vulnerability to corruption, lower transparency of decision-making and so forth. Decentralisation, apart from security, brings however also other profits. For instance, "there is some international evidence that decentralization can be closely tied to democratization (. . .) the commitment to decentralization as a means of countering the democratic deficit and bringing the decision-making process 'closer to the people.'" (Brown, 2009) This is an important element of the adoption of blockchain technology, which is often bottom-up directed and driven by the need of people to fight for more freedom, privacy or fighting against the government and "banksters" (recall the notes in Bitcoin Genesis Block). From macroeconomic point of view, Oates (1993) based on the analysis of over 50 countries has confirmed a positive relationship between decentralisation and economic growth.

Blockchain technology, thanks to introducing a solid set of rules written info immutable code[1] and through other solution (like synchronisation of nodes), solves, for example, the Byzantine Generals Problem. Thus, some of the traditional

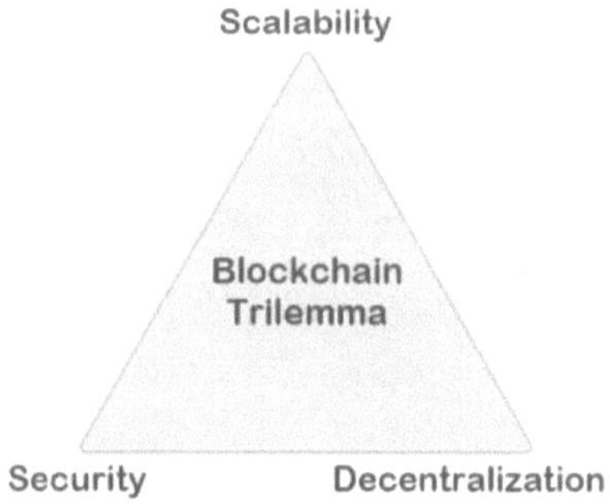

Figure 9.2 The scalability/blockchain trilemma

Source: Karaarslan & Konacakli, 2020.

problems with management, especially when some information is missing or counterfeited is solved. However, some other problems still exist.

Moreover, the scalability trilemma that exists in distributed-ledger technologies. Namely, there is a trade-off between three of their properties: decentralisation, scalability and security. It is a well-known problem in blockchain technology first described during the early works on Ethereum by VitalikButerin. It is nearly not possible to meet all three requirements at the same time.

The scalability is one of the major key problems of Ethereum and other blockchains. So far, different solutions have been proposed, including, for example, sharding, application of Directed Acyclic Graph (DAG), lightning network, increase of the size of blocks or the second layer solutions (like side chains, payment channels) – see Figure 9.3.

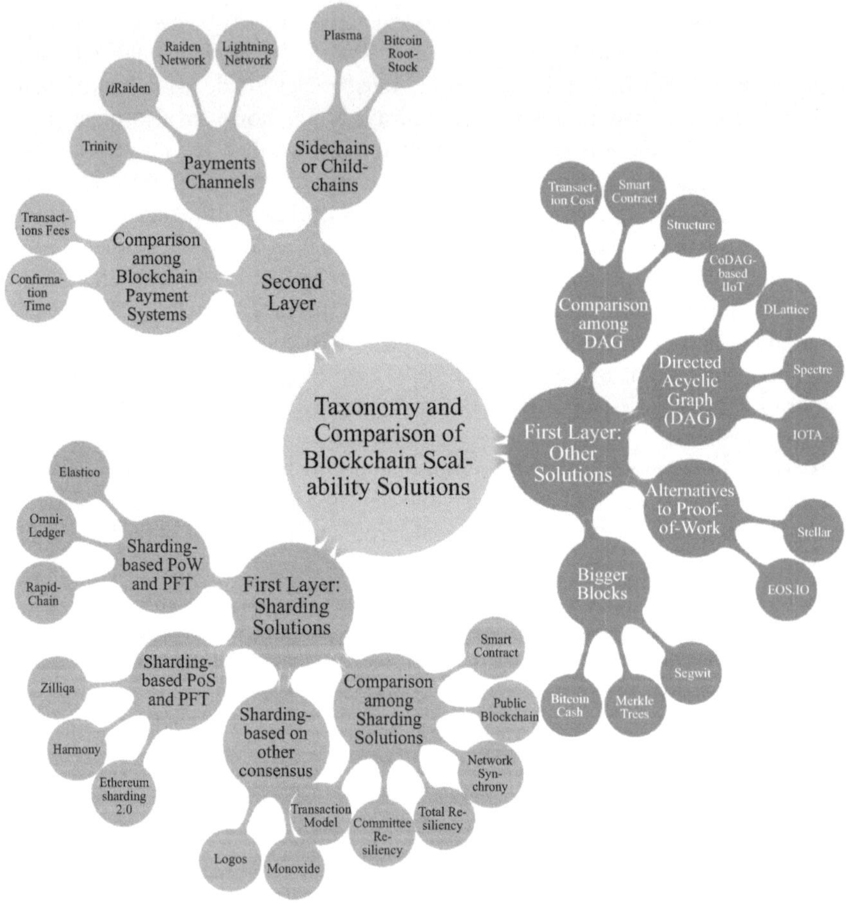

Figure 9.3 Taxonomy and comparison of blockchain scalability solutions

Source: Hafid et al., 2020

Buterin (2021) believes that sharding is the solution to the Scalability Trilemma. As he wrote:

> A sharded blockchain is:
>
> - Scalable: it can process far more transactions than a single node
> - Decentralised: it can survive entirely on consumer laptops, with no dependency on "supernodes" whatsoever
> - Secure: an attacker can't target a small part of the system with a small amount of resources; they can only try to dominate and attack the whole thing.

There are, however, also other solutions (see, e.g. Solana, IOTA, to name a few).

Types of decentralisation

The literature usually provides four dimensions of decentralisation. Often the following ones are mentioned:

- political (decision-making) – "transfer of state administration, legislative authority and judicial autonomy to local governments," "more authority to citizens" (Ozmen, 2014), democracy; in decentralised systems, all three different levels of government (national, regional and local) have independent decision-making power (Brancati, 2006, p. 654);
- fiscal (economic or financial); intergovernmental fiscal relations in countries where, constitutional and statutory powers of taxation, budget and expenditure rights are given to federal units within the federal state (Ozmen, 2014) or the assignment of funds to local levels;
- administrative – transferring of some typical functions of the government (e.g. planning, management, allocation of resources) to autonomous public institutions; usually, its three major forms are mentioned: deconcentration, delegation and devolution;
- market (or economic), and the two forms are usually mentioned: privatisation and deregulation, "because they shift responsibility for functions from the public to the private sector" (World Bank, 2005) or to the market.

This division is different from the more narrow one proposed by Buterin (2017), the blogpost of whom became seminal for the blockchain industry. He then enumerated the following "axes" of decentralisation:

> - Architectural (de)centralization – how many physical computers is a system made up of? How many of those computers can it tolerate breaking down at any single time?
> - Political (de)centralization – how many individuals or organizations ultimately control the computers that the system is made up of?

- Logical (de)centralization – does the interface and data structures that the system presents and maintains look more like a single monolithic object, or an amorphous swarm? One simple heuristic is: if you cut the system in half, including both providers and users, will both halves continue to fully operate as independent units?

His typology, however, neglects some aspects of blockchain technology implementations that became important in the next years. It concentrates on the technical side without recognising different groups of interests behind cryptocurrencies. As decentralisation is about sharing/transferring the power, those who have them should be identified first. In the case of major cryptocurrencies like Bitcoin or Ethereum, it is proposed to distinguish between the following groups of interests: initiator – author of the project, code developers, miners (validators of transactions), big investors ("whales," investment funds), big companies (esp. exchanges), influencers (e.g. VitalikButerin and Elon Musk) and users (usually retail investors at the same time). This differs from the traditional typology of decentralisation found in the literature. Hence, for the purpose of this chapter, it needs to be distinguished the following types of decentralisation: political, economic (with fiscal, market and financial) and technical. It is suggested grouping and naming them in the following way:

a) political decentralisation: main author of the project, code developers;
b) administrative decentralisation: miners and transaction validators, masternode holders;
c) market decentralisation: investors, companies and users; and
d) technological decentralisation: nodes, pools, core client, wallets, testnets.

(De)centralisation of blockchain

Below, the typology will be extended by using the authors' knowledge of the field to identify different elements that need to be analysed from the point of view of decentralisation. For each dimension, the following questions can be raised:

1. Political decentralisation:

    - Who is the SPoF? Is it the author of the project, chief executive officer or chief technology officer, or maybe the main sponsor or investor?
    - The main author of the project – is he known? How large is his influence on the project? Can he take the decisions alone? Can he be manipulated (bribed, threatened, blackmailed)?
    - Core developers – who are they? Are they from the same company? Is there a person who controls them and gives them the orders? Who pays them?
    - Other developers – do they belong to the same company? Is there one company responsible for software? Who controls it?

- Regulators Anti-money Laundering (AML) – is there one major regulator whose decisions have a deep impact on the project? Can any political body/regulator outlaw the project and make it disappear?
- Voting – how decisions are taken? (through voting? Is there a DAO? – are there any larger voters there?). Is there a hierarchy of decisions making or is the power distributed (or delegated)?

2. Administrative decentralisation:

   - Legal entity – is there any? Is it responsible for code development? Are the IPRs legally separated from finances? Which jurisdictions are used (if any) and how reliable they are? (autocratic vs. democratic, how strong is there the rule of law?)
   - Miners and transaction validators – how many of them there are? Is known any collusion among them or can happen in the future? How the network is protected against possible conspiracy?
   - Reward – is it distributed automatically by the code among major mining pools? How are the mining pools managed? Is solo mining possible and can be profitable?
   - Pools – how many mining pools there are? Is any of them close to having 50% of the hashrate? Who controls the pools?
   - Masternode holders – how many masternode holders there are? Is there a threat of a conspiracy among them?

3. Market decentralisation:

   - Investors – their concentration (coin/token distribution across TOP-100 and TOP-10 addresses). Is there a dominating one – or a few of them? How many persons control top addresses (including exchanges)?
   - Companies – the scale of oligopolisation of the market, top exchanges, the role of DEXes (share in total exchange markets), payment gateways fiat-crypto-fiat (how many there are?).
   - Influencers – is there one person who can manipulate the coin/token price with his actions? Are there more of them (and how many)? Can they be manipulated (paid/bribed etc.)? Are the opinions of larger influencers neutral or biased and why?
   - Users – where are they located? How many of them there are? What is the proportion of fake accounts on social media (Telegram, Twitter, Instagram and YouTube) versus the real activity of the community? Who generates the content on social media and how easily the community can be manipulated?

4. Technological decentralisation:

   - Are there any SPoFs? Are they identified? Were external auditors employed to find them?
   - Nodes – how many are there? (only one or just a few? If so, who controls them: one person/company? Can it influence the other node keepers?).

How high is the (de)concentration of nodes (ownership, geographical distribution – does one country dominate? How centralised is the political power there?) Usage of own server versus cloud services (cloud services dependency): how many cloud providers, what is the concentration of nodes there?

- Pools – how many pools there are and who controls them? What is the hashrate distribution among top mining pools? Is there one that has over 50% of hashrate? Are there any procedures/examples of processes introduced in the case of getting close to the 50% limit?
- Core client – is there only one such full client? How much is it reliable? How many people develop it?
- Wallets – how many of them exist (only one or more)? Are they based on original invention or were adopted from other, proven solutions?
- Testnets – is there a testnet or the changes are introduced directly to mainnet? How many testnets there are? Are they updated together with the upgrades of mainnet? Do people use it or only a very limited number of core developers? How many wallets can use testnets?

As it can be seen earlier, decentralisation of blockchain is a much more sophisticated issue than, for example, Buterin (2017, 2021) coined. In order to estimate and measure the real level of decentralisation of any blockchain, many of the aforementioned questions have to be asked first and many answers evaluated then.

As blockchain is the basis of decentralised finance, it is not possible to analyse the latter term without giving the prior answers on the scope of (de)centralisation of a particular blockchain it is based on. In most cases so far, DeFi uses the Ethereum blockchain. However, given the dynamic development of this market, more blockchains have been gradually employed, with Stellar outpassing many others in terms of the number of transactions (over 7.2 million per day compared to 2.2 m in Ripple, 1.3 m Ethereum and only 0.2 m in Bitcoin; see: Forexsuggest, 2022).

DeFi concept

There are still no clearly defined, universally recognized boundaries of the concept of DeFi. Many projects and startups use the "DeFi" notion for marketing purposes, in fact, neither meeting any of the definitions nor recognized features of DeFi. One of the largest problems with decentralisation of finance is the centralisation of its management or provision of centralised services despite being based on blockchain, which is a decentralised technology, although some blockchains are controlled by one legal entity only (hence its governance is centralised). Similar applies to so-called decentralised applications (dApps) which may be provided by one entity and its owners control them. Thus, it can be seen how ambiguous the concept of decentralisation is.

Review of approaches in the literature

In order to delineate the unambiguous limits of the concept of decentralised finance, various definitions of this notion and finally authors' definition of DeFi will be proposed, which will include the commonly recognised distinguishing features of DeFi. Table 9.1 summarises 21 sources related to DeFi.

Table 9.1 Definitions and descriptions of the concept of DeFi

Definition or a description of the concept	*Source*
DeFi refers to a movement that includes a collection of financial services (e.g. trading, lending, borrowing, payments). These services utilize decentralized infrastructure to operate in the form of a blockchain network and smart contracts.	Amanai, 2019
The term DeFi refers to the financial applications run by smart contracts on a blockchain, typically a permissionless (i.e. public) chain. . . . DeFi provides financial services without centralised intermediaries, by operating through automated protocols on blockchains. The DeFi ecosystem revolves around two elements: (i) novel protocols for trading, lending and investing, and (ii) stablecoins, which are cryptoassets that facilitate fund transfers and aim to maintain a fixed face value vis-à-vis fiat currencies, mainly the US dollar.	Aramonte et al., 2021
DeFi can be described as an experimental form of financial praxis that is removed from dependence on centralized financial intermediaries, which in this context might include banks, exchanges and brokerages. As such, DeFi purports to disintermediate financial activity from the traditional mechanisms of finance, and it does so through the use of a blockchain substitutive architecture. Oftentimes, the most commonly utilized architecture platform in DeFi applications is Ethereum, which has become a mainstay platform for many blockchain-based innovations in the past five years.	Chohan, 2021
DeFi (or "decentralized finance") is an umbrella term for financial services on public blockchains, primarily Ethereum. With DeFi, you can do most of the things that banks support – earn interest, borrow, lend, buy insurance, trade derivatives, trade assets, and more – but it's faster and doesn't require paperwork or a third party. As with crypto generally, DeFi is global, peer-to-peer (meaning directly between two people, not routed through a centralized system), pseudonymous, and open to all.	Coinbase, 2022
Decentralized finance – DeFi – refers to the shift from traditional, centralized financial systems to peer-to-peer finance enabled by the Ethereum blockchain.	Consensys, 2021

(*Continued*)

Table 9.1 (Continued)

Definition or a description of the concept	*Source*
[*According to DeFi Llama's methodology – DeFi project is what the community decides.*]	DeFi Llama, 2022
Decentralized Finance (DeFi) is the movement that leverages decentralized networks to transform old financial products into trustless and transparent protocols that run without intermediaries.	DeFiPrime, 2022
DeFi is a collective term for financial products and services that are accessible to anyone who can use Ethereum – anyone with an internet connection. With DeFi, the markets are always open and there are no centralized authorities who can block payments or deny you access to anything. Services that were previously slow and at risk of human error are automatic and safer now that they're handled by code that anyone can inspect and scrutinize.	Ethereum Foundation, 2022
DeFi is a set of tools and applications, the so-called "Dapps" (Distributed Apps) operating in the blockchain network (currently mostly on the Ethereum blockchain) and allowing the user to use a number of financial services that we know from the traditional financial sector, but implemented mostly without the participation of a central institution (e.g. a bank). The functioning of the service is coordinated by the so-called smart contracts, i.e. contracts written and programmed in the form of computer code located on the blockchain network.	FinTech Poland, 2021
Decentralized Finance (DeFi) – a peer-to-peer financial system, which leverages distributed ledger-based smart contracts to ensure its integrity and security.	Gudgeon et al., 2020
Decentralized finance (DeFi) is an emerging financial technology based on secure distributed ledgers similar to those used by cryptocurrencies. The system removes the control banks and institutions have on money, financial products, and financial services.	Investopedia, 2022a
DeFi = Short for Decentralised Finance. Peer-to-peer software-based network of protocols that can be used to facilitate traditional financial services like borrowing, lending, trading derivatives, insurance, and more through smart contracts. DeFi consists of financial services enabled by public blockchains and smart contracts executing rules set by developers and governance token-holders, with no ability for a central party to intervene or manipulate users' assets.	KPMG, 2021

Definition or a description of the concept	*Source*
Decentralised Finance or 'DeFi' is an effort to replicate certain functions of the traditional financial system in an open, decentralised, permissionless and autonomous way, based on blockchains. As with any distributed ledger technology (DLT)-based application, DeFi could potentially offer efficiencies driven by automation and disintermediation powered by blockchains and smart contracts. . . . DeFi is the latest trend in the crypto-asset space, and promises to replicate various activities in the traditional financial system in an open, decentralised, permissionless and autonomous way. DeFi applications allow for the provision of financial products and services built as decentralised applications on the blockchain. . . . Although there is no widely accepted definition of DeFi, this report defines the key features differentiating DeFi from traditional financial markets as follows: Non-custodial . . ., Self-governed and community-driven . . ., Composable.	OECD, 2022
Decentralized platforms that offer financial services similar to those of banks and similar organizations to their users. This sector of the market has grown to be called Decentralized Finance.	Ramos & Zanko, 2020
The term decentralized finance (DeFi) refers to an alternative financial infrastructure built on top of the Ethereum blockchain. DeFi uses smart contracts to create protocols that replicate existing financial services in a more open, interoperable, and transparent way. . . . Decentralized finance (DeFi) is a blockchain-based financial infrastructure that has recently gained a lot of traction. The term generally refers to an open, permissionless, and highly interoperable protocol stack built on public smart contract platforms . . . . It replicates existing financial services in a more open and transparent way. In particular, DeFi does not rely on intermediaries and centralized institutions. Instead, it is based on open protocols and decentralized applications (DApps). Agreements are enforced by code, transactions are executed in a secure and verifiable way, and legitimate state changes persist on a public blockchain. Thus, this architecture can create an immutable and highly interoperable financial system with unprecedented transparency, equal access rights, and little need for custodians, central clearing houses, or escrow services, as most of these roles can be assumed by "smart contracts."	Schär, 2021

(*Continued*)

Table 9.1 (Continued)

Definition or a description of the concept	*Source*
[DeFi] is a new market industry in which financial or para-financial services are delivered in a decentralized environment. Decentralized finance can fall under the broader category of 'DEcentralized Services', that is, services that are delivered using decentralized applications. Decentralized applications include a collection of related smart contracts entered into the blockchain and the user interface along with an appropriate API that allows you to interact with the contract.	Sobiecki, 2021
DeFi is a set of decentralized applications (dApps) that automate financial services based on the blockchain technology without any centralized control. DeFi is sometimes called "Money Lego" because it offers unlimited combination opportunities. DeFi includes 3-D (Digitalization, Decentralization, and Democratization) concepts of sustainable development that motivate the users to employ the blockchain technology in financial services.	Stepanova & Erins, 2022
Decentralized finance . . . is implemented through smart contracts (DApps) which are stored on a public distributed ledger (such as a blockchain) and can be activated to automate execution of financial instruments and digital assets. The immutable property of blockchains guarantees that these DApps are also tamper-proof and the content could be publicly audited.	Wang, 2020
DeFi is . . . is a category of blockchain-based decentralized applications (DApps) for financial services. DeFi encompasses a variety of technologies, business models and organizational structures, generally replacing traditional forms of intermediation. DeFi transactions involve digital assets and generally operate on top of base-layer settlement platforms.	WEF, Wharton, 2021
DeFi is a general term for decentralized applications (Dapps) providing financial services on a blockchain settlement layer, including payments, lending, trading, investments, insurance, and asset management. DeFi services typically operate without centralized intermediaries or institutions, and use open protocols that allow services to be programmatically combined in flexible ways. . . . DeFi takes advantage of various technologies developed in the blockchain sphere. All have applications outside of DeFi, but play essential roles within the DeFi ecosystem: Blockchains . . ., Digital Assets . . ., Wallets. . ., Smart Contracts . . ., Decentralized Applications (Dapps) . . ., Governance Systems . . ., Decentralized Autonomous Organizations (DAOs) . . . Stablecoins . . ., Oracles.	Wharton, 2021

Definition or a description of the concept	*Source*
"Decentralized Finance" (DeFi) is neither a legal nor a technical term. It is nonetheless increasingly used in the context of discussions about the future evolution of finance and its regulation. Common usage incorporates one or more elements of: (i) decentralization; (ii) distributed ledger technology and blockchain; (iii) smart contracts; (iv) disintermediation; and (v) open banking.	Zetzsche et al., 2020

Source: Authors' own elaboration.

Distinguishing features of the concept

In accordance with the definitions quoted, DeFi is framed as

- a financial system, an area of the financial market, an alternative financial infrastructure,
- a phenomenon, a movement, a trend of decentralisation of financial systems,
- a set of financial services and products,
- a set of tools and applications, technology, technological stack, and
- a set of activities, practices and business relations.

DeFi as such is a space for new economic phenomena, but the "phenomenon" does not define the essence of this concept. Even though DeFi develops new products and services, it is not actually creating a new financial system. DeFi provides both traditional (loans, exchanges, insurance) and completely new services (liquidity pools[2], staking[3]), all using new tools, mainly based on blockchain technology. It is new, but cannot be defined as an "alternative", because of the difficulty in assessing, what it is an alternative to[4] and whether it is an alternative or a complement?

An industry is a part of the economy (a type of activity including enterprises, production processes, distribution, markets or business relations) in which closely related products or services are produced (products and services with a similar purpose, produced using similar technology). Therefore DeFi should be treated as a "new branch of the industry" within the area of finance and insurance (in most economic classifications, the highest level of grouping covers the same area), which are a part of the services sector of an economy.

Most common features of DeFi mentioned in the definition collected earlier are:

- decentralised nature (no intermediaries, no central control over the service, non-custodial, autonomy);
- open nature: public, open networks, not requiring top-down access rights, open source protocols and applications;
- service delivery automation available in the 24/7/365 schema;

- embedded in the digital world (digital goods, digital value transfer, algorithms);
- use of blockchain technology and related utilities (integrity, security, transparency) and elements characteristic of the blockchain ecosystem: tokens (including stablecoins), smart contracts, decentralised autonomous organisations (DAO), wallets, oracles;
- and providing financial services (loans, trading, insurance etc.).

These features can be grouped into three dimensions (3D):

1. Digitization
2. Democratisation
3. Decentralisation

DeFi services are embedded in the technological stack of "digital technology" – blockchain. Due to the fact that it is based on blockchain technology, DeFi inherits all its properties. Therefore, DeFi services are made of or take advantage of the utility of the same elements (Sobiecki, 2021):

1. **Data structure** (blockchain – the current entry in the data register depends on the previous ones) – ensures data integrity.
2. **Decentralised p2p network** (distributed in the sense of Paul Baran) – a virtual network (not physical) formed between autonomous and sovereign nodes that follow the same protocol and which communicate directly with each other. As a rule, DeFi uses protocols that do not require infrastructure authorizations or use (open networks, public).
3. **Consensus mechanism** – nodes synchronisation mechanism in conditions of continuous data flow, independence of nodes' decisions and lack of a central coordinator – complements the aforementioned elements, resulting in non-repudiation (evidence) and invariability (durability) of data recording. Due to invariability, it is possible to maintain a decentralised register of holdings of digital goods (tokens), which are characterised by absolute scarcity.
4. **Identification and authentication mechanisms** – specific mechanisms of identifying network users by network address, which is also an element of the mechanism of their authentication in the network and ensuring the security of data (and resources).
5. **Incentive mechanisms** – mechanisms granting specific real benefits to the co-creating the ecosystem (especially nodes maintaining the network infrastructure) ensuring the survival of the system (network) as a whole.
6. **Virtual decentralised machine** – generalisation of a decentralised registry to a decentralised "computer", thanks to which it is not only possible to maintain a transaction registry in a decentralised environment, and the mechanisms stored in the protocol enable token transfer, but it also becomes possible to automate in a decentralised environment of business relations.

DeFi services are by nature platforms, as they connect different entities of business relations. DeFi automates those business relations using the functionality of smart contracts and a specific, new type of digital goods – tokens that have (may have) the trait of absolute scarcity, which is the key foundation of their value, and it was not obtainable in a decentralised environment before. Digital goods and services are available globally without interruption and allow operation without unnecessary formalities while maintaining a high level of privacy.

DeFi services transfer the burden of service provision and the associated risk to the broadly understood ecosystem – the community of service stakeholders:

- **Platform users** – prosumers (consumers who can turn into producers/ providers), who independently control their funds (funds are not entrusted to any single entity).
- **Members of a decentralised autonomous organisation (DAO)** – decentralised group regulating the operation of the service and undertaking decisions on matters related to the operation of the service.
- **System operators**– initiating the service, proposing changes to the functioning, usability.
- **External service providers**– to which a given service depends, and those whose operation depends on a given service, including: blockchain infrastructure providers for DeFi applications, providers of payment units (including stablecoins), keepers intermediating between the decentralised application and the market, oracles receiving signals from the applications and providing data to the applications, data storage providers (as blockchain networks are usually not adapted to the storage of traditional data types), decentralised exchanges, liquidity service providers and so on.

This makes DeFi services network-based and network-generating or a chain-service, compositional. Sometimes this feature is called "Money Lego", but it simplifies DeFi's flexibility and narrows down potential functionalities. In the previous section, we discussed what "decentralisation" means in a broad sense. In the context of DeFi, the decentralisation of service delivery processes entails the democratisation of management – there is no (as a rule) a single "owner" of the service (in fact the service itself is put in to a public domain), the is no one single control centre for all service processes. In practice, they are often separated from each other and, at the same time, independently democratised: control over the regulation of service parameters, control over the use of funds allocated to the development of the service and control over the acceptance of a new service code (new processes, error correction). Automation and decentralisation of service processes means no entity legally, organisationally and financially is responsible for the provision of the service that operates on finances. This usually means the lack of typical assets of the organisation responsible for the service to be used as a resource of production potential or a resource of liquidity in settlements. While the production potential-intangible assets in the form of code can be transferred to the public domain, there is still a need to obtain liquidity needed for settlements and the functioning of services. Hence, for example, a specific independent service arose – liquidity pools. Each service functions as long as it benefits the entity responsible for it. When there is no such entity, the functioning of incentive mechanisms becomes of key importance so that each of the service stakeholders has a real benefit.

DeFi definition

Taking into account the above features of DeFi, we propose to adopt the following definition of DeFi. DeFi is a new industry that includes financial services:

- that provided automatically in virtual peer-to-peer networks with highly decentralised control,
- that use public permissionless networks (do not require centrally granted permission to use the service nor to create a service infrastructure or provide the service),
- that use smart contracts and blockchain technology in the processes of: service provision, creation and digital goods (tokens) and the units of account (including stablecoins), clearing and settlements, address identification and transaction authentication, and coordination of service provision.

DeFi services classification

By analogy to financial services, next we have distinguished the categories of DeFi services, covering the full-known services spectrum.

[1] **Payment tokens systems.** These services enable the generation and handling of payment tokens and the transfer of cryptoassets. These services (systems) are the foundation of the DeFi industry. They enable the generation of cryptocoins on individual terms and contain mechanisms for their transfer to other entities. These can be infrastructure solutions that provide cryptocurrencies as units of account within the blockchain network (e.g. Bitcoin, Ethereum and Dash), derivative solutions (e.g. second-layer solutions) or higher-level solutions (second generation) – generating tokens within smart contracts.

[2] **Digital token trading platforms.** These are the services most often collectively referred to as "decentralised exchanges" (DEX). We distinguish four types of exchanges:

   - Decentralised exchanges based on an order-book-based (OBB) table– under which automatic mechanisms collect sales and purchase orders on an ongoing basis and execute exchange transactions in the DVP model, at the rate resulting from the collected orders (e.g. MerleX, Dex blue and StellarX).
   - Decentralised exchange offices (automated market makers, AMM) – algorithmic token exchange platforms based on pooled liquidity/

liquidity pools – liquidity reserves entered the system by independent users instead of on order tables; the originators of the transaction trade with the pool and not with other principals (e.g. Bancor protocol and the Uniswap protocol).

- P2P market platforms – similar to distributed exchanges based on the order table, but with greater control of order conditions. The exchange takes place on the basis of individual direct p2p relations – the ordering party (buyer or seller) carries out the selected offer, exchanging according to the parameters specified in the individual offer (example of Local Cryptos).
- Trading platforms – extensive solutions that allow you to take long, short positions, including leveraged positions – often combined with lending platforms that provide the missing capital for leverage or include such functionalities in their own protocol. They also include mechanisms such as escrow or margin call (brokerage call to replenish capital) (e.g. the bZx protocol and related Fulcrum or Torque services).

[3] **Loan and deposit platforms.** These allow users to borrow for interest and deposit tokens in loan instruments. Loans can:

- have a p2p nature – that is, be granted individually by specific investors from a dispersed network, to selected borrowers according to the parameters specified individually in their offer (e.g. Lendoit or Nitrogen);
- use a common liquidity pool – often combined with other services (stablecoins, trading platforms); within this group, there are secured loan platforms (e.g. the Dharma project using the Compound or Definer protocol) or unsecured loans (TrueFi); they can be used as part of some algorithmic stablecoins to stabilise the rate (for example DAI/SAI tokens under MakerDAO).

The vast majority of loan services (or loan functionalities as part of services whose essence is a different functionality or combining various functionalities, e.g. MakerDAO) require liquid funds collateral (in the form of cryptocurrencies), which often significantly exceed the current market value of the borrowed cryptocurrency. The so-called over collateral can range from 150% to 200% of the value of the borrowed cryptocurrency. Examples of projects offering secured loans are Aave, Compound and MakerDAO.

The blockchain technology along with the functionality of smart contracts, thanks to its flexibility, made it possible to create solutions that made it possible to effectively grant loans without collateral (or with partial collateral), including low-value loans. Unsecured loans provide lenders with the opportunity to obtain higher long-term returns than secured loans and provide borrowers with the opportunity to maximise capital efficiency (primarily reducing the cost of capital). However, unsecured loans require, as in traditional financial markets, to test the borrowing capacity in order to estimate the risk associated with granting it to the creditor and calculate the interest rate on this basis. In a decentralised, anonymised environment, this was a key challenge, as was debt collection or bailiff enforcement in the event of loan default. However, a number of solutions to this problem have been developed (Clear Chain Capital, 2021).

[4] **Investment services (asset management services).** The following services can be distinguished among investment services:

- oracle-based investment funds – semi-automatic mechanisms that allow the use of the dispersed "wisdom of the crowd" in the form of DAO to receive and manage collected cryptoassets (an example is Betoken, PowerPool);
- mutual funds based on automatic rules – they enable the automatic implementation of a crypto resource management strategy (example Set)

[5] **Staking.** Staking funds (pools) are used for the implementation of infrastructural processes that require the accumulation of large amounts of assets, e.g. by nodes in networks using the Proof-of-Stake consensus algorithm. Staking services are a cryptocurrency equivalent of a service similar to a joint venture mechanism and an investment fund at the same time, it consists in the deliberate accumulation of cryptoassets in return for specific benefits.

[6] **Liquidity pools.** These pools are staking-like mechanisms embedded in smart contracts to receive, store and spend cryptoassets to enable services that need available 'operational' cryptoassets to function. What distinguishes them from staking is primarily the way they use blocked cryptoassets. Liquidity pools may be part of integrated services but are sometimes also distinguished as independent aggregation services ("liquidity-as-a-service"). They enable the integration of various liquidity pools operating on different platforms and the accumulation of funds in one pool used by other DeFi services (e.g. BlockFills and Ren). The investment process by blocking cryptoassets in a liquidity pool is called "liquidity mining" to distinguish it from cryptocurrency mining or staking.

[7] **Token rental platforms.** Rental services (leasing) make it possible to separate the possession of tokens from their utility. The leasable tokens are usually:

- tokens representing a certain value or rights (e.g. voting rights in a given platform),
- tokenized digital assets (e.g. game artefacts) in the form of NFT tokens,
- tokenized physical assets (e.g. Chintai).

Token rental is a way for token holders to earn passive income while still owning their digital assets. For those, who only want to use assets for temporary or one-time access to a service, it is more profitable to lease these assets than to buy them, and then to keep them and to worry about price fluctuations and storage options.

[8] **Mutual bets and prediction markets.** Mutual bets (bookmakers' bets), including the so-called prediction markets; implement mechanisms

similar to those used in distributed exchanges, enriched with a mechanism of rewarding correct forecasts (incentive mechanism, reputation mechanism), which enable the execution of bets related to various events and their automatic settlement and settlement. These platforms include automatic or semi-automatic mechanisms called distributed oracles that feed factual information into the web. The result of their operation can be an assessment of the likelihood of certain events occurring in the future (within fact betting) – hence the term "forecast markets" (e.g. Helena, Augur, Bitcoin Hivemind or Gnosis).

[9] **Insurance services.** These services enable protection against various events of the real world or (more often) of the DeFi industry (e.g. Nexus Mutual, Unslashed – protection against errors of smart contracts, oracle errors, portfolio errors, risk of trustees and improper actions of validators).

[10] **Hedging and derivatives.** These are often combined with DEX exchanges – services enabling automatic protection against, for example, changes in cryptocurrency prices, based on derivative instruments – for example, cryptofutures, including the so-called perpetual contracts – perpetuals (e.g. Opyn or the dYdX exchange) or physical world events: flight delays, hurricanes, crop failure, health and life insurance (e.g. Ethersc protocol).

[11] **Payment requests services.** These services make it possible to relieve the payer from monitoring payments, especially cyclical ones, thanks to which. Such services are available in traditional banking finance.

[12] **Factoring.** Factoring platforms make it possible to increase the credibility of bidders, faster access to liquidity and at the same time are an investment vehicle (e.g. partially dispersed Clear Factor).

[13] **Letter of credit services** speed up commercial processes, reduce disputes thanks to the guarantee of durability of entries, reduce costs, reduce exchange rate risks, automatically and precisely perform all contract entries, automate settlements and settlements, and transparently record the history of operations (e.g. Contour/previously Voltron).

Legal challenges of decentralised finance

The causes of legal challenges of decentralised finance

Apart from all the potential benefits of decentralised finance, it also comes with many risks and challenges including inter alia downscaling the investor's protection and high exposure to frauds and money laundering. Legal uncertainty in this sphere appears to be one of the leading causes for that. Despite being an issue of great significance to the world's financial stability, activities related to providing DeFi services are not explicitly subject to legal provisions in any country. Furthermore, a high degree of the technological advancement of DeFi applications significantly impedes the application of existing legal provisions to them. Earlier is given a source of many theoretical and practical problems considering the fact that DeFi services in large part resemble the activity of regulated financial institutions, that is, entities obliged to fulfil very restrictive legal requirements and falling under the supervision of competent financial authorities.

There is no doubt in legal doctrine that the financial supervisory system aims primarily at ensuring an adequate level of quality and professionalism among supervised entities. Effective supervision and control over financial institutions is one of the most important factors influencing the proper functioning of financial markets (Caruana, 2015). The lack of appropriate mechanisms guaranteeing the safety of transactions on DeFi market poses a threat to the proper functioning of this market, its stability, security and transparency, as well as to the protection of the interests of market participants. The existing regulatory gap regarding DeFi applications may result, for example, in offering investment products that are inappropriate or unsuitable for a specific group of investors, considering their knowledge and experience in investing in the capital market, financial situation or risk acceptance.[5]

It should be highlighted that there is general agreement that the law shall remain technologically neutral (Hildebrandt & Tielmans, 2013). It means that provisions should set forth rights or obligations without referring to technology or technological means required to fulfil these rules. In this context, decentralised services or products should not be classified other than centralised ones. For instance, if DeFi service meets the definition of investment service under the Directive 2014/65/EU (EU, 2014) it should remain regulated under the general legislation on providing investment services, regardless of the underlying technology. A different approach would result in occurrence of two different regulatory regimes for the same or similar financial services. A technologically neutral approach is also visible in the proposal for a regulation of the European Parliament and of the Council on Markets in Crypto-Assets (MiCAR). The newest version of the proposal adopted the so-called same business, same risks, same rules principle which means imposing the same requirements upon all active players in a cryptoassets market, regardless of the legal nature of those entities.[6] As a consequence, according to MiCAR cryptocurrencies issued by decentralised autonomous organisations (DAO) should be admitted to trading on platforms based in the European Union only if such cryptocurrencies are compatible with all the legal requirements and do not pose a risk to investor protection, market integrity or financial stability.

However, difficulties arise not only with determining the scope of applicable regulations but also at the stage of identifying an entity responsible for ensuring the compliance of DeFi services with law. Most regulators agree that the qualification of a DeFi application should be the same as the legal qualification of the software program, Internet or mobile network (FATF, 2021). However, person or persons who maintain control or sufficient influence in the DeFi arrangements might be subject to particular legal and regulatory requirements[7]. Due to the fact that DeFi projects are not controlled by certain individuals in the sense known from the traditional financial market (there is no legal entity formally established to manage and represent a particular project), it is not clear who is liable for it. An answer to this question is a matter of great significance not only from the regulator's perspective but also investors' and consumers' who suffered injury as a result of DeFi application malfunction.

Liability for DeFi application

Although there is no consensus among regulators who should be held responsible in the event of the infringement of law or third-party rights in the provision of DeFi services, two concepts seem to be dominant.

The first concept assumes that liability for the DeFi project should be held by governance token's holders. Governance tokens are distributed among the users of a particular application to represent each user's stake in this project. The ownership of governance tokens might be concentrated in hands of particular investors or groups (e.g. software development team or the venture capital investors) who are colloquially referred to as 'whales' (OECD, 2022a, p. 34). The powers denoted by the governance tokens may include traditional management roles and the authority to change the project's protocol, that is, its foundation in code (George, 2022). As a result, 'whales' might be able to control the project and make decisions regarding main directions of development similar to the company's shareholders. This concept however has some significant drawbacks. Firstly, governance token's holders may admittedly make an impact on the project's future, but rather in the technological sphere. In practice, investors may not have any possibility to ensure the compliance of the project with applicable regulations. Secondly, in a fully decentralised DeFi project, there might not be any entity (or groups of entities) holding more than 51% stake of the project.

The second concept implies that the responsibility should be held by software operators or programmers who have provided the first cut of the protocol to the community (OECD, 2022, p. 34) or persons on behalf of which such activities were undertaken. This approach is based on the assumption that going public with a particular project requires prior completing all requirements prescribed by law for such project. It appears that this concept is easier to apply in practice. Interestingly, one of the few proceedings regarding violation of the law in connection with the activity of a DeFi platform was based on similar premises. In 2018, Securities and Exchange Commission (SEC), considering the case of EtherDelta's (a decentralised trading platform) violations of the Exchange Act deemed appropriate to impose the sanctions on Zachary Coburn, who founded EtherDelta, wrote and deployed the EtherDelta's smart contract to the Ethereum Blockchain, and exercised complete and sole control over the platform (SEC, 2018).

However, regardless of the adopted concept, the identification of the entity who should be responsible for ensuring the compliance of DeFi services with all applicable provisions may in practice pose many difficulties, due to anonymity (or pseudonymity[8]) of the transactions made on permissionless protocols. In order to rectify the problem of identifying responsible entities in DeFi systems, some industry participants propose a so-called gatekeeper approach, which involves regulating entry and exit points (often referred to as 'on-and-off ramps') to DeFi applications (OECD, 2022, p. 54). This approach imposes particular obligations on cryptoassets exchanges or other financial and non-financial service providers at the edges of DeFi, when cryptoassets are converted into fiat money and vice versa. There is no doubt, however, that this approach may be used solely as a supplementary tool in the fight with tax evasion or money laundering and terrorism financing.[9] Tightening up on-and-off ramps would only have an impact on the first and last transactions, leaving other transactions out of control. This approach would not also be effective in the process of seeking remedy for damages caused by the DeFi application or imposing sanctions due to law infringement.

It should also be noted that, in general, the use of DeFi application is not limited to a specific jurisdiction or geographical location, which generates additional doubts regarding applicable provisions. Providing a regulatory framework for decentralised finance in a particular country would not be sufficient to ensure legal certainty in this field. Therefore, close cross-border collaboration and discussion between regulators are crucial to eliminate legal risks and challenges regarding DeFi applications and keep financial stability in the international market.

Conclusion

Decentralised finance without doubt is a new trend in both financial services and information technology. It still needs to be clarified, hence the authors aimed at describing trying to categorise it. It departed from the meaning of decentralisation, especially of blockchains, and went through various definitions of DeFi concluding that none of them is well enough for clarification purposes. Moreover, most of them lacked elements that were provided by other authors and others. The problem with the precise definition is not helping with pursuing any further scientific attempts of analysis of DeFi. Having definitions collected and analysed, the authors' own definition was elaborated.

The four dimensions of decentralisation of blockchain were defined (going much beyond its meaning provided by Buterin 2017), and also the authors' definition of DeFi was formulated and identified its 13 areas. Further research of the DeFi area is necessary starting from a clear point of departure, as, for instance, proposed in this chapter.

Decentralised finance currently falls outside of the legal framework. There are no explicit provisions for services related to decentralised finance, which raises doubts about the scope of applicable regulations. Moreover, the lack of such provisions leaves market participants exposed to various risks, including in particular downscaling the investor's protection and precludes the unambiguous identification of an entity responsible for DeFi application malfunction. We have presented two dominant views on determining a person holding responsibility in the event of the infringement of law or third-party rights in the provision of DeFi services (i.e. governance tokens holders and software operators or programmers). An alternative approach was presented, which involved regulating entry and exit points of DeFi services rather than identifying a particular person liable for a project. However, without cross-border cooperation and the consistency of the regulatory approach at global level, eliminating legal challenges of decentralised finance is not feasible.

Notes

1 This, however, may be changed, and we could see a lot of code updates so far resulting in "soft" and "hard" forks of the blockchain ledger.
2 Accumulating liquidity for the operation of services provided by decentralised applications.
3 Collecting liquidity as part of the implementation of infrastructure functions of blockchain networks in networks based on proof of stake.
4 The designation of the phrase "traditional finance" is too ambiguous to describe anything as an "alternative" to "traditional finance."
5 According to research performed by finder.com, crypto-assets are mostly used by younger generations. The studies have shown that of all crypto-assets investors, 44.3% are millennials, 28.6% are Gen X, 17.8% are Gen Z, and 8.2% are Baby Boomers. It means that there is a high probability that investment in crypto-assets is the first or one of the firsts investments of a particular investor. See Laycock & Choi (2021).
6 See the recital (6) of the proposal for a regulation of the European Parliament and of the Council on markets in crypto-asset and amending Directive (EU) 2019/1937 (COM(2020)0593 – C9-0306/2020-2020/0265(COD). (EU, 2020).
7 Such a thesis can be interpreted, inter alia, from the FATF official statements. According to (FATF, 2021), the DeFI application itself is not a Virtual Asset Service Provider (VASP), as the guidance does not apply to underlying software or technology. This does not preclude recognition as a VASP creators, owners and operators or some other persons who maintain control or sufficient influence in the DeFi arrangements, even if those arrangements seem decentralised.
8 The term "pseudonymity" is more accurate for describing the transactions made on permissionless protocols, due to the fact that these transactions are traceable and coded in the public address. See Cryptopedia, 2021.
9 According to Chainalysis (2021b), in 2021, DeFi protocols received 17% of all funds sent from illicit wallets in, up from 2% the previous year. That translates to a 1964% year-over-year increase in total value received by DeFi protocols from illicit addresses, reaching a total of $900 million in 2021. Increasing the effectiveness of counteracting illicit transactions is therefore a matter of a great significance.

10 Toward an European central bank digital currency

Chances and problems

Andreas Bielig

Introduction

Digital transformation during the past decade did not only change our lives drastically in terms of goods and services consumption or in personal communication but also seriously impacted the financial sector at global scale. Traditional financial intermediaries undertook strong efforts in products and services digitization to meet increasing client demands in convenience and promptness as well as in high security levels. Digitization converges previous analog information into digital form, hence, aims on data format changes to ease or accelerate data processing (Bogush, 2021). On the contrary, new actors from the fintech sector invested huge resources in digitalization of innovative payment solutions that suit more to customer's needs in the digital world. Digitalization creates products, services or processes in solely digital codes, hence is based on information processing in digital form. Finally, large software tech players with their large reach of internet market places, social networks or information and communication services created technological ecosystems for economic transactions with the potential to supersede traditional forms of market exchanges. In this dynamic development not only traditional financial business models increasingly got squeezed but also central banks run risks of long-term marginalization if clients drastically reduce demand for cash as only publicly available form of central bank money. Technological advancements of digital transformation (Bogush, 2021) provided scope for development of cryptoassets, with Bitcoin as first introduced in 2008 (Peneder, 2021, p. 13 f.), a pioneer's achievement of anonymous software developer with pseudonym Satoshi Nakamoto (2008). Cryptoassets are pure electronic assets based on digital programming and algorithms without material representation or form. These digital tokenized assets are hold by economic subjects mainly for investment purposes. Private so-called crypto currencies are only one type of them, however, with dramatically increasing importance (Investopedia, 2022b). Crypto currencies, like the Bitcoin, allow for electronic payments by solving the "double spending problem" (Bitpanda, 2022) with specific algorithms, many of them on basis of blockchain principle use (Halaburda, 2016, pp. 81–85). Since 2008, crypto markets exploded in terms of privately issued crypto currencies available for clients, for example, on April 22, 2022, on coinlore.com platform were 9,186

DOI: 10.4324/9781003310365-10

crypto currencies listed with a total market cap of $1,825,863,848,263 from which 1,431 were in coin and 7,046 in token form with remaining not assigned to previous categories (Coinlore.com, 2022). Also if many private crypto currencies currently available on global markets still jointly suffer on partially extreme price volatilities, hence not provide monetary value stability, central banks recognize challenges deriving from private electronic money for their future role in national and international financial system. The Meta Platform (previously Facebook) project of a stablecoin digital currency issued under working title Diem (previously Libra) headed for solution of instability problems inherent to unbacked private digital currencies. The ambitious project's end in February 2022 caused by eminent regulatory uncertainties retarded ongoing transition processes toward broad dissemination and market penetration of crypto currencies. (ABC News, 2022) In combination with Facebook user network's global footprint exist enormous potentials to leverage digital currency benefits against prevailing traditional payment instruments and change financial architectures worldwide radically. In this mélange of reducing cash demand, emergence of new powerful competitors with innovative payment services and, finally, increasing popularity of crypto currencies central banks are forced, first, to rethink their role in future financial systems and, second, to reassort and redesign adequate instruments of monetary policy as response to challenges by private crypto currencies. The European Central Bank (ECB) in past opposed introductions of an European central bank digital currency (CBDC) (Mersch, 2017, 2018):

> Overall, there is currently no convincing motivation for the Eurosystem to issue DBM to the general public. It is unnecessary at present and, when the likely negative impacts on the financial system are taken into account, such a move appears disproportionate to the aims put forward by its proponents.... If anything, one could imagine a digital representation of cash that replicates the features of cash in the reasonably distant future, if citizens demanded it. Such an approach seems more appropriate for jurisdictions whose currencies face domestic regress as they are also not widely accepted beyond their territory – which is certainly not the case for the euro.
>
> (Mersch, 2018)

However, ECB policy changed attitude toward a future digital euro during the push for digitalization in pandemic crisis in 2020 to a proponent position:

> What is at stake is nothing short of the future of money. As private money goes digital, sovereign money also needs to be reinvented. This requires central bank money to remain available under all circumstances – in the form of cash, of course, but also potentially as a digital euro.
>
> (Panetta, 2020b)

Based on these facts, the contribution analyses in front of monetary theory potential designs of a future digital euro with respect to impacts on monetary characteristics, payment systems and innovation aspects. With caution, it tries to answer the question what monetary characteristics a potential digital euro could have and which economic implications derive for actors in monetary and financial system? For this purpose, analysis is structured as follows: The second chapter outlines economic aspects of money and currencies relevant also for digital currencies. In the third chapter, specific economic problems of digital currencies are analyzed. The fourth chapter examines ECB's role and situation in CBDC development and asks for potential digital Euro designs. Finally, the contribution closes by concluding remarks.

Money, currency and forms of money

Economic literature indicates a differentiation between money and currency (Vollmer, 2005, p. 6).Money is an abstract economic term defined by fulfillment of three monetary functions: First, the transactions function as a medium of exchange; second, the function as unit of account for calculations and transaction settlements; and third, the function as store of value. For most economies in principle several assets can fulfill these aspects to different extents. Examples are, for example, coins and banknotes, sight deposits at banks, crypto currencies but also physical assets like precious metals, gems or rare works of art. Currency is by origin a legal term describing by sovereign established payment instruments of public monetary system with legal tender character and in a broader sense the public monetary system. Hence, money and currency categories are similar but not inevitably congruent as Figure 10.1 indicates. If under normal circumstances by central banks issued coins and banknotes fulfill monetary functions well, then money and currency terms are in this case congruent (overlapping area). During economic or political crises, public money's monetary functions can be weakened and official currency by tendency crowded out of economic transactions by other money forms (right area). Alternative assets with monetary functions can adopt public money's role although not having legal tender characteristics (left area), for example, sight deposits, precious metals or crypto currencies. In economic sense, crypto currency is "no" currency but crypto money.

During crises in history, often currency substitutes were created by economic actors as printed or minted tokens or in form of physical goods with monetary functions that were commonly in economies accepted as means of payment (e.g. for GDR see Huschka, 2013). An alternative form of crisis money is emergency money that is officially issued by public authorities or also by private entities in

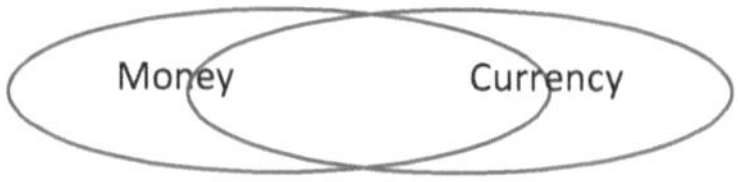

Figure 10.1 Money and currency scopes according to term definitions

Source: Own depiction on the basis of Vollmer (2005, p. 6).

case of public currency scarcities (e.g. for Thuringia in Germany, see Bubeck, 2007). Beside crises, in many economic regions are diverse forms of so-called regional money in permanent use for economic transactions as supplementary payment instruments to official currency (Fachverb and Regiogeld, 2022). They are mainly used for regional development purposes and rooted in certain skepticism against public currency, sometimes combined also with normative aspirations, like aiming on sustainability. As a specific alternative form of almost moneyless economic exchanges work regional or local barter circles, where participants exchange products and services directly in closed loops without using a central medium of exchange, however, often with central units of account (Tauschwiki, 2022). The short outline indicates that public currency issued by central banks always competes at least potentially with various forms of money concerning the fulfillment of monetary functions in the economy. Digitalization intensifies this competition by enabling crypto money in utilizing the advantages of digital technologies and networks in terms of small transaction costs, big data basis, real-time information processing and global reach. So, Chinese WeChat Pay leverages with about 800 million active users on monthly basis competitive advantages of WeChat's dominant internet platform (Plantin & de Seta, 2019) to boost platform's internal but also external payment services on global scale (WeChat Pay, 2022). Currently available crypto money forms can be differentiated into inside money and outside money. Issuance of inside money is related with claims of money holders on assets of issuing private entities (Brunnermeier et al., 2019, p. 4), hence liabilities of issuer's balance sheet, for example, bank deposits and e-money forms like WeChat Pay wallets in app form. Digital wallets are applications on mobile devices for financial transactions and using digital money units, making economic transactions more convenient by storing various required personal information of device holders (Kagan, 2022). In contrast to this is outside money not related to claims on issuer's assets. It has no liability impacts on balance sheet of the issuing entity and is a positive net supply, regardless if it comes in a backed version (e.g. by other money forms) or unbacked (without backing of money value). Many forms of crypto money are outside money with no claims on issuers assets, like modern public currencies issued as fiat currencies. In the past, many public currencies were issued as commodity currency, that ensured a convertibility of money into a unit of a valuable assets, mostly precious metals like gold or silver. At the latest, by end of international Bretton-Woods System, national currencies abandoned convertibility into commodities and transitioned to fiat currencies, that derive exchange value without reference to valuable assets. From economic perspective, crypto money is, like todays public currency, fiat money, hence, faces analog challenges in value anchoring to central bank money. Whereas in past history, the latter developed suitable monetary instruments to solve this problem in terms of internal and external currency value, most crypto money values not only show high volatilities but, even more, are in economic perspective also in the medium run not supposed to overcome central fiat money problems as euphemistic notions would suggest (e.g. Dapp, 2021). An important aspect of money design related to the commodity-fiat distinction is convertibility into other payment instruments. Full convertibility binds the issuing entity to ensure exchanges of own monetary units at fixed exchange rates into other money forms (Brunnermeier et al., 2019, p. 3f.). Strict convertibility between different payment instruments results in uniformity of money properties despite of their different forms. Issuers of crypto money can bind their hands by self-commitments to full convertibility in order to harmonize monetary characteristics of their payment instruments for improving market acceptance and penetration; however, most digital money still fails at this point. As alternative, money issuers can back payment instruments with other assets to stabilize money's value. Without full convertibility, the entity's value management reveals an in-built flexibility allowing for discretionary adjustments by issuance or redemptions of money units to hold a currency peg or band. Earlier mentioned Meta Platform's Diem project initially aimed on full backing of issued digital money by a basket of international currencies and short-dated government bonds (Beer, 2022). After intensive discussions with supervising authorities in the European Union (EU) and the USA, the revised version limited itself to a US-dollar currency peg and US applications of the monetary. At first glance, of rather organizational nature is a distinction of money forms according to outer appearance between account-based and token-based money. However, different technical characteristics determine also diverse economic money properties (Brunnermeier et al., 2019, p. 4f.). Utilization of account-based money in economic transactions requires an authentication of users concerning legitimated account access. It is mostly designed in form of inside money and usually allows for potential functioning as credit basis. Bank sight deposits are traditional phenotypes of account based money but also crypto money can take this form. ECB representative Bindseil (2020, p. 4) argues in favor of account-based solutions for a future digital euro and tests potential monetary implications of this scenario for the financial system. The use of token-based money in economic transactions requires in contrast no user but token authentications. It is mostly designed in outside money form and rather difficult to use as credit basis. Public currency in form of banknotes and coins are traditional forms of token money but also most crypto money representations have token characteristics. Concerning convertibility properties of money, Brunnermeier et al. (2019, p. 5f.) introduce the term of independence of money, based on a retain of issuer's commitment to convertibility into other forms of money. Each payment instrument of this money form uses same unit of account, hence, is full convertible within this money but has no external convertibility. Dependent money, in contrast, reveals a binding issuer commitment to convertibility into other money forms. It triggers of external claims of money holders on own issuer's assets in case of breaking the convertibility promises made before. Therefore, money's dependence degree is conditional on issuer's commitment intensity. Most current forms of crypto money are independent money, using own units of account and lacking of binding issuer's convertibility commitments, like Bitcoin or Ether. However, in absence of reliable fiscal anchors, money's store of value function is in most cases limited. Meta Platform's Diem stablecoin project finally failed at this point with the concept of asset backing in international (later only US) reserves to ensure stable pegs of money value to reference currencies. Prospects of success to ensure full convertibility of crypto money base on reliable issuers commitments with the abandonment of money value management on own private discretion, thus, a major obstacle in private digital money development. Such in a money dependence resulting commitment fulfill current Chinese WeChat Pay wallet services that are bound on Chinese public currency and linked to Chinese deposit accounts as well as the stablecoin Tether with its 1:1 peg to USdollar. Brunnermeier et al. (2019, p. 8f.) hint on the fact that increasing diversification of digitalized payment instruments contributes to overcome the traditional competition barriers between money and currency forms; however, it induces also contrary effects with respect to monetary functions. In a constellation of perfect competition different money forms use their own units of account, for example, in public currencies competition between different countries (like USdollar vs. euro), between different crypto money forms (like Bitcoin vs. Ether) or crosswise between traditional analog and crypto money (like Euro bank deposits vs. Bitcoin). In imperfect competition, each money uses same units of account but compete with different technical and economic characteristics for potential users as payment instruments, for example, Euro Banknotes versus Euro bank deposits or WeChat Pay wallets versus Chinese yuan banknotes. Moreover, recent research in reference markets, like China, shows that digital mobile payments significantly impact patterns of economic transactions, hence change also consumer behavior (Xi & Ng, 2021). A future digital euro, most likely, would have same units of account as ECB's traditional cash, hence compete with the latter on basis of new innovative technical and economic characteristics.

Digital currencies

Forms and characteristics of CBDC

Because CBDC is (still) not a clearly defined term but rather refers to diverse concepts, as the Committee on Payments and Market Infrastructures and Markets Committee (CPMI-MC, 2018, p. 3f) states, it can be described in a negative formulation as a new (third) digital form of central bank's base money that has different characteristics than existing balances in traditional reserve or settlement accounts. Set into relation to other money forms, it can be differentiated on basis of four main money properties, visually depictable in Venn-diagram form as so called "money flower" (CPMI-MC, 2018, p. 4f): (1) issuer (central bank or others), (2) form (digital or physical), (3) access (widely or restricted) and (4) technology (token or account-based). Following this classification, diverse potential CBDC forms derive (Bindseil, 2020, p. 5), for example

1. as pure wholesale CBDC or as general purpose CBDC (available for all households),
2. as deposit account CBDC or as digital token CBDC,

3. as central ledger CBDC or as distributed ledger CBDC,
4. with permissioned ledgers (with ex ante access regulation) and with unpermissioned ledgers (open access regime) or
5. as transactions account or as transactions wallet.

Based on 2020 report results of leading Central Banks Working Group on CBDC,14 core properties according to three main aspects of instrumental, systemic and institutional features can be distinguished as Table 10.1 indicates (BIS, 2020, p. 11). For major central banks worldwide, these central requirements will constitute the bar for their own CBDC development projects; however, between diverse features are trade-offs, for example, convenience and security.

Still in a 2018 worldwide BIS survey among central banks, 70 per cent of respondents covering jurisdictions of 80 per cent of world population or 90 per cent of global GDP answered that their institutions run theoretical or conceptual work on CBDC issue but about 85 per cent not intended to issue a CDBC in the shortterm. No central bank intended issuance of a wholesale CBDC in shortrun; however, central banks of two emerging market economies planned a short-term introduction of retail CBDC forms (Barontini, 2019, p. 11). At this stage, CBDCs are in function in some small economies only (the Bahamas, Cambodia, Venezuela and Marshall Islands) with varying success records (Blockchaincenter, 2022). Since 2020, a promising Chinese pilot project is in progress, fostered by Chinese leading position in mobile payments. For recent research findings on national CBDC projects outside euro area, see among others Allen et al. (2022), Armelius et al. (2018), Cheng (2022), Li and Huang (2021), Samudrala and Yerchuru (2021) and Teichmann and Falker (2021).

Table 10.1 Central bank digital currency core properties

Properties	*Features*
Instrumental	Convertibility
	Convenience
	Acceptance and local availability
	Low cost level
Systemic	Security
	Promptness
	Resilience
	Permanent availability
	Throughput
	Scalability
	Interoperability
	Flexibility and adaptability
Institutional	Robust legal framework
	Technical standards

Source: Own depiction based on BIS (2020, p. 11).

Monetary aspects of digital central bank currencies

Along with introduction of CBDC's goes a variety of potential advantages from monetary perspective that are key drivers in CB's motivation to engage in CBDC development (Bordo, 2021, pp. 7–9). First, CBDC's can contribute to significant cost reductions of cash issuance and operation. Second, in times of national cash disappearance CBDC can function as suitable substitute with cash near properties at reduced susceptibility to frauds and loss. Simultaneously CBs are enabled to preserve control power of monetary policy in a cashless environment. Third, CBDCs can promote financial inclusion in underbanked economies or within social population segments with restricted access to traditional financial services. Fourth, CBDCs can serve as digital alternative to private stablecoins that are by nature subject to credit risk and defaults. Fifth, CBDC can provide a secure and reliable digital base money, ensuring protection against fraud, hacking, money laundering and terrorism financing. Finally, key motivations for CBDC issuance predominantly derive from economic argumentation of money as a public good that should provide public authorities due to inefficient provision by market forces (Bordo, 2021, p. 9). However, economist hint also on the fact that real economic CBDC benefits are highly conditional upon framework conditions (Bindseil, 2020, pp. 5–8). The size of potential efficiency improvements by CBDC depends on cash demand reductions for central Bank banknotes and coins. They are also larger if broader population segments have only restricted access to commercial banking services and in case of unstable or highly concentrated payment infrastructure in a national economy. A reduction of illicit transactions is bound to reductions of banknotes in circulation and strict limitations of economic transactions with anonymous digital tokens. One aspect of enhancement of CB's control power in monetary transmission process derives from possibilities to overcoming the zero-lower bound of interest rates in CB's monetary policy. To benefit from negative rates CBs must cope with challenges of "flights into cash", hence reduce incentives to change digital currencies into cash by fees or caps. However, such "sand in the wheels" approaches (Bordo, 2021, p. 11) come at cost of inefficiency. If variable interests on CBDCs can be regarded as additional instruments of CB's monetary policy depends on policy designs applied in specific jurisdictions and, of course, on concrete CBDC design. For the ECB case, CBDC's additional instrumental character is rather in question due to doubtful impacts on monetary transmission channels (Bindseil, 2020, p. 6). An expansion of central banks' monetary base and, first, resulting redirections of substantial seigniorage shares to the public sector as well as, second, potential stability improvements of the financial system and reductions of moral hazards of banks by downscaling the banking sector depend on large absorptions of bank sight deposits by the central bank. Resulting banking disintermediation could transform banks-based financial systems to sovereign money financial systems, hence, undesirable drawbacks of CBDC in case of ECB (Bindseil, 2020, p. 8). In contrast of private households substitution of cash against CBDC with no effect on central banks' and commercial banks' balance sheets, an intensive substitution of banks sight deposits with

CBDC would entail serious risks for systemic financial stability requiring again substantial support engagement of CBs and assign them an unintended role of central credit allocators (Bindseil, 2020, pp. 8–13). For further recent research findings on monetary aspects of CBDC, see among many others in a tremendous literature, for example, Agur et al. (2022), Barrdear and Kumhof (2021), Chen and Siklos (2022), Fegatelli (2022), Fernández-Villaverde et al. (2021), Kumhof and Noone (2021) and Ferrari et al. (2020b).

Monetary independence, dollarization trends and CBDC

A challenge for central banks at drastically reduced cash utilization by economic subjects is the diminishing role of Central Bank money as monetary anchor in financial system (Brunnermeier et al., 2019, p. 26f). In result, other payment instruments (bank deposits and private digital money forms) by tendency transition to free-floating prices and exchange rates. On the other hand also monetary discipline motivation of money issuers weakens caused by orientation of value management toward own self-interest. This potential decrease in substitutability of money forms in a nearly cashless economy is counteracted by CBDC introduction. It can contribute to re-establish missing substitutability by mutual convertibility and, with this, to provide potentials for uniformity of monetary payment instruments properties. Furthermore, a CBDC introduction facilitates preservation of public monetary power of control without going seductive ways of strict regulation of emerging sectors with innovative private digital money forms. In modern platform-based economies, central bank money experiences by tendency a shrinking role as medium of exchange (Brunnermeier et al., 2019, p. 27f). Networks allow for simple substitution by internal platform-based forms of money and settlement of transactions, dependent on network size and used technologies, for example, tokens. Economic subjects are encouraged toward use of platform-internal money forms as unit of account in contracting. In future, at large-scale shifts, transformed financial system would potentially center around large providers of digital platforms and public monetary authorities heavily had lost influences on liquidity and risk allocation in banking's credit business. Precautionary introduction of CBDC may inhibit public money's loss of unit of account function, also in the minimum case of being only a parallel currency beside of private money forms. However, essential for this is interoperability between CBDC and digital platforms. Also with respect to perspectives of European banking industry prospects are rather mixed (Bechtel et al., 2020): In case of CBDC introduction in business-to-consumer relations (B2C) banks still can rely on their safe role as gatekeepers to private clients with supply of deposits as long as it concerns payments in form of central bank money. In business-to-business relations (B2B) banks currently have two options of business model transition: first, they can strengthen the role of the SEPA-Inst system for transactions and settlements, but there is currently no offer for new payment forms as future interface to their customers. This option requires intensive financial efforts in future, is hard to amortize and associated with marginal returns. The second option uses CBDC for transactions settlement and the development of new payment services on basis of existing customer systems, hence links industry 4.0 transformations with new digital financial services of banks.

ECB and digital Euro: The Euro and ECB policy

The euro area was established in 1999 where 11 European member states adopted the Euro as "book money" (EC, 2022). In 2002, the cash euro was introduced as legal means of payment for euro member states. Today's euro area consists of 19 EU member states plus four minor states outside of EU (Andorra, Monaco, San Marino and the Vatican City) that adopted euro as their national currency by agreements with the EU. Monetary policy in the euro area is governed by Eurosystem consisting of ECB and national central banks of euro area members. With this, the euro covers today jurisdictions of 342.87 million European inhabitants with an economic output of €12,244.17 billion measured by GDP (current prices, calendar and seasonally adjusted data) in 2021 (ECB Statistical Data Warehouse, 2022a, 2022b). In international comparison, euro area ranks in terms of inhabitants paying with same national currency on third place worldwide (after China and India) as well as in terms of economic transactions (after the Unites States and China, measured in euro's current prices). Monetary policy decisions made in ECB's tower headquarter in Frankfurt/Main factually impact also many economies outside of euro area worldwide. The monetary policy is since first adoption of ECB's monetary policy strategy in 1998 guided and bound by the primary aim of maintaining price stability (ECB, 2022a). The term "monetary policy" describes central banks' decisions to influence costs and availability of money in the economy, for ECB case, in the euro area. Due to ECB's specific supra-national character – the Governing Council as decision-making body consists of six Executive Board members plus 19 governors of Euro National Central Banks – monetary policy outcome was in past mainly heading for compromises as best solutions for the euro area by balancing national interests and perspectives in its policy decisions. As other major central banks, also ECB uses a set of conventional monetary policy instruments, based on open market operations, standing facilities, minimum reserve requirements and the soft factor-based forward guidance (ECB, 2022b). Also in October 2014, the ECB followed other major CBs to a Quantitative Easing in European monetary policy in form of four long-term asset purchase programs APP (corporate sector purchase programme [CSPP], public sector purchase program[PSPP], asset-backed securities purchase programme [ABSPP] and third covered bond purchase program[CBPP3]) to provide more liquidity for the currency area. In March 2022, remaining ECB asset holdings of this APPs still amount to €26,992 million (ECB, 2022c). Just in 2012, ECB decided for an Outright Monetary Transactions program (OMT) to stabilize financial markets and prevent anticipated exits of highly indebted Euro member states with large risks of default (Draghi, 2012; Cœuré, 2013). Since 2008 joint loose monetary policy of ECB with other majors has let to exceptional amounts of excess liquidity in financial markets, driving in this unnormal liquidity situation some euro short-term market rates below deposit facility rates for banks (Bindseil, 2020, p. 16). As result, the initial pre-crisis corridor interest rate system of the Eurosystem evolved since 2015 to a de facto floor system structure (Resinek, 2019, p. 3f.). In this situation, the zero lower bound problem not only becomes relevant but advanced to an additional challenge for ECB's monetary policy that could mastered by CBDC.

Euroarea payment attitudes

Primary role of future European CBDC is its prevalence as accepted and convenient payment instrument, hence payment patterns of euro area citizens matter. Here, potential CBDC properties are measured in especially against standard payment instruments, like cash or cards. Many Euro member states reported a reduction of cash as payment instrument during the past years; hence, in 2019, ECB carried out a survey among euro area consumers concerning their payment attitudes (SPACE). Following the results, cash payment is in the euro area still predominantly used in Point of sale (POS) and peer to peer-transactions (P2P) (ECB, 2020a, pp. 17–20). In 2019, 48% of POS and P2P transactions in terms of value were made in cash, but 78% in terms of transaction numbers. Card payments were responsible for 41% of POS and P2P transactions in terms of value (30.2% debit cards and 10.5% credit cards) but only 24% in terms of numbers (18.4% debit cards and 5.3% credit cards). Mobile phone transactions accounted together with remaining cash-less instruments for less than 1% of transactions. In terms of transaction value, mobile applications accounted together with direct debit and other cash-less instruments (without credit transfer and cheques) for less than 4%. Hence, ECB issuance of CBDC has to consider the still strong adherence to cash and its specific money properties among euro area residents. Also if the general finding of cash's predominance holds true for nearly all euro area economies in terms of transactions (with exception of Finland with 35% and the Netherlands with 34%), cash shares there varied substantially between 88% in Malta and 48% in Estonia. In terms of total value cash shares varied even more between 73% in Cyprus and 22% in the Netherlands. In comparison with 2016 survey results of the previous SUCH study (Esselink & Hernández, 2017), cash shares in transactions value in the euro area declined by 6%-points, indicating reducing importance as payment instrument. But here also transition processes vary among euro economies: in terms of transaction numbers, cash shares decreased most substantially in Finland (−19%-points) and in terms of transaction value in Greece (−13%-points). In contrast, Estonia, Latvia and Ireland recorded cash use increases in terms of transaction value. However, COVID 19-pandemic impacted European payment patterns leading to shifts from cash to cash-less payment instruments, like results of IMPACT-survey in 2020 show (ECB, 2020a, pp. 21–24). According to IMPACT, 40% of respondents used contactless cards more often, whereas 40% used cash less than before the pandemic. Further SPACE study results indicate also considerable contrasts between real payment patterns and revealed payment preferences (ECB, 2020a, p. 57): 27%

of respondents prefer cash and 49% cashless payments, whereas payment patterns show a cash/cashless relation of 78% to 22% in terms of transaction numbers. Also in case of declining cash usage, results show that the preference for an "option" of cash payments remains important in euro area (ECB, 2022a, p. 60f.), even at current trends toward "single homing" in cashless payments in comparison with a "multi homing" in individual use of diverse payment instruments by private households. Beside payment purposes, cash importance derives also from the store of value function, like the so-called paradox of banknotes in the euro area indicates, leading to increasing banknotes demand despite of decreasing use for transactions payments (Zamora-Pérez, 2021).

Challenges of digitalization for ECB

Current challenges of digitalization for ECB derive from interrelations of euro area payment patterns, innovation potentials of digital money forms, aspects of financial system and monetary policy (Panetta, 2020a). Ongoing digital transformation increases public and private demands for both convenience and security. Needs for payments with promptness and uncritical integration of complex technological solutions are confronted with increasing demands for privacy, internet security and end user solution's reliability. Innovative payment solutions can fill the gap between properties of existing payment instruments and new characteristics required by society. Here, the pandemic supports just previously existing trends toward digital payments. Cash is regarded as a secure and inclusive payment instrument but not allows for digital applications. Cards enable digital contactless payments, but still lack in prevalence and acceptance at many European points of sale. The European market for card payments is currently highly dependent on international card schemes of non-European providers, like VISA or Mastercard (MC), with large market segment concentrations, for example, in deposit account and online transactions VISA and MC are responsible for two-thirds of the EU market. Economic dependency and large market concentrations cause a set of negative implications, like potential restraints of competition, limited consumer choices, excessive prices, lower resilience of payment systems and the weakening of supervisors control power. Other challenges derive from new innovative enterprises. Many fintechs with data-driven business models offer diverse free of charge payment services in exchange for personal data of clients. Increasing numbers of banks cooperate with fintechs and adapt their technical solutions or payment services to get near to modern clients, thereby moderately transition their business model. Global tech enterprises (Thomson Reuters, 2022) enter payment services markets by scaling of data-driven business models to new dimensions, using substantial firm resources (large client basis, real time data processing and analysis, control of decisive infrastructures, e.g., online market places, social media and mobile technologies), immense financial power and their global presence. Their expansion into new financial services, like payment services or credit granting, intensifies competition with the banking sector. A specific economic challenge brings the combination of global techs with stablecoins issuance. Their fast dissemination advantage by substantial resources efforts accompany also potential risks deriving from no ensured value stability of payment instruments, missing protection by deposit insurance schemes, currently no diligent control by supervision authorities or lacking access to reserve system and standing facilities of central banks. Holders of these private payment instruments bear large credit, market and liquidity risks. Private money in form of stablecoins has "club good-characteristics and is in practice available only for network members in exchange for fee payments or platform memberships bound on private data access."

ECB's public consultation on digital euro

To match ECB research findings on CBDC and related payment instruments with broader public perspectives on European payment needs the ECB carried out in 2020 a public consultation about benefits and challenges of a future digital Euro and potential designs (ECB, 2021, p. 2) Also if survey results lack on representativity for total euro area due to demographic biases (ECB, 2021, p. 2, 7), they reveal important insights into money properties to be fulfilled by ECB's CBDC. In ranking of respondents desired aspects of privacy is with 43% at first place, security with 18% at second, comprehensive usability across euro area with 11% at third, absence of additional user's costs with 9% at fourth and offline utilization possibilities with 8% at fifth place (ECB, 2021, p. 10). In simple terms, respondents expect a future digital euro to have cash-near properties on non-material basis. Concerning potential choices between an offline euro with more emphasis on privacy issues and an online euro coming with innovative applications private persons revealed main preferences for offline solutions, whereas firms revealed mixed preferences between online and offline CBDCs (ECB, 2021, pp. 10–28). The most important challenges of ECB's CBDC for private persons are privacy, utilization potentials and simplicity of usage. Enterprises address same aspects but see also weak internet coverages as problematic. Another important challenge for firms constitute integration issues in existing banking and payments infrastructures. Concerning possible technological solutions applied by ECB's CBDC, private persons prefer more enduser hardware solutions (25% voted for solutions on cards or hardware integrated secure elements), whereas firms prefer end user-solutions on software or hardware basis (33%), but also combinations of end user solutions and back end infrastructure (33%). Survey results show that ECB's future CBDC design has to balance different expectations of private households and enterprise sector.

ECB requirements and work streams for digital euro

Against backgrounds of potential users' revealed preferences, private crypto money markets' dynamic development, existing challenges in the financial sector and monetary policy considerations EBC formulate general requirements for the digital euro(Panetta, 2020b). It defines the primary CBDC function as payment instrument only. Neither is an investment purpose intended nor desired. In comparison with usability of other digital money forms, the benchmark for the ECB's digital euro is a cash-like prevalence. A second functional requirement is improvement of data security in digital payments. Based on mixed past and current experiences in crypto money markets and revealed users preferences the future digital euro should mainly emphasize privacy and secure holders against frauds and losses. The ECB currently analyzes in cooperation with Bank of Japan for diverse potential CBDC designs adequate privacy enhancing technologies (PET) for future application in the digital euro (ECB, 2020b; ECB & Bank of Japan, 2020). At third, the CBDC must have necessarily compliance to regulations, here, that is, against illicit transactions, that fulfils substantially higher standards than most private digital money forms. Fourth, and essentially from CB perspective, CBDC issuance should avoid interferences with central bank policies, in particular, with regard to monetary policy and financial stability. Beside of those fundamental requirements, ECB aspires with respect to support and stabilization of financial system by CBDC issuance a frictionless interoperability with private payment technologies. In simplified terms, a future digital euro should function as a basic commodity and an input factor of private-based end user services of supervised financial intermediaries (Panetta, 2020b). To reach these targets, ECB actually works on four main areas for its CBDC project: First, compatibility between digital euro and existing payment settlement systems, second, linking of decentralized technologies (like distributed ledgers) with centralized systems, third, utilization of payments focused blockchains with electronic identity and fourth, functionalities analysis of hardware for offline transaction purposes for privacy enhancement and data security.

Conclusion

In 2021, ECB committed to future introduction of a digital euro (Siedenbiedel, 2021). At present, discussions about CBDC designs of the euro have speculative nature. Digital euros could adopt diverse token forms for use with end user device electronic wallets, or, on contrary technological solution side, an account-based form as suggested by ECB representatives to keep concept and related technological challenges straightforward. In design aspects, ECB is urged to consider several dimensions ranging from present payment attitudes and user expectations via privacy and data security issues to financial system stability or present and future monetary policy. Furthermore, ECB with its responsibility for unitary monetary policy in 19 euro area economies is bound to compromises for adequate solutions that find political support also at supranational level. The digital Euro will be in particular respond to increased existing and potential competition by private digital payment instruments (with previous Facebook/Meta Platforms stablecoin Libra/Diem as largest project at present). Compared with challenges by global tech giants potential threats by other national CBDC projects seem secondary. However, ECB also has to consider their potential implications carefully. U.S. Fed's digital dollar project is strongly motivated by standard setting to allow American firms for innovative payment services development by creation of incentivizing technological ecosystems. After experiencing euro area's heavy reliance in traditional forms of digital payments, ECB is called for adequate counteraction of potential threats in new financial services with the digital euro to provide a level playing field also for European fintech enterprises, and here, that is, for small- and medium-sized enterprises (SMEs) to ensure sufficient diversity of potential market solutions. Here, a token-based CBDC form would widen scopes of private innovation activities. In future cases of massive cash crowding-outs by private digital payments, an European CBDC would raise an additional defense line to preserve control power in financial system. In present situation of ECB's quantitative easing, a digital euro with negative interest rates could contribute to overcome traditional zero-lower bound of monetary policy, but at costs of potential flights into cash at low transaction costs and insufficient transactions limits. In principal, reduction of transaction costs, one of original major CBDC benefits, tend to increase dynamics during banking system instabilities and bank runs. Nevertheless, negative interest rates on CBDC holdings could support an ECB's exit strategy from current quantitative easing in monetary policy, but digital euro introduction is scheduled not before 2026. A crucial aspect for CBDC dissemination is endusers acceptance that is not controlled by ECB. However, strategic CBDC concept and operational design are key factors of money utilization. Future prospects indicate mixed prevalence of cash and digital payment instruments and the digital euro being one of them. During next years, euro area citizens' strong focus on cash probably will continue, what holds in particular for regions and population segments with non-electronic payment adherence. For this, in particular, properties of money proved to be crucial. So, for instance, is strict payment anonymity provided only by cash use but not by digital tokens that leave information tracks at points of sales or in networks. For innovation-friendly economies but also for still underdeveloped national financial markets, digital money forms provide immense future economic potentials. A digital euro as euro area's technological standard could support European enterprises to exploit market chances by digital data-driven business models and innovative financial services. So allow, for example, combinations of digital money with self-fulfilling crypto contracts (smart contracts) for many new application fields. For future, however, remain many questions, for instance: Will private digital money issuers reach faster dissemination and dominant positions in payments than the digital euro? (Schäffler, 2022). Do end users accept digital currencies and money forms as medium of exchange on broader basis? Here, differences of payment attitudes not only between countries and regions, urban-rural relationships and dependencies on culture mentalities but also in quality of infrastructures (mobile devices vs. bank branches) are crucial. Or, last but not least, are essential payment and settlement infrastructures provided, that can be used by privates enterprises to develop innovative payment services on basis of the digital euro? First steps toward a digital European currency are done by ECB, but there is still a long way to go to the target line.

11 CBDC design and implementation in the context of differences between advanced and emerging economies

Paweł Pisany

Introduction

Central bank digital currency (CBDC) is defined by Bank for International Settlements (BIS) and the coalition[1] of six central banks (BIS et al., 2020) as "digital payment instrument, denominated in the national unit of account, that is issued by a monetary authority and remains a direct liability of the central bank." Retail CBDC is essentially the new form of central bank money that will be available to the general public, similarly to the physical cash, that is, coins and banknotes. In this chapter, the retail (or general purpose) CBDC is the main topic of the investigation. The retail CBDC may be described as digital equivalent of cash and it is meant to be used by households and enterprises. The CBDC may also exist in its wholesale form, which is also a direct liability of the central bank, but the user circle is limited to certain financial intermediaries.

The ambition of this chapter is to show that retail CBDC should be and – fortunately – starts to be perceived as a solution for some specific challenges that some economies are facing nowadays, rather than the natural step forward in the evolution of financial system for all. CBDC indeed may be beneficial in a given country on the condition that it is designed in line with specific needs and characteristics of this economy. Digital currency is not a panacea, but a potentially effective solution, however only when used as prescribed.

CBDC: Motives and needs in emerging and advanced economies

In 2021, BIS published the report on the survey related to CBDC made in 2020 (Boar & Wehrli, 2021). Sixty-five central banks – from economies representing 72% of the global population and 91% of the global GDP – replied to that questionnaire. Finally, BIS gathered answers from 22 advanced economies and 44 emerging markets. In 2020, 56 central banks were actively involved in CBDC, and some of them even conducted pilot programs. In subsequent in-depth studies, BIS focused more on emerging economies (Chen et al., 2022), but the Boar and Wehrli's (2021) remains more complex elaboration and gives a very good insight into the motives and some differences between emerging and advanced

DOI: 10.4324/9781003310365-11

economies as far CBDC is concerned. In 2022, IMF estimated that around 100 countries all over the world are exploring the idea of CBDC; however, those economies present very different levels of advancements in their CBDC projects (Georgieva, 2022). Furthermore, IMF (2022b) published in-depth case analyses of six countries that are actively exploring the retail CBDC: (i) during final implementation for use (the Bahamas), (ii) during advanced pilot programmes (China, Eastern Caribbean Currency Union – ECCU, Sweden and Uruguay) and (iii) conducting wide, but pure analytical activities related to CBDC, like research and tests (Canada).

In the survey analysed by Boar and Wehrli (2021), financial inclusion was one of the most important drivers for CBDC projects in emerging markets and developing countries, especially when compared to developed countries. Advanced economies underlined the role of payment systems robustness and efficiency, including cross-border efficiency. Those drivers were assessed as roughly equally important by both emerging and advanced economies. Other factors, particularly financial stability protection and monetary policy implementation, were significantly more important for central banks from emerging economies compared to the scores declared in the questionnaires from developed markets. This shows that emerging markets and developing countries perceived CBDC as a chance to boost socio-economic development by enhancing financial inclusion, moreover as a way to develop payment systems and – last, but not least – improve the quality of monetary policy and financial stability protection. The goals declared by the emerging economies correspond to the level of economic development and reflect the need for investing in institutional quality improvement. This justifies a more proactive attitude in the case emerging economies and developing countries in the area of CBDC.

Motives and concerns regarding CBDC have been also the subject of investigation in the BIS Emerging Market Economies Deputy Governors survey (Chen et al., 2022). The 26 countries participated in this survey and most of them can be classified as emerging economies.[2] Results of the survey show that four motives are playing the crucial role in surveyed markets, namely (i) the need to provide cash in the digital form along with changing customer preferences, (ii) financial inclusion enhancement, (iii) improving efficiency, diversity and competition in payment services, and (iv) programmable money. Other potential motives, like privacy considerations, boosting anti-money laundering and anti-tax avoidance procedures and monetary policy effectiveness, were of lesser importance. The most important concern, indicated by twelve out of twenty-six central banks as the top one, was the risk of bank disintermediation.

Furthermore, we need to be aware that retail CBDC may be an answer to a very specific needs of a given economy, including those of geographic nature. Auer et al. (2022) indicated that countries with vast remote territories (like Canada, China, but Nigeria as well) or large number of small islands (like the Bahamas and ECCU) may benefit from CBDC because banks and other private financial intermediaries may not be interested in providing services for those remote areas due to relatively low profitability of this business. In other cases, institutional factors, like lack of effective country-wide ID system, for example, in Malawi, South Sudan, Chad or Armenia (Demirgüç-Kunt et al., 2017), may be important obstacle for development of banking offer. In general, the data by World Bank (Findex) is the best source of information to assess barriers for financial inclusion worldwide (Demirgüç-Kunt et al., 2017). Kowalewski and Pisany (2021) underline, referring to the Findex data, that many obstacles for financial inclusion (costs and lack of proper market offer, physical distance, low trust towards banks and institutional shortages) may really be addressed by technology-driven solutions, potentially also by solutions based on CBDC.

Against this background, the responses of central banks from developed countries regarding the rationale for working on retail CBDC, summarized by Boar and Wehrli (2021), seem to suggest less needs and less interest in CBDC. A look at the policy papers and statements of central banks from developed economies allows us to observe that their approach to retail CBDC is more reactive, secondary to what the actions of market entities interested in issuing private money will look like. One of the main reasons for interest in retail CBDC in advanced economies that emanate from central banks research, policy papers and speeches given by executives is the need to be ready for potential further development of private money, in particular stablecoins[3] issued by the largest e-commerce or social media platforms.

Federal Reserve of the United States (2022) in the policy paper, that is a background for wide public consultation on retail CBDC, openly states that emergence of financial technology innovations, particularly cryptoassets and stablecoins, was one of the main drivers for undertaking the topic of CBDC. Similarly, Bank of Canada (2020) declared in its principal policy paper *Contingency Planning for a Central Bank Digital Currency* (still valid in 2022) that – however Canada had no plans for issuing retail CBDC – it is worth to be prepared for making such a decision if one day it becomes beneficial or even necessary. According to Bank of Canada, it would happen in two potential scenarios, namely, when (i) the use of physical cash decreases to the point, where banknotes and coins will not allow for wide range of transactions in Canada and (ii) alternative digital currencies issued by the private sector are widely used for payment, as a store of value or as unit of account.

Similar approach *be ready, wait and see* has been adopted by Bank of England,[4] while the UK parliament, namely House of Lords (2022), presented an even more distanced approach in a study under the suggestive title: *Central bank digital currencies: a solution in search of a problem?* The analysis by Monetary Authority of Singapore (2021) presents the retail CBDCin a more favourable way and emphasizes its potentially positive impact on innovation and ensuring the level-playing field in the financial market; however, here there is also an unequivocal statement that there is no urgent need for issuing CBDC in Singapore, and research activities are only about understanding the topic and being ready without establishing any road map to actual implementation. Sweden, that is one of the most engaged European countries in CBDC research and tests, also has not made final decision, whether e-krona will be issued or not.[5]

European Central Bank (ECB) is very active in exploring the idea of retail CBDC (digital euro). ECB (2020a) in its primary policy paper *Report on a digital euro* indicates examples of possible scenarios, when issuance of CBDC becomes even essential, that is: (i) use of cash declines significantly; (ii) some other digital payment methods become unavailable due to materialisation of operational risk (in this logic: payment system with CBDC and all the other forms of money is simply more robust as it is more diversified); and (iii) foreign digital money is getting the popularity as a mean of payment or saving instrument.

The third scenario presented by ECB refers both to CBDC issued by other central banks and to private money projects, in particular global stablecoins issued by large corporations, including those outside the regulated and supervised financial system, that is, e-commerce and social media platforms. At the moment, there is no decision whether the CBDC issue in the euro zone will ever take place, or even pilot project and the design assumptions are also not known. Economic and consumer research as well as technological tests are ongoing.[6] While looking into scenarios indicated by ECB (that made CBDC issuance needed or even essential), one could easily see the aforementioned *be ready, wait and see* approach.

Central banks from advanced economies do not treat CBDC as development chance, especially in euro area, if one takes into consideration the effectiveness and features of currently developed payment schemes based on existing forms of central bank money, for example, TARGET Instant Payment Settlement (TIPS)[7] – the extension of TARGET2, which opens for financial institutions the possibility to offer customers (individuals and firms) instant money transfer at any time. Potential issuance of CBDC is rather treated in advanced economies as an answer to the upcoming challenges and structural changes, provided they really occur. As the challenges of digital age in the financial system are difficult to forecast (e.g. future role of big techs on the credit markets), it seems very advisable for central banks to be ready to provide citizens with digital cash.

The aspect of private money issuance and associated financial stability risks should be underlined. We have seen some attempts to design and issue global stablecoin by leading international technology company, that is, social media platform, that is generating huge network effects and can build competitive advantage (also in financial and payment services) thanks to its big and well-known userbase. This potentially refers also to global e-commerce firms, which collet unprecedented amount of information on final customers, products and merchants, including transaction details. Availability of those data opens the new possibilities for financial product distribution and – even more importantly – for credit risk assessment. The empirical investigations showing the strength and mechanism of this competition are already available in the economic literature (Kowalewski & Pisany, 2022). The first, kind of natural, reaction of authorities is simply regulation and enhanced supervision that answer new challenges.

Currently, there is a very interesting debate about what financial regulations should look like in the digital age. The role of the technology neutrality and technology agnosticism approaches is emphasized, as well as a wise balance between: the standards addressed by the type/industry of the enterprise (entity-based regulation) and the standards addressed by the type of activity undertaken (activity-based regulation) (Bains, 2022). The need for increased regulatory coordination, even on a global scale, is often emphasized, and this is also happening – just to mention achievements of institutions such as: BIS, Financial Stability Board[8] (FSB) or Financial Action Task Force[9] (FATF). The last one – in the area of anti-money laundering and counter-terrorist financing policies.

Moreover, European Union is undertaking a large and well-targeted regulatory effort. First, the proposed Markets in Crypto-Assets Regulation[10] (MiCA) introduces regulatory schemes for stablecoins (depending on the type as: asset-referenced tokens[11] and e-money tokens[12]). In addition, other acts of the EU Digital Strategy[13] have a chance to cover subsequent regulations gaps and the options for regulatory arbitration are being closed.

On the other hand, it seems that the regulation itself may turn out to be insufficient. Discussion, research and tests on CBDC may be treated in developed economies as a preparation for financial stability protection by actively coming out with a new offer concerning central bank money for the general public. The official policy papers of the euro area as well as scientific publications show that, apart from monetary stability, maintaining an undisturbed monetary transmission mechanism and financial stability, it is also very important to focus on appropriate level of competition on the financial markets and ethical issues, especially regarding individuals and customers of financial services. These issues will be easier to tackle when the role of the state in the monetary sphere remains untouched in the digital age. Using the example of the euro area, it can be concluded that developed economies will decide to issue retail CBDC, if it turns out to be necessary to ensure access to central bank money for citizens in digital age with respect for safety, fairness, privacy, openness, accessibility and maintaining level-playing field (Bindseil et al., 2021; Assenmacher & Bindseil, 2021; ECB, 2020a).

CBDC: Design choices

CBDC design is a weighing of various aspects and benefits, while mitigating potential risks related to such a significant change as issuance new type of central bank money. In some areas, we may see consensus among central banks, and in others, we can expect different decisions due to the fact that CBDC projects have different goals and tasks, and will reflect the characteristics of various economies and financial systems as well as distinct preferences of decision-makers. Design choices that need to be made during CBDC project can be summarized into the following aspects:

- architecture (direct versus intermediated model) and interoperability (both domestic and cross-border functionality),
- technology (centralized versus decentralized ledgers) and offline functionality,
- remuneration and limits,
- data governance and privacy protection.

Architecture (direct versus intermediated model) and interoperability (both domestic and cross-border functionality)

In most jurisdictions, in both emerging and advanced economies, one declares that intermediated model (with active role of commercial banks and payment institutions in providing financial services for the general public using the CBDC issued by central bank) is preferred. This is due to the fact that most authorities strive to ensure that the possible introduction of CBDC does not cause significant shocks in the traditional financial system, where commercial banks and deposit money play a key role alongside the central bank. Risk of commercial banks' deposits disintermediation is indicated as the most serious threat related to retail CBDC issuance and it is quite common in both emerging and advanced economies (Chen et al., 2022; Assenmacher & Bindseil, 2021).

Moreover, the assessment of the credit risk of private entities or individuals, as well as the assessment of the attractiveness of investment projects, remains the competence of the private sector financial intermediaries, for example, banks that grant loans to households and entrepreneurs. The involvement of banks and other financial institutions in the CBDC project also guarantees that the central bank will not bear excessive operational and reputational risk stemming from direct accounts keeping and everyday service. Finally, commercial banks and payment institutions will compete in the market and provide innovative solutions for the customers. The entrepreneurial attitude of the private businesses will not be wasted in the intermediated model of CBDC. In the broad context, the central bank, by issuing digital money, contributes to the maintenance of the level-playing field in the financial market. This is particularly important in today's conditions, where the financial services, apart from banks or payment firms, are also offered by large technological entities from e-commerce and social media industries, that are using very significant information advantages coming from their large customer network from core business line.

The second area of design choices related to CBDC, about which some consensus among different countries can be observed, is interoperability: domestic and cross-border. BIS (2021b) defines domestic interoperability as "the ease with which funds flow between CBDC and other payment systems." This refers, for example, to the possibility of direct transfer between CBDC and private e-money non-bank solutions without the necessity of having a bank account. Wide domestic interoperability has a lot of advantages – it fosters trust among users of different types of money and potentially creates the chances to build diversified and competitive financial system. On the other hand, it brings additional costs and risks, for example, operational ones and an appropriate regulation and careful supervision are needed as well. Cross-border and cross-currency interoperability, that is, between CBDC issued by different central banks is also advisable and international coordinating bodies are working on enhancing the debate and potentially setting the appropriate standards[14] in the future (BIS, 2021a).

Technology (centralized versus decentralized ledgers) and offline functionality

The underlying technology may be based on both central and decentralized ledgers. It is probably easier to maintain control over the central ledgers and some central banks of advanced economies, namely United States[15] and euro zone[16] are still exploring and testing both ways. Decentralized ledgers (permissioned) have already been used for the CBDC project, for example, in Nigeria (Central Bank of Nigeria, 2021).

On top of that, offline functionality is something that is often discussed and presented as an important and desired feature of retail CBDC. First, it strengthens inclusive role of CBDC and more importantly it boosts the operational resilience in the face of IT infrastructure breakdowns. In the light of the recent BIS survey (Chen et al., 2022), offline functionality is perceived among emerging economies as the element of inclusive design by the largest number of respondents.

Remuneration and limits

Remuneration is the key feature of CBDC that positions the digital currency issued by the central bank against other types of money available to the general public. In the financial system, as it stands today, individuals and real sector enterprises may use: non-remunerated cash (which is a direct liability of the central bank) or remunerated deposits (which are a liability of a commercial bank). For cash, payment function is predominant, while bank deposits serve also in many cases as saving tools. Therefore, if the CBDC brings interest, it becomes a kind of an equivalent of bank deposits, and when it is not remunerated, it can be considered a cash equivalent, however in a very modern digital form. Most central banks involved in CBDC projects, including Federal Reserve, ECB and Bank of Sweden as well as Central Bank of Nigeria, underline pros of non-remunerated scheme. CBDC that is not generating any interest income becomes a cash equivalent and consequently the disintermediation risk (risk of deposits outflow from the banking sector) is significantly restricted. Limits on the CBDC may play an analogous role. Certain restrictions imposed on the transaction volumes or cumulative balances support using CBDC as a medium of exchange (payment function) and hamper potential use of digital central bank money as a vehicle for storing value. Those kind of limits are present, for example, in both CBDC projects already implemented in emerging economies, that is, in Nigeria – eNaira (Central Bank of Nigeria, 2021) and the Bahamas – Sand Dollar.[17]

Data governance and privacy protection

CBDC, due to its digital form, seems to be traceable in each and every case. Token-based systems are usually considered to be more anonymous in comparison to account-based ones, but in reality, it is matter of a cost to keep track of all transactions. China, for example, declares to follow the principle of "anonymous small transactions and traceable and transparent large volume transactions" (Chen et al., 2022). There is still, however, no international standards in terms of privacy protection and data governance in broad context. As far as CBDC is concerned, probably for some people, the fact that in the end of the day, the central bank (essentially the state), not the private sector, is in the possession of their personal and transactional data, may be treated as a some kind of protection.

Conclusion

The analysis carried out in this chapter shows that emerging and advanced markets differ significantly in their motives for exploring the subject of CBDC. Emerging markets treat CBDC as a tool for financial inclusion enhancement and socio-economic development in a broad context. It also happens that CBDC addresses the specific needs of a given economy, for example, resulting from certain geographic limitations, for example, insular territory. Some developing countries also declare their interest in the possibility of programming money, for example, limiting its use for certain purposes. Hence, emerging economies are more proactive and the first full implementations can be found among them (the Bahamas and Nigeria), or very advanced pilot projects (China). On the other hand, developed economies declare their interest in increasing the effectiveness of payment systems, especially in cross-border use. In addition, they adopt a *wait-and-see* approach, that is, they conduct research on CBDC, but with the reservation that possible implementation will take place only if it is needed for social reasons or to maintain monetary sovereignty in the digital age. The perceived risk of retail CBDC issuance is similar in emerging and advanced economies, that is, commercial bank deposits disintermediation is indicated as the most severe risk; in other words, the risk of deposits outflow from the banking sector with all its consequences for the stability of banks and the availability of credit in the economy. Hence, we observe a consensus regarding the desired design of retail CBDC in the shape of cash, so as not to create competition for deposits. In most countries, intermediated CBDC models with the role of banks and other financial intermediaries in servicing clients, as well as non-remunerated solutions with additional transaction limits for CBDC users are more appreciated. On the other hand, countries differ in their assessment of the technology that may be useful (centralized versus decentralized ledgers) and will likely differ when it comes to data protection and user privacy solutions. All in all, the aforementioned analysis indicates that retail CBDC should be treated as a solution for economies that really need it, and not the next stage in the development of the financial system for everyone. CBDC, at least in the current global economy, does not fit all. Moreover, one size of CBDC does not fit all and careful design in the case of CBDC is absolutely crucial. It should be preceded by the in-depth research and a precise definition of the needs of a given economy.

Notes

1 BIS has coordinated efforts of six central banks, namely Bank of Canada, European Central Bank, Bank of Japan, SverigesRiksbank (Sweden), Swiss National Bank, Bank of England and Board of Governors Federal Reserve System during the policy research project *Central bank digital currencies: Foundational principles and core features.*
2 The 26 central banks took part in the survey 2022 EME Deputy Governors survey: Algeria, Argentina, Brazil, Chile, China, Colombia, the Czech Republic, Hong Kong SAR, Hungary, India, Indonesia, Israel, Korea, Malaysia, Mexico, Peru, the Philippines, Poland, Russia, Saudi Arabia, Singapore, South Africa, Thailand, Turkey, the United Arab Emirates and Vietnam.
3 Stablecoins are the specific crypto-assets, that is, stablecoins are digital units of value that use blockchain cryptography, but they also rely on tools to maintain a stable value relative to: (i) one fiat currency or (ii) several fiat currencies or other assets or commodities, including crypto-assets. One of the tools to maintain the stable value is when the issuer holds the reserves against which the stablecoins holding can be redeemed (ECB, 2021).
4 Based on the official website dedicated for CBDC in the UK: www.bankofengland.co.uk/research/digital-currencies
5 Based on official website of Riksbank: www.riksbank.se/en-gb/payments–cash/e-krona/
6 Based on official website of ECB: www.ecb.europa.eu/paym/digital_euro/html/index.en.html
7 Based on official website of ECB: www.ecb.europa.eu/paym/target/tips/html/index.en.html
8 Institution website: www.fsb.org/
9 Institution website: www.fatf-gafi.org/about/
10 The proposal for MiCA is available at: https://eur-lex.europa.eu/legal-content/EN/TXT/?uri=CELEX%3A52020PC0593
11 Asset-referenced token – a type of crypto-asset that purports to maintain a stable value by referring to the value of several fiat currencies that are legal tender, one or several commodities or one or several crypto-assets, or a combination of such assets (MiCA, Article 3, 1(3)).
12 E-money token – a type of crypto-asset the main purpose of which is to be used as a means of exchange and that purports to maintain a stable value by referring to the value of a fiat currency that is legal tender (MiCA, Article 3, 1(4)).
13 https://ec.europa.eu/info/strategy/priorities-2019-2024/europe-fit-digital-age_en
14 BIS is also conducting (and coordinating) ambitious experiments and test in this area: www.bis.org/about/bisih/projects.htm?m=3102
15 Information on the project Hamilton conducted by Boston Fed and Massachusetts Institute of Technology: www.bostonfed.org/publications/one-time-pubs/project-hamilton-phase-1-executive-summary.aspx
16 Key learnings of ECB tests experimentations: www.ecb.europa.eu/pub/pdf/other/ecb.digitaleuroscopekeylearnings202107~564d89045e.en.pdf
17 Based on information from Sand Dollar official portal: www.sanddollar.bs/individual

12 Advent of central bank digital currency and the future of monetary sovereignty

Vishal Sarin and Ranjan Aneja

Introduction

The concept of central bank digital currencies (CBDCs) is generally credited to Nobel laureate James Tobin, who recommended that the Federal Reserve Bank in the United States might make available to the public an extensively accessible "medium with the convenience of deposits and the safety of currency".[1] Just a decade-old concept of digital currency is gaining currency among central banks, economists, and various governments.

With the advent of the new era of financial technology (fintech), except paper currency, all other financial instruments in the contemporary financial system whether it is gilt-edge security, bonds, and other have now been replaced by their equivalent digital and electronic versions. It is evident also that physical cash in transactions to has been dwindling down in recent times, and during COVID-19 period, this notion was further reinforced that the world is moving away from paper-based currency transactions to electronic money transactions Sankar (2021). Hence, recent developments moot central banks and governments to step up the efforts towards discovering the idea of a 'digital version of fiat currency. A CBDC could be termed as a mix of the deposit in digital form with the usability in peer-to-peer cash-like transactions. But would it also be similar to deposits like a regular account at the central bank, or would it be near cash, materializing as a digital token? Would it generate interest rates like a bank deposit or would nominal returns be fixed at zero, like cash.[2]

The survey by Boar et al. (2020) and Barontini and Holden (2019) observed that most of the Central Banks are fascinated by the idea of CBDC but find themselves more in a research or experimentation state but less in an implementation state. Clarity on the objectives followed by CBDC has not yet been available. Bindseil (2020) summarized the whole ruckus on the shift to the CBDC debate by stating that most economists and central bankers are confident that this mechanism will provide secure and efficient banking to one and all and will enhance the contestability of retail payments.

But before proceeding to appreciate the idea of CBDC, one needs to revisit the idea of currency and money. We all know how money evolved from a barter system to a standardized barter system driven by metals and cowrie shells. Metals

DOI: 10.4324/9781003310365-12

were used because of their intrinsic values and shells were attractive for their exquisiteness. Later this system transit into a more sophisticated system, where silver and gold coins became the pertinent part of settling financial transactions because silver and gold had money as well as intrinsic value. During this journey, people improvised the standardized barter system into a more novel and complex system by introducing the concept of a bill of exchange, which later lead to the creation of paper currency. Hence, historically, money carries two facts: (1) money has been used in the form of either commodity with intrinsic value or in terms of the instrument of debt. For example, paper currency acts as representative money and it is a debt instrument too. The currency's owner knows who owes him or who has the basic liability and there exists the issuer of representative money. (2) Sovereign issue money. Paper currency comprises seigniorage, that is, the difference between the intrinsic value and the representative value which accrues to the issuers and is then used for public spending (Bofinger & Haas, 2020). Hence, as per modern economics, the definition of currency elucidates that paper currency is a money kind exclusively issued by the autonomous or sovereign (i.e. central bank). It is a liability of the dispensing central bank and an asset of the public. Currency is fiat, a legal tender. But the currency of paper is not the defining character of money.

Defining CBDC

CBDC should satisfy certain primary functions to be categorized as such. One of the frequently used definitions of CBDC is that it is a kind of digitally formed legal tender. This definition is forwarded by International Monetary Fund (IMF) (Kiff et al., 2020). Although CBDC may have the capability to replace the existing physical cash in the coming future if it preserves most of the desired characteristics. It may also complement electronic money (M_1) and performs analogous functions or act as a fully backed reserve.[3] In a narrow definition, the CBDC is a new sort of liability in the electronic mode of the central bank, which can be used as a means of payment and storage value, and yet maintain most of the required characteristics of M_0 and M_1 (Lee et al., 2021). Bjerg (2017) foresees CBDC as a universally accepted e-money. Bordo and Levin (2017) went further to assume two mediums of exchange by assuming CBDC Tokens and CBDC Accounts. Kumhof and Noone (2018) define it as widely accessible, interest-bearing money with all functionalities of retail transactions. It carries all components that money has like an electronic version of fiat liability of a central bank which can be used as a medium of exchange and to settle future payments. It will be a digital representation of sovereign currency (Kiff et al., 2020; Allen et al., 2020). Auer et al. (2020b) assume CBDC as digital currency which is different from balances in traditional reserves.

Hence, CBDC is a kind of legal digitally formed tender; CBDC must have four elementary functions of currency: medium of exchange, store of value, unit of account, and standard of deferred payments (Lee et al., 2021).

Review of Literature

A vast array of studies has been conducted on CBDC ever since this concept gained currency. The usability and accessibility aspect of CBDC has captured the attention of researchers across the world and various dimensions are being studied, which CBDC can facilitate. These dimensions include financial inclusion, the central bank's functions and objectives, its welfare effect and its role in the macroeconomic stability of the country, and lastly, the future of banking with CBDC.

A survey conducted by Boar and Wehrli (2021) about CBDC adoption found that about 86 per cent of central banks were actively researching the potentialities of CBDC, 60 per cent of central banks were working on the technology aspect of CBDC and 14 per cent of central banks were almost reached at pilot stages of using CBDC. Náñez et al. (2021) while studying the status of CBDC for countries like China, Uruguay, and the Bahamas found that these countries are at different stages of the CBDC development. While studying the adoption of CBDC in the African continent, Ozili (2021a) observed that so far only seven African countries have shown interest in the central bank-based digital currency, in which four African countries are at the pilot testing stage while Nigeria, the only African country, has adopted the CBDC. The study also highlighted that West African countries are lagging far behind as far as the adoption of CBDC is concerned. Apart from the idea of adoption, many studies highlighted the strong relationship between financial inclusion and CBDC. Ozili (2021b) eulogized the role of CBDC in augmenting financial inclusion as the study further elaborated that CBDC will improve access to financial services and with reduced transactions cost, it will further spread the financial literacy in the country. Foster et al. (2021) further supported this idea by proving that more excluded populations will come under the ambit of digital platforms and their inclusion will alleviate their living standard. Andolfatto (2021) argues that CBDC, in the future, will reduce the cash demand and may lead to financial inclusion as fintech may help them to hold cash without having a bank account. Engert and Fung (2017) reasoned that primarily countries are supporting CBDC because it will increase financial inclusion. But Maniff (2020) points out that the presence of CBDC will increase financial inclusion, but it may not be very effective in achieving other goals. Didenko and Buckley (2021) while studying the financial inclusion aspect of CBDC in the Pacific region cautioned the authorities to take more time in analysing the various facets of CBDC before launching the same.

While studying the CBDC and its effectiveness on macroeconomic and financial policy, Cukierman (2019) strongly supported the central bank-backed digital currency over the private digital currencies. Schilling et al. (2020) argue that the central bank's three goals – financial stability, efficiency goals, and price stability– seem impossible to achieve with the advent of CBDC, as the central bank can manage to attain any two at a given point of time. Further, Bjerg (2017) cast doubt over the co-existence of the central bank and the commercial bank, as both shall become competitors. However, many studies favour the welfare aspects of CBDC; Auer and Boehme (2020) argued the CBDC will offer two important features (i) case like safety and (ii) convenience for peer-to-peer payments. While studying the Canadian case, Davoodalhosseini (2021) examined a monetary design with three scenarios (i) where only cash, (ii) only CBDC, or (iii) both cash and digital currency are available to economic agents. The study proved that cost of using CBDC is not too high as compared to cash and hence economic agents will prefer CBDC over cash. It is further observed that in presence of both, cash and CBDC, lower welfare will be attainable than in the other two scenarios. Ward and Rochemont (2019) highlighted that despite the aggressive promotion of CBDC by central banks, the international community is divided on the issue of prospective benefits of CBDC. Many studies were conducted to understand the effect of CBDC on macroeconomic and financial stability. In this direction, Yao (2017) found that the very presence of CBDC will make money more stable in value, which eventually becomes an effective tool to control macroeconomic stability. Williamson (2019) claimed that CBDC will help to mitigate financial crime. Williamson (2019) further elucidates that allowing deposits in CBDC accounts will reduce the supply of private credit by commercial banks, which further will raise the nominal interest rate and lower the reserve to deposit ratio of commercial banks. This will put pressure on financial stability as commercial banks will find themselves short of cash. Ferrari et al. (2020a) further elaborated the argument and forecasted that the presence of CBDC can amplify the global shocks and it will solely depend on the risk mitigation process laid down by a particular central bank to safeguard its economy, but other central banks fail to arrest this spillover than global shocks may affect economies where central banks have strong control over the risk mitigation system. Many studies observed that central bank controlled digital currency and there are many challenges of existence of commercial banks, Andolfatto (2021) analysed that interest-bearing CBDC can diminish the cash demand in the economy and may not disintermediate banks rather it can extend their deposit-based and in the presence of competition will compel banks the raise interest on deposits. Grym et al. (2017) evaluated that in the future, CBDC will replace the banknotes and will make them outdated. Even on the issue of choice of privacy with the advent of CBCD, many studies were conducted. Rennie and Steele (2021), Grothoff and Moser (2021), Darbha and Arora (2020) outline the issue of choice of privacy and argue that governments can track the payments system of the individual via blockchain technology, which is one way that will affect the right of privacy but in parallel could control the financial crimes too. It has been observed that in the recent past research on CBDC has been gaining momentum and steadily lots of new aspects of CBDC have been emerging.

Methodology

A vast array of literature has emerged on CBDC in the recent past as this idea has been gaining momentum among the central banks of the world and governments are also taking interest in this concept and have started sensitizing people about the accessibility and usability of CBDC. Prior research in this area was predominantly conducted by major central banks of the world and in the recent past, some empirical research papers are emerging, citing various facets of CBDC. The present research is based on the methodology of narrative review as the purpose was to identify a problem of interest and describe them as the narrative has been emerging. Wide segments of research reports, working papers, and research papers were studied to capture the true narrative about the advent of CBDC.

Why CBDC?

1. Public access to legal tenders: One of the prime intentions of introducing CBDC is to ensure that the public has proper access to legal tenders in case of extraordinary circumstances when cash were no longer available. Hence, both case and CBDC would be treated as a legal tender by both central bank and the government (McBride, 2015). Due to ease of payments using care, or other digital modes, the use of cash has been reduced. It is difficult to trace cash in the economic system, hence it becomes an attractive instrument for tax evasion, illegal transactions, and money laundering, hence the removal of cash would help to reduce such money-related crime and improve tax receipts.
2. Reduce settlement risk: CBDC has a clear advantage over other digital payment systems. It will reduce settlement risk in the financial system. By enabling a more real-time payment settlement system, CBDC would be the more preferred choice among people. Currency settlements would make the time zone immaterial and it would mitigate the "Herstatt" risk too. The CBDC could mend the effectiveness and safety of both small- and large-value payment systems. Payment efficiency will enhance at the point of sale, online, and peer-to-peer. CBDC could also help countries to remove small value coins via delivery of electronic change. For example, Bank of Korea in 2017 initiated a coinless society trial by allowing customers to deposit their change onto prepaid cards instead of accepting small change from purchases and by virtue of this idea, country notionally saved 53.7 billion won, which is spent on producing coins.
3. Road to a less-cash society: In times to come, the digital money will replace coins and notes, which will move countries to a less-cash society, which has its own benefits. Less cash society saves a lot of cost of printing, transporting, distributing, and storing currency.
4. Efficient cross-border payments: A joint study of Central Banks of Canada, the U.K., and Singapore[4] found CBDC improves counterparty credit risk for cross-border interbank payments and settlement. The current system based on real-time gross settlement (RTGS) is a multi-layered system marred by time lags, generating friction and lags in settlements, and CBDC is incapable to erase such issues with ease.
5. Challenges of virtual currencies (VCs) and CBDC– a safety measure: The urgency of CBDC is also required to meet the challenges brought up by virtual currencies (like cryptocurrencies etc.). If in times to come, VCs start gaining attraction, Randal Quarles (BIS, 2021d) argues that national currencies with some degree of convertibility are likely to come under threat. He further argues that the US dollar may not be affected much as most of the VCs are denominated in the US dollar. Rather, the use of VCs will further

encourage the use of US dollars worldwide. But if the Central bank creates its own CBDC, it could help the local currency to remain in preference and further protect the public from abnormal volatility that VCs hold. As Ms Christine Legarde, president of the European Central Bank, once stated in the BIS Annual Report (2020):"central banks have a duty to safeguard people's trust in our money. The central bank must complement their domestic efforts with close cooperation to guide the exploration of CBDC to identify reliable principles and encourage innovation."

6. Transaction demand for money: CBDC, if used extensively, can reduce the transaction demand for bank deposits, that is, reduction in the liquidity needs for settlement of the transaction. This subsequently will reduce the requirement for government guarantees on bank deposits (Dyson & Hodgson, 2016).
7. CBDC and financial inclusion: With the increased accessibility of internet services and enhanced digital literacy, central banks of many countries are assuming CBDC as a key driver to improving financial inclusion (Boar et al., 2020). Many countries across the world are in search of cost-effective and easily accessible measures to improve financial inclusion and CBDC could be one of the important instruments to achieve financial inclusion.
8. Facilitating fiscal transfer: During COVID-19, the need for an efficient and quick fund transfer system was felt across the world for providing benefits to identified people. CBDC, if properly linked with a digital identity system, could prove to be a boon to countries where pilferage in monetary transfers of benefits is quite common.

Challenges Posed by CBDC

1. Potential disintermediation of banks: There is a risk of disintermediation in banks or enabling destabilizing runs into central bank money, thereby, commercial banks' financial stability would be at risk. Disintermediation of banks will directly undermine the credit creation ability. Moreover, due to the loss of a noteworthy volume of low-cost transaction deposits, their interest margin will fall which subsequently will enhance the credit cost (Sankar, 2021).
2. Issues of liquidity with commercial banks: A banking system predominately based on CBDC will enhance cash withdrawals in the blink of an eye. In case of banking stress, account holders will take no time to withdraw their money by electronic transactions, which will further push the commercial banks to hold a large level of liquidity which will translate into lower returns for commercial banks.
3. Cyberrisk and technology up-gradation: Cyber risk is a big cause of concern for the existence of CBDC and it invites a serious discussion on cyber security to pave the way for unhindered expansion of CBDC. Stringent cyber security laws along with concerted efforts on financial literacy are essential for any country dealing with CBDC. The success of CBDC also depends upon the technology preparedness of the country. A high-scaled digital currency system to cater to the need of every citizen requires heavy investment in telecommunication technology.

In the aforementioned discussion, it was proved that CBDC has the potential to provide significant benefits by reducing settlement risk, being less reliant on cash, and allowing the government to run cash benefit schemes efficiently. Introduction to CBDC would possibly lead to a more robust, trusted, efficient, regulated, and legal tender-based payment option. The attached risk also poses critical issues but the potential benefit of CBDC overweighs the threat it poses, for which a careful calibration and nuanced approach are required. In order to overcome matters pertaining to CBDC issuance, a detailed report on CBDC published by the Bank of International Settlement (BIS, 2020) guided central banks to follow three foundational principles before embarking on the idea of CBDC. These foundational principles include the concept of "Do no harm", Coexistence, and Innovation and efficiency.

1. "Do not harm"– CBDC should preserve and emphasize the homogeneity of a currency, allowing the public to use a different forms of money interchangeably.
2. Co-existence – Different types of money offered by the central bank, including CBDC, should complement one another and co-exist with robust private money (i.e. commercial bank accounts) to support public policy objectives.
3. Innovation and Efficiency – The payment ecosystem that includes both public authorities and private agents would need continued innovation; otherwise, it will jeopardize the payment transfer system.

In order to fulfil the foundational principles, a potential CBDC would need to fulfil 14 core features. These core features are in Figure 12.1:

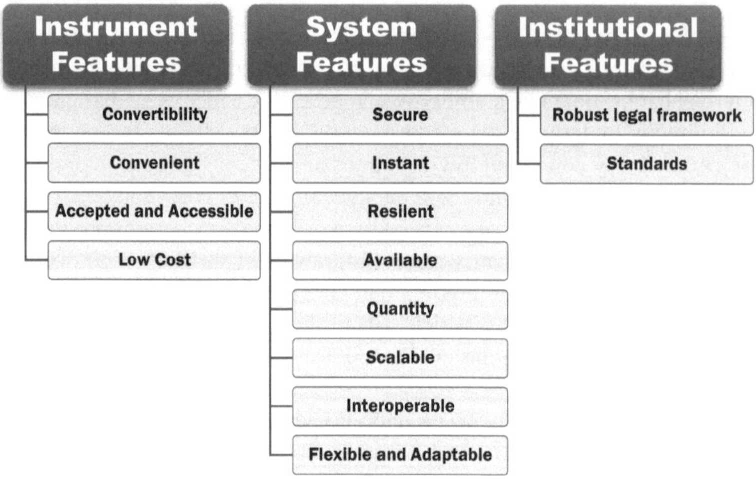

Figure 12.1 Core CBDC features

Source: CBDC: Foundational Principles and Core Features, Report no. 1, Bank of International Settlement (BIS), 2020.

The explanation of these 14 features shall further enhance our understanding of the CBDC. As the feature of convertibility explains, CBDC should ensure singleness of the currency means at the exchange it should be traded at par with private money and cash. Conveniences state that CBDC payments should complement cash. No difference in the transaction of CBDC whether it is a point of sale or person-to-person. Provision to ensure offline transactions, such feature indicates accessibility and acceptance of CBDC and it should carry low cost, that is, low or no transaction cost for CBDC payments along with a minimal requirement of investment in technology. As far as system features are concerned, first, it should be secure, which means the system should ensure effective protection and security from counterfeiting as stakeholders shall be prone to cyberattacks. Second, immediate payment settlements should be available to the endusers. Third, in case of unforeseen circumstances, CBDC system should have the ability to ensure offline payment, that is, a resilient system is an important condition. Fourth, 24×7 payment available should be ensured to endusers. Fifth, the system should be capable process enormous transactions simultaneously. Sixth, scalability warrants a system flexible enough to cater to future volume. Seventh, uninterrupted integration with privately managed payment systems to ensure smooth fund flows between the two systems, and eighth, the system must ensure flexibility and adaptability for future policy changes. Institutional features include a robust legal framework where Central Bank should have clear-cut authority to issue CBDC and along with it, the system should be based on stringent standards as guided by a suitable regulatory authority. These foundational principal are capable to ensure an exclusive set of requirements from CBDC to make this system relevant in the times to come.

CBDC and Monetary Sovereignty

The world is at a crossroads in monetary history. New financial instruments are developing because of technological advancements. The innovations in money and money-like assets are changing the way monetary policies works. This part of the work is discussing the most relevant issues of CBDC in the context of monetary sovereignty:

1. CBDC and monetary policy transmission: Debate swirls over how the presence of CBDC would affect the working of monetary policy. Goodfriend (2016) and Bordo and Levin (2017) maintained that using the interest rates on CBDC as its policy tools, along with the reduction in cash holding would eradicate the effective lower bound (ELB) as a limitation on monetary policy. This action will enable the central bank to maintain macroeconomic parameters and price stability. Studies conducted by Barrdear and Kumhof (2016), Meaning et al. (2018), Williamson (2018), and IMF (2020) found that adding the interest rate on CBDC as a new policy tool will increase the transmission mechanism and fortifies the lending channels. The interest rate on CBDC

could be used to foster true price stability by following the price level target following a Taylor-type rule (Bordo & Levin, 2017).

2. CBDC and Efficiency in Monetary System: CBDC could optimally be used by central banks to pursue their public policy objectives. An efficient payment system, properly linked with a unique identification number, could prove to be a boon for the government's direct subsidy transfer and direct benefit transfer programme without any friction. The idea of financial inclusion will gain momentum. Issues pertaining to tracking of transactions, and money laundering could be curbed without bearing any extra administrative cost (Payment Canada, 2021).
3. CBDC as a safe alternative to private digital monies: With the advent of private digital monies like crypto and stablecoins, the public has been allured towards them, but these private digital monies exist without any sovereign agency, thus these currencies become more vulnerable to risk and volatility. The introduction of CBDC by the central bank will provide digital monies with monetary sovereignty and subsequently, CBDC become the legal tender that will be a risk-free asset.
4. CBDC as an alternative to other online payment methods: It is now quite evident that the uses of alternative payment services offered by private entities have become dominant among the public. China, for example, has seen nearly universal adoption of digital payment with nearly 94 percent of mobile transactions supported by Alibaba and Tencent (Niepelt, 2020a). Though these players leverage economies of scale and pass the cost efficiencies to the consumers but on the other side, they also pose a risk of monopoly, misuse of data, and safety and security of the technology. CBDC could address these concerns by continued retail access to central bank money.
5. CBDC will redefine central banks: By introducing CBDC, direct access to central bank liabilities for households and businesses may, however, lead to an enlarged role of the central bank. The central bank will complement the role of the commercial bank. Hence, central banks enhance phenomenal capabilities which will cut the role of commercial banks, and many face liquidity shortages along with rising lending costs.
6. Disintermediation of commercial banks: CBDC provides a direct channel for a central bank to transmit interest rates to households and businesses and the economy will see a smooth monetary transmission. If households and businesses find CBDC more attractive than commercial bank deposits, this would result in the disintermediation of the banking sector. The banking sector may also become relatively less important as a transmission channel (Ferrari et al., 2020a).

Conclusion

It is quite evident that the presence of cryptocurrencies and which is slowly but steadily growing in acceptance is disrupting the traditional payment system and posing a direct challenge to Central banks either to innovate or to face the music. CBDC is the answer to such an immediate threat. One estimate by IMF indicates that almost 100 countries are either considering or rolling out the idea of CBDC in their respective regions. CBDC is quite different from online payment and the difference lies in the concept of ownership of liabilities. Online digital payments are actually the liabilities of commercial banks, whereas CBDC is a direct liability of the country's central bank. Although this notion poses serious questions about the relevance of commercial banks in the presence of CBDC (but this puzzle is still unsolved), another apprehension is arising about CBDC that if payment tracking will become easy via this system, which actually is impossible in the existing system, then the possibilities of tracking down the economic activities of citizens will become easy, which certainly pose threat to cannon of privacy. Presently, only small nations are experimenting with near to CBDC ideas, as it is easy for them to manage unforeseen circumstances on the monetary front, but the same issues may turn up into a catastrophe in the case of big nations. Hence, the idea of CBDC is mostly at the study or experimentation stage where many facets of its implication on monetary sovereignty are yet to be validated. But one thing is sure with the advent of CBDC, the working of monetary policy and the role of central banks will change once and for all.

Notes

1 https://law.stanford.edu/projects/central-bank-digital-currencies-a-transatlantic-perspective
2 See Mancini-Griffoli et al. (2018) for other relevant design aspects of CBDCs, which are mostly of an operational in nature, such as the means to disseminate, clear and secure CBDCs.
3 CBDC is crafted to act as both reserve and can create replacement of bank deposits created by commercial banks. But CBDC also create confusion that whether it is a liability of the central bank of its own country or of another.
4 Bank of Canada, Bank of England, Monetary Authority of Singapore, Cross-border Interbank Payments and Settlements, 2018, 68. www.mas.gov.sg/-/media/MAS/ProjectUbin/Cross-Border-Interbank-Payments-and-Settlements.pdf, accessed 10.04.2022.

Acknowledgements and conclusion

We would like to give full respect and thankfulness to all professors and researchers from Estonia, India and Poland who decided to share their knowledge and thoughts to write this book, which is concentrated on digital currencies and New Global Financial System.

The twelve chapters give the answers to the questions formulated in preface of the book. Relevant case studies and econometric models were also presented to underline that the digital currencies and New Global Financial System are one of the main concerns of Central Banks. The world cannot exist without finance, but it can be much different when New Global Financial System with its digital currencies will be fully implemented.

The important question raised in this book is: how the New Global Financial System will look like and how it will be implemented globally? The answer is stated in this book highlighting the dimension of post-pandemic COVID-19 challenges for central banks, the impact of money supply, central bank digital currency design and implementation in the context of differences between advanced and emerging markets, the retail investors' strategies, the efforts of ECB to establish digital euro, and also inequality and poverty dimension regarding digital currency use. The book gives the order in understanding the concept of digital currencies and New Global Financial System with its all most important instruments which are governed by the international organizations such as the International Monetary Fund, United Nations, European Central Bank and Federal Reserve Bank (FED). The success of implementing the New Global Financial System depends much on international governance which creates the framework and implementation policy requirements for all countries which are United Nations members. Currently the situation is dynamic due to the war in Ukraine which definitely has its impact on the design of the system and the time of the implementation.

References

ABC News. (2022). The end: Facebook-backed digital currency. Diem sold to bank. *ABC News*. https://abcnews.go.com/Business/wireStory/end-facebook-backed-digital-currency-diem-sold-bank-82603571, accessed 29.04.2022

Adelmann, F., Elliott, J., Ergen, I., Gaidosch, T., Jenkinson, N., Khiaonarong, T., Morozova, A., Schwarz, N., Wilson, C. (2020). *Cyber risk and financial stability: It's a small world after all*. IMF Staff Discussion Note, SDN/20/07. IMF.

Ağan, B. (2020). The impact of covid-19 pandemic process on digital payment system: The case of turkey. *Eurasian Journal of Researches in Social and Economics (EJRSE)*. www.researchgate.net/profile/Buesra-Agan/publication/343524730_The_Impact_of_Covid-19_Pandemic_Process_on_Digital_Payment_System_The_Case_of_Turkey/links/5f2e7316a6fdcccc43b31ceb/The-Impact-of-Covid-19-Pandemic-Process-on-Digital-Payment-System-The-Case-of-Turkey.pdf?origin=publication_detail, accessed 04.04.2022

Agur, I., Ari, A., Dell'Ariccia, G. (2022). Designing central bank digital currencies. *Journal of Monetary Economics*, vol. 125, pp. 62–79. https://doi.org/10.1016/j.jmoneco.2021.05.002, accessed 29.04.2022

Ajello, A., Laubach, T., López-Salido, D., Nakata, T. (2019). Financial stability and optimal interest rate policy. *International Journal of Central Banking*, vol. 15(1), pp. 279–326.

Akana, T. (2021). Changing US consumer payment habits during the COVID-19 crisis. *Journal of Payments Strategy & Systems*, vol. 15(3), pp. 234–243.

Aldasoro, I., Frost, J., Gambacorta, L., Whyte, D. (2021). Covid-19 and cyber risk in the financial sector. *BIS Bulletin*, vol. 37, pp. 1–9.

Aldasoro, I., Gambacorta, L., Giudici, P., Leach, T. (2020). *Operational and cyber risks in the financial sector*. BIS Working Papers No. 840. BIS.

Aldasoro, I., Gambacorta, L., Giudici, P., Leach, T. (2022). The drivers of cyber risk. *Journal of Financial Stability*, vol. 60. https://doi.org/10.1016/j.jfs.2022.100989.

Alfani, G., Gierok, V., Schaff, F. (2022). Economic inequality in preindustrial Germany, ca. 1300–1850. *The Journal of Economic History*, vol. 82(1), pp. 87–125. https://doi.org/10.1017/S0022050721000607

Alfonso, V., Boar, C., Frost, J., Gambacorta, L., Liu, J. (2021). E-commerce in the pandemic and beyond. *BIS Bulletin*, vol. 36, 12 January.

Al-Kandari, A., Abul, S. (2019). The impact of macroeconomic variables on stock prices in Kuwait. *International Journal of Business and Management*, vol. 14(6). https://doi.org/10.5539/ijbm.v14n6p99

Allen, F., Gu, X., Jagtiani, J. (2022). Fintech, cryptocurrencies, and CBDC: Financial structural transformation in China. *Journal of International Money and*

Finance, vol. 124, June 2022. www.sciencedirect.com/science/article/abs/pii/S0261560622000286?via%3Dihub, accessed 29.04.2022

Allen, S., Čapkun, S., Eyal, I., Fanti, G., Ford, B.A., Grimmelmann, J., Juels, A., Kostiainen, K., Meiklejohn, S., Miller, A., Prasad, E., Wüst, K., Zhang, F. (2020). *Design choices for Central Bank digital currency: Policy and technical considerations*. Brookings. www.brookings.edu/research/design-choices-for-central-bank-digital-currency-policy-and-technical-considerations/

Amanai. (2019). *Diving into DeFi: A beginner's guide, AltCoinMagazine*, 25 September. https://medium.com/the-capital/diving-into-defi-a-beginners-guide-5bbbb5dfc4aa, accessed 19.04.2022

Amendola, A., Braione, M., Candila, V., Storti, G. (2020). A model confidence set approach to the combination of multivariate volatility forecasts. *International Journal of Forecasting*, vol. 36, 873–891. https://doi.org/10.1016/j.ijforecast.2019.10.001

Andersson, B., Claussen, C. A. (2017). Alternatives to inflation targeting. *SverigesRiksbank Economic Review*, vol. 1.

Andolfatto, D. (2021). Assessing the impact of Central Bank digital currency on private banks. *The Economic Journal*, vol. 131(634), pp. 525–540. https://doi.org/10.1093/ej/ueaa073

Aramonte, S., Huang, W., Schrimpf, A. (2021). DeFi risks and the decentralisation illusion. *BIS Quarterly Review*, December. www.bis.org/publ/qtrpdf/r_qt2112b.htm, accessed: 19.04.2022

Ardakani, O. M., Kishor, N. K., Song, S. (2018). Re-evaluating the effectiveness of inflation targeting. *Journal of Economic Dynamics and Control*, vol. 90, pp. 76–97. https://doi.org/10.1016/j.jedc.2018.01.045

Armelius, H., Boel, P., Claussen, C. A., Nessén, M. (2018). The e-krona and the macroeconomy. *SerigesRiksbank Economic Review*, vol. 3, pp. 43–65. www.riksbank.se/globalassets/media/rapporter/pov/artiklar/engelska/2018/181105/20183-the-e-krona-and-the-macroeconomy.pdf, accessed 29.04.2022

Arnold, M. (2020). ECB confident it can overcome challenges to create a digital euro. *Financial Times*, 02 October. www.ft.com/content/b6f0c233-0b35-45d1-896f-1c6599558d9b, accessed 28.01.2022

Artner, A. (2020). Can China lead the change of the world?, *Third World Quarterly*, vol. 41(11). https://10.1080/01436597.2020.1793664

Assenmacher, K., Bindseil, U. (2021). The Eurosytem's digital euro project: Preparing for a digital future. In D. Niepelt (Ed.), *Central Bank digital currency: Considerations, projects, outlook*. https://voxeu.org/content/central-bank-digital-currency-considerations-projects-outlook

Aste, T. (2019). Cryptocurrency market structure: Connecting emotions and economics. *Digital Finance*, vol. 1(1–4), pp. 5–21. https://doi.org/10.1007/s42521-019-00008-9

Atıcı, G. (2019). Bitcoin and blockchain: A threat or opportunity for the financial system. *European Journal of Economics and Business Studies*, 4(3). https://10.2478/ejes-2018-0063

Atkinson, A. B. (1970). On the measurement of inequality. *Journal of Economic Theory*, vol. 2(3), pp. 244–263. https://doi.org/10.1016/0022-0531(70)90039-6

Atkinson, A. B. (2015). *Inequality: What can be done?* Harvard University Press.

Atkinson, A. B., Brandolini, A. (2009). On analysing the world distribution of income. *SSRN Electronic Journal*. https://doi.org/10.2139/ssrn.1357268

Atkinson, A. B., Piketty, T., Saez, E. (2011). Top incomes in the long run of history. *Journal of Economic Literature*, vol. 49(1), pp. 3–71. https://doi.org/10.1257/jel.49.1.3

Auer, R., Banka, H., Boakye-Adjei, N. Y., Faragallah, A., Frost, J, Natarajan, H., Prenio, J. (2022). *Central Bank digital currencies: A new tool in the financial inclusion toolkit?* FSI Insights on Policy Implementation No. 41. FSI.

Auer, R., Böhme, R. (2021). *Central Bank digital currency: The quest for minimally invasive technology*. BIS Working Papers No. 948. www.bis.org/publ/work948.pdf, accessed 01.02.2022.

Auer, R., Cornelli, G., Frost, J. (2020a). Covid-19, cash, and the future of payments. *BIS Bulletin*, vol. 3, pp. 1–6.

Auer, R., Cornelli, G., Frost, J. (2020b). *Rise of the central bank digital currencies: Drivers, approaches and technologies*. BIS Working Papers, No. 880. BIS, August, p. 3.

Auer, R., Frost, J., Gambacorta, L., Monnet, C., Rice, T., Shin, H. S. (2021). *Central Bank digital currencies: Motives, economic implications and the research frontier*. BIS Working Papers No. 976, Bank for International Settlements, Monetary and Economic Department, November, p. 5. www.bis.org/publ/work976.pdf, accessed 04.04.2022

Auer, R., Frost, J., Gambacorta, L., Monnet, C., Rice, T., Shin, H. S. (2021). *Central bank digital currencies: Motives, economic implications and the research frontier*. BIS Working papers, No 976. Bank for International Settlements.

Auer, R., Boehme, R. (2020). The technology of retail Central Bank digital currency. *BIS Quarterly Review*, March. Banks of International Settlement. www.bis.org/publ/qtrpdf/r_qt2003j.htm

Azarenkova, G., Shkodina, I., Samorodov, B., Babenko, M., Onishchenko, I. (2018). The influence of financial technologies on the global financial system stability. *Investment Management and Financial Innovations*, 15(4), https://10.21511/imfi.15(4).2018.19

Badarau, C., Popescu, A. (2014). Monetary policy and credit cycles: A DSGE analysis. *Economic Modelling*, vol. 42, pp. 301–312. https://doi.org/10.1016/j.econmod.2014.07.016

Bailey, A. M., Rettler, B., Warmke, C. (2021). Philosophy, politics, and economics of cryptocurrency II: The moral landscape of monetary design. *Philosophy Compass*, vol. 16(11). https://doi.org/10.1111/phc3.12784

Bailliu, J., Meh, C., Zhang, Y. (2015). Macroprudential rules and monetary policy when financial frictions matter. *Economic Modelling*, vol. 50, pp. 148–161. https://doi.org/10.1016/j.econmod.2015.06.012

Bains, P. (2022). *International monetary fund blockchain consensus mechanisms: A primer for supervisors*. Note 2022/003. IMF.

Baker, S. R., Bloom, N., Davis, S. J., Kost, K., Sammon, M., Viratyosin, T. (2020). *The unprecedented stock market reaction to COVID-19*. Working Paper. https://bfi.uchicago.edu/wp-content/uploads/ BFI_White-Paper_Davis_3.2020.pdf

Balvers, R., McDonald, B. (2021). Designing a global digital currency. *Journal of International Money and Finance*, vol. 111. https://10.1016/j.jimonfin.2020.102317

Balz, B. (2020). *Zunehmend smarter: Zahlungsverkehr in der Digitalisierung*. Banken Dialog Karlsruhe, 27 October. www.bundesbank.de/de/presse/reden/zunehmend-smarter-zahlungsverkehr-in-der-digitalisierung-849008, accessed 04.04.2022

Banerjee, A. V., Duflo, E. (2003). Inequality and growth: What can the data say? *Journal of Economic Growth*, vol. 8(3), pp. 267–299. https://doi.org/10.1023/A:1026205114860

Bank of Canada. (2020). *Contingency planning for a Central Bank digital currency*. www.bankofcanada.ca/2020/02/contingency-planning-central-bank-digital-currency/

Banque de France. (2021). *Digital Euro experiment combined feasibility – Tiered model*, July. www.banque-france.fr/sites/default/files/media/2021/08/02/821220_digital_euro_en.pdf, accessed 05.02.2022

Baran, P. (1962). *On distributed communications networks*. RAND Corporation Papers, Document P-2626. RAND Corporation.

Barnebeck, T., Malchow-Møller, N., Nordvig, J. (2015). Inflation targeting and macroeconomic performance since the great recession. *Oxford Economic Papers*, vol. 67(3), pp. 598–613. https://doi.org/10.1093/oep/gpv024

Barontini, C., Holden, H. (2019). *Proceeding with caution – A survey on central bank digital currency*. BIS Papers No. 101. Bank for International Settlements, January. www.bis.org/publ/bppdf/bispap101.pdf, accessed 29.04.2022

Barrdear, J., Kumhof, M. (2016). *The macroeconomics of central bank issued digital currencies* (July 18, 2016). Bank of England Working Paper No. 605, Available at SSRN: https://ssrn.com/abstract=2811208 or http://dx.doi.org/10.2139/ssrn.2811208

Barrdear, J., Kumhof, M. (2021). The macroeconomics of Central Bank digital currencies. *Journal of Economic Dynamics and Control*, vol. 10(1), pp. 41–48. https://doi.org/10.1016/j.jedc.2021.104148, accessed 29.04.2022

Bataev, A., Plotnikova, E., Gladkova, S. (2019). *Multiparametic forecast model with variable cryptocurrency capitalization assessment framework*. SPBPU IDE'19: Proceedings of the 2019 International SPBPU Scientific Conference on Innovations in Digital Economy October 2019, Article No. 4, pp. 1–8. https://doi.org/10.1145/3372177.3373090, accessed 02.03.2022

Baur, D. G., Hong, K., Lee, A. D. (2018). Bitcoin: Medium of exchange or speculative assets? *Journal of International Financial Markets, Institutions and Money*, vol. 54, pp. 177–189. https://doi.org/10.1016/j.intfin.2017.12.004

Baxa, J., Plašil, M., Vašíček, B. (2015). Changes in inflation dynamics under inflation targeting? Evidence from Central European countries. *Economic Modelling*, vol. 44, pp. 116–130. https://doi.org/10.1016/j.econmod.2014.10.028

Bean, C. (2009). The meaning of internal balance' thirty years on. *The Economic Journal*, vol. 119(541), pp. 442–460. https://doi.org/10.1111/j.1468-0297.2009.02315.x

Beau, D. (2021). *LabexRéfi conference "The new challenges of financial regulation", the challenges of the digital euro*. Speech by Denis Beau, First Deputy Governor, Banque de France Eurosysteme, 19 November. www.banque-france.fr/sites/default/files/medias/documents/2021_11_19_speech_labex_d._beau_vf.pdf, accessed 01.02.2022

Bechtel, A., Forster, M., Katilmis, S. (2020). *Der digitale Euro als Basis der Digitalisierung der Wirtschaft, payment and banking*. https://paymentandbanking.com/der-digitale-euro-als-basis-der-digitalisierung-der-wirtschaft/, accessed 29.04.2022

Będowska-Sójka, B., Kliber, A., Rutkowska, A. (2021). Is Bitcoin still a king? Relationships between prices, volatility and liquidity of cryptocurrencies during the pandemic. *Entropy*, vol. 23(11), p. 1386. https://doi.org/10.3390/e23111386

Beer, K. (2022). *MetasStablecoin Diem – vormals Libra – angeblich vor dem Aus, heise online*, 26 January. www.heise.de/news/Metas-Stablecoin-Diem-vormals-Libra-angeblich-vor-dem-Aus-6338511.html, accessed 29.04.2022

Behringer, J., Kowall, N., Theobald, T., van Treeck, T. (2020). Inequality in Germany: A macroeconomic perspective. *German Politics*, vol. 29(3), pp. 479–497. https://doi.org/10.1080/09644008.2019.1621297

Belay, H. (2019). Global financial regulation in the "New International Economic Order": The unfulfilled promise of equitable economic governance. *Journal of Financial Regulation and Compliance*, 27(1). https://10.1108/JFRC-10-2017-0086

Belke, A., Polleit, T. (2007). How the ECB and the US fed set interest rates. *Applied Economics*, vol. 39, pp. 2197–2209. https://doi.org/10.1080/00036840600749623

Beniak, P. (2019). *Central bank digital currency and monetary policy: A literature review*. Narodowy Bank Polski, Western Australian Treasury Corporation, MPRA Paper No. 96663, 24 October. https://mpra.ub.uni-muenchen.de/96663/, accessed 04.02.2022

Beyer, A., Nicoletti, G., Papadopoulou, N., Papsdorf, P., Rünstler, G., Schwarz, C., Sousa, J., Vergote, O. (2017). *The transmission channels of monetary, macro- and microprudential policies and their interrelations*. Occasional Paper Series, No. 191. ECB.

Bianco, J. (2021). A new global monetary order threatens the dollar. *Bloomberg Opinion*, 12 May. www.bloomberg.com/opinion/articles/2021-05-12/new-global-monetary-order-threatens-the-dollar, accessed 18.02.2022

Biewen, M. (2000). Income inequality in Germany during the 1980s and 1990s. *Review of Income and Wealth*, vol. 46(1), pp. 1–19. https://doi.org/10.1111/j.1475-4991.2000.tb00388.x

Bindseil, U. (2020). *Tiered CBDC and the financial system*. Working Paper Series, No 2351, ECB, January. www.ecb.europa.eu/pub/pdf/scpwps/ecb.wp2351~c8c18bbd60.en.pdf, accessed 29.04.2022

Bindseil, U., Panetta, F., Terol, I. (2021). *Central Bank digital currency: Functional scope, pricing and controls*. ECB Occasional Paper Series No. 286. www.ecb.europa.eu/pub/pdf/scpops/ecb.op286~9d472374ea.en.pdf, accessed 01.02.2022

BIS (2021d). *Randal K Quarles: The FSB in 2021 – addressing financial stability challenges in an age of interconnectedness, innovation, and change*. https://www.bis.org/review/r210331b.htm

BIS, Bank of Canada, European Central Bank, Bank of Japan, SverigesRiksbank, Swiss National Bank, Bank of England, Board of Governors Federal Reserve System (2020). *Central bank digital currencies: Foundation principles and core features*. www.bis.org/publ/othp33.pdf, accessed 31.01.2022.

BIS, Committee on Payments and Market Infrastructures, Innovation Hub, International Monetary Fund, World Bank Group. (2021). *Central Bank digital currencies for cross-border payments: Report to the G20*. www.bis.org/publ/othp38.pdf, accessed 01.02.2022.

BIS, The Bank of International Settlements, Committee on Payments and Market Infrastructures. (2021). *Covid-19 accelerated the digitalisation of payments*, 09 December. www.bis.org/statistics/payment_stats/commentary2112.pdf, accessed 04.04.2022

BIS. (2019). *Green bonds: The reserve management perspective, quarterly review*. BIS, September.

BIS. (2020). *CBDC: Central Bank digital currencies: Foundational principles and core features*. BIS Innovation Hub Report No. 1 in a series of collaborations from a group of Central Banks, Bank of Canada, European Central Bank, Bank of Japan, Sveriges-Riksbank, Swiss National Bank, Bank of England, Board of Governors Federal Reserve System, Bank for International Settlements. www.bis.org/publ/othp33.pdf, accessed 29.01.2022

BIS. (2020). *CBDC: Central Bank digital currencies: Foundational principles and core features* (Innovation Hub Report No. 1). Bank of International Settlements. www.bis.org/publ/othp33.htm

BIS. (2021a). *Central bank digital currencies for cross-border payments, report to the G20*. www.bis.org/publ/othp38.pdf, ISBN 978-92-9259-476-3

BIS. (2021b). *Central Bank digital currencies: System design and interoperability*. BIS, September.

BIS. (2021c). *CBDCs: An opportunity for the monetary system*. BIS Annual Economic Report 2021. BIS. www.bis.org/publ/arpdf/ar2021e3.pdf, accessed 01.02.2022.

Bitpanda. (2022). *Was ist "double spending" und warumist es ein Problem?* www.bitpanda.com/academy/de/lektionen/was-ist-double-spending-und-warum-ist-es-ein-problem/, accessed 29.04.2022

Bjerg, O. (2017). *Designing new money – the policy trilemma of Central Bank digital currency.* CBS Working Paper. https://doi.org/10.2139/ssrn.2985381

Blanc, J. (2006). *Silvio Gesell's theory and accelerated money experiments.* HAL SHS, Sciences Humaines et Sociales, HAL Id: halshs-00119192. https://halshs.archives-ouvertes.fr/halshs-00119192, accessed 21.02.2022

Blau, B. M., Griffith, T. G., Whitby, R. J. (2021). Inflation and bitcoin: A descriptive time-series analysis. *Economics Letters*, vol. 203. https://doi.org/10.1016/j.econlet.2021.109848

Blockchain.com. (2022). *Explorer*. www.blockchain.com/explorer

Blockchaincenter. (2022). *CBDC*. www.blockchaincenter.net/cbdc/, accessed 29.04.2022

Bloomberg. (2020). *Money supply*. Bloomberg.

Boar, C, Holden, H., Wadsworth, A. (2020). "*Impending arrival – a sequel to the survey on central bank digital currency*", BIS Paper No 107.

Boar, C., Wehrli, A. (2021). *Ready, steady, go? – Results of the third BIS survey on central bank digital currency*. BIS Working Papers No. 114. Bank for International Settlements. www.bis.org/publ/bppdf/bispap114.htm

Boar, C., Holden, H., Wadsworth, A. (2020). *Impending arrival: A sequel to the survey on central banking digital currency*. BIS Paper No. 107. Bank of International Settlements. www.bis.org/publ/bppdf/bispap107.htm

Board of Governors of the Federal Reserve System. (2022). *Money and payments: The U.S. dollar in the age of digital transformation.* www.federalreserve.gov/publications/files/money-and-payments-20220120.pdf, accessed 31.01.2022.

Bofinger, P., Haas, T. (2020). *CBDC: A systemic perspective*. Würzburg Economic Paper No. 10. University of Würzburg, Department of Economics. www.econstor.eu/handle/10419/222980

Bogush, P. (2021). Digitalization vs digitization – knowing the difference. *Bussinesstech Weekly*, 22 June. www.businesstechweekly.com/operational-efficiency/digital-transformation/digitalization-vs-digitization/, accessed 29.04.2022

Bohr, J., Bashir, M. (2014). *Who Uses Bitcoin? An exploration of the Bitcoin community*, Conference: 2014 Twelfth Annual Conference on Privacy, Security and Trust (PST). https://10.1109/PST.2014.6890928

Bolt, W., Lubbersen, V., Wierts, P. (2022). *Getting the balance right: Crypto, stablecoin and CBDC*. DNB Working Paper No. 736. www.dnb.nl/media/jo3h1dlu/working_paper_no-_736.pdf, accessed 07.02.2022

Boneva, L., Ferrucci, G., Mongelli, F. P. (2021). *To be or not to be "green": How can monetary policy react to climate change?* Occasional Paper Series, No. 285. ECB.

Bordo, M. D. (2021). *Central Bank digital currency in historical perspective: Another crossroad in monetary history*. NBER Working Paper Series, Working Paper 29171, August. www.nber.org/papers/w29171, accessed 29.04.2022

Bordo, M. D., Levin, A. T. (2017). *Central Bank digital currency and the future of monetary policy*. Working Paper No. 23711. National Bureau of Economic Research. www.nber.org/papers/w23711

Botta, A., Bruno, P., Galvin, J. (2021). *The 2021 McKinsey global payments report*. McKinsey, pp. 6–7, October.

Botzen, W. J. W., Marey, P. S. (2010). Did the ECB respond to the stock market before the crisis? *Journal of Policy Modeling*, vol. 32, pp. 303–322. https://doi.org/10.1016/j.jpolmod.2010.03.001

Bouoiyour, J., Selmi, R. (2017). *The Bitcoin price formation: Beyond the fundamental sources*, pp. 1–28. http://arxiv.org/abs/1707.01284

Bouri, E., Gupta, R., Raubaud, D. (2018). *Herding behaviour in the cryptocurrency market*. University of Pretoria. RePEc:pre:wpaper:201834

Bouri, E., Molnár, P., Azzi, G., Raubaud, D., Hagfors, L. I. (2017). On the hedge and safe haven properties of bitcoin: Is It really more than a diversifier? *Finance Research Letters*, vol. 20, 2017, pp. 192–198.

Bouveret, A. (2018). *Cyber risk for the financial sector: A framework for quantitative assessment*. IMF Working Paper, No. 18/143. IMF.

Brancati, D. (2006). Decentralization: Fueling the fire or dampening the flames of ethnic conflict and secessionism? *International Organization*, vol. 60, pp. 651–685, Summer.

Brauneis, A., Mestel, R. (2019). Cryptocurrency-portfolios in a mean-variance framework. *Finance Research Letters*, vol. 28, pp. 259–264. https://doi.org/doi:10.1016/j.frl.2018.05.008

Brosens, T. (2021). *Why banks need to pay attention to where a digital euro is heading*. Atlantic Council, European Union Focused CBDC Analysis, 15 April. https://think.ing.com/articles/where-next-with-the-digital-euro/, accessed 04.02.2022

Brown, T. (2009). Health services restructuring. In R. Kitchin, N. Thrift (Eds.), *International encyclopedia of human geography*. Elsevier, pp. 51–57. https://doi.org/10.1016/B978-008044910-4.00341-2

Broz, L., Frieden, J. (2001). The political economy of international monetary relations. *Annual Review of Political Science*, vol. 4, pp. 317–343.

Brunnermeier, M. K., James, H., Landau, J. P. (2019). *The digitalization of money*. NBER Working Paper Series, Working Paper 26300, September. www.nber.org/papers/w26300, accessed 29.04.2022

Brzeziński, M. B. (2013). *Income polarization and economic growth*. Working Paper, No. 147. National Bank of Poland. https://doi.org/10.2139/ssrn.2244858

Bubeck, I. (2007). *Geldnot und Notgeld in Thüringen*.Erfurt.

Buterin, V. (2017). *The meaning of decentralization*, 06 February 2017, https://medium.com/@VitalikButerin/the-meaning-of-decentralization-a0c92b76a274

Buterin, V. (2021). *Why sharding is great: Demystifying the technical properties*, 07 April. https://vitalik.ca/general/2021/04/07/sharding.html, accessed 19.04.2022

Candila, V. (2021). Multivariate analysis of cryptocurrencies. *Econometrics*, vol. 9, p. 28. https://doi.org/10.3390/economterics9030028

Caporale, G. M., Zekokh, T. (2019). Modelling volatility of cryptocurrencies using markov-switching GARCH models. *Research in International Business and Finance*, vol. 48, pp. 143–155. https://doi.org/10.1016/j.ribaf.2018.12.009, accessed 01.03.2022

Caporale, G., Plastun, A. (2019). Price overreactions in the cryptocurrency market. *Journal of Economic Studies*, vol. 46, pp. 1137–1155. https://doi.org/10.1108/JES-09-2018-0310

Carbo-Valverde, S., Cuadros-Solas, P., Rodriguez-Fernandez, F. (2018). *How Do Bank Customers Go Digital? A Machine Learning Approach*. https://dx.doi.org/10.2139/ssrn.3195286

Carbo-Valverde, S., Cuadros-Solas, P., Rodriguez-Fernandez, F. (2018). How do bank customers go digital? *A Machine Learning Approach*. http://dx.doi.org/10.2139/ssrn.3195286, accessed 27.02.2022

Carney, M. (2014). *Rebuilding trust in global banking.* Lawrence National Centre for Policy and Management, University of Western Ontario.

Carr, J., Glied, S., Mathewson, F. (1989). Unlimited liability and a free banking in Scotland: A note. *Journal of Economic History*, vol. 49(4), pp. 974–978.

Caruana, J. (2015). *Keynote address by Mr Jaime Caruana, General Manager of the BIS.* At the Tenth High-level Meeting on Global Banking Standards and Supervisory Priorities in the Americas, jointly organised by the Association of Supervisors of Banks of the Americas (ASBA), the Basel Committee on Banking Supervision (BCBS) and the Financial Stability Institute (FSI), Montevideo, 28 October.

Castro, V. (2011). Can Central Banks' monetary policy be described by a linear (augmented) Taylor rule or by a nonlinear rule? *Journal of Financial Stability*, vol. 7(4), pp. 228–246. https://doi.org/10.1016/j.jfs.2010.06.002

Catania, L., Grassi, S., Ravazzolo, F. (2018). Predicting the volatility of cryptocurrency time series. In *Mathematical and statistical methods for actuarial sciences and finance*. Springer, pp. 203–207.

Cebrian-Hernandez, A., Jimenez-Rodriguez, E. (2021). Modelling of the bitcoin volatility through key financial environment variables: An application of conditional correlation MGARCH models. *Mathematics*, vol. 9, p. 267.

Central Bank of Nigeria. (2021). *Design paper for the eNaira.* www.enaira.gov.ng/download/eNaira_Design_Paper.pdf

Chaim, P., Laurini, M. P. (2019). Nonlinear dependence in cryptocurrency markets. *The North American Journal of Economics and Finance*, vol. 48, pp. 32–47. https://doi.org/10.1016/j.najef.2019.01.015

Chainalysis. (2021a). *Introducing the chainalysis global DeFi adoption index*. https://blog.chainalysis.com/reports/2021-global-defi-adoption-index/, accessed 21.02.2022

Chainalysis. (2021b). *The chainalysis 2021 crypto crime report*. https://go.chainalysis.com/2021-Crypto-Crime-Report.html, accessed 11.04.2022

Chainalysis. (2021c). *The 2021 geography of cryptocurrency report*. Chainalysis.

Chancel, L., Piketty, T., Saez, E., Zucman, G. (2022). *World inequality report 2022*. World Inequality Lab.

Cheah, J., Fry, J. (2015). Speculative bubbles in Bitcoin markets? An empirical investigation into the fundamental value of Bitcoin. *Economics Letters,* vol. 130. https://doi.org/10.1016/j.econlet.2015.02.029

Chen, H., Engert, W., Huynh, K. P., Nicholls, G., Nicholson, M., Zhu, J. (2020). *Cash and COVID-19: The impact of the pandemic on the demand for and use of cash*. Staff, Discussion Paper 2020–6. Bank of Canada, July.

Chen, H., Siklos, P. (2022). Central bank digital currency: A review and some macro-financial implications. *Journal of Financial Stability*, vol. 60, June, available at https://doi.org/10.1016/j.jfs.2022.100985, accessed 29.04.2022

Chen, S., Goel, T., Qiu, H., Shim, I. (2022). *CBDCs in emerging market economies*. BIS Papers No. 123. BIS.

Cheng, P. (2022). Decoding the rise of Central Bank digital currency in China: Designs, problems, and prospects. *Journal of Banking Regulation*. https://doi.org/10.1057/s41261-022-00193-5, accessed 29.04.2022

Chiu, J., Davoodalhosseini, S. M., Jiang, J., Zhu, Y. (2019). *Bank market power and central bank digital currency: Theory and quantitative assessment*. Staff Working Paper No. 2019–20. Bank of Canada.

Chohan, U. W. (2021). *Decentralized finance (DeFi): An emergent alternative financial architecture*. Critical Blockchain Research Initiative (CBRI) Working Papers, 26 January. http://dx.doi.org/10.2139/ssrn.3791921

Choudhury, B. (2021). Climate change as systemic risk. *Berkeley Business Law Journal*, vol. 18(2). https://doi.org/10.15779/Z381J9783Q

Chowdhury, R., Rahman, M. A., Rahman, M. S., Mahdy, M. R. C. (2020). An approach to predict and forecast the price of constituents and index of cryptocurrency using machine learning. *Physica A: Statistical Mechanics and Its Applications*, vol. 551, p. 124569. https://doi.org/10.1016/j.physa.2020.124569

Christiano, L. J., R. Motto, R., Rostagno, M. (2010). *Financial factors in economic fluctuations*. ECB Working Paper Series, No. 1192. ECB.

Chu, J., Chan, S., Nadarajah, S., Osterrieder, J. (2017). GARCH modelling of cryptocurrencies. *Journal of Risk and Financial Management*, vol. 10(4), p. 17. https://doi.org/10.3390/, accessed 27.02.2022

Chuen, D. L. K., Guo, L., Wang, Y. (2017). Cryptocurrency: A new investment opportunity? *The Journal of Alternative Investments*, vol. 20(3), pp. 16–40. https://doi.org/doi:10.3905/jai.2018.20.3.016

Clear Chain Capital. (2021). *The current state of undercollateralized DeFi lending – 2021*. https://medium.com/coinmonks/the-current-state-of-undercollateralized-defi-lending-2021--1f84e14527b5, accessed: 04.05.2022

Coase, R. (1974). The lighthouse in economics. *Journal of Law and Economics*, vol. 17(2), pp. 357–376.

Cœuré, B. (2013). *Outright monetary transactions, one year on*. Speech by Benoît Cœuré, Member of the Executive Board of the ECB, at the conference "The ECB and its OMT programme", organised by Centre for Economic Policy Research, German Institute for Economic Research and KfW Bankengruppe Berlin, 02 September. www.ecb.europa.eu/press/key/date/2013/html/sp130902.en.html, accessed 29.04.2022

Coinbase. (2022). *What is DeFi?* www.coinbase.com/pl/learn/crypto-basics/what-is-defi, accessed 19.04.2022

Coinlore.com. (2022). *Cryptocurrency list*, 22 April. www.coinlore.com/all_coins, accessed 29.04.2022

Coinmarketcap.com. (2022). *Coin market cap*. https://coinmarketcap.com

Consensys. (2021). *The Q1 2021 DeFi report: An analysis of Ethereum's decentralized finance ecosystem in Q1 2021*. https://consensys.net/reports/defi-report-q1-2021/, accessed 19.04.2022

Corbet, S., Cumming, D. J., Lucey, B. M., Peat, M., Vigne, S. A. (2020a). The destabilising effects of cryptocurrency cybercriminality. *Economics Letters*, vol. 191. https://doi.org/10.1016/j.econlet.2019.108741

Corbet, S., Larkin, C., Lucey, B. (2020b). The contagion effects of the COVID-19 pandemic: Evidence from gold and cryptocurrencies. *Finance Research Letters*, vol. 35. https://doi.org/10.1016/j.frl.2020.101554

Corbet, S., McHugh, G., Meegan, A. (2017). The influence of Central Bank monetary policy announcements on cryptocurrency return volatility. *Investment Management and Financial Innovations*, vol. 14(4), pp. 60–72. https://doi.org/doi:10.21511/imfi.14(4).2017.07

CPMI-MC. (2018). *Central bank digital currencies, committee on payments and market infrastructures and markets committee*. Bank for International Settlements, March. www.bis.org/cpmi/publ/d174.pdf, accessed 29.04.2022

Cremades, R., Surminski, S., Máñez Costa, M., Hudson, P., Shrivastava, P., Gascoigne, J. (2018). Using the adaptive cycle in climate-risk insurance to design resilient futures. *Nature Climate Change*, vol. 8(1), pp. 4–7. https://doi.org/10.1038/s41558-017-0044-2

Crisanto, J. C., Prenio, J. (2017). *Regulatory approaches to enhance banks' cyber-security frameworks*. FSI Insights on Policy Implementation, No. 2. FSI.

Cryptopedia. (2021). *Anonymity vs. pseudonymity in crypto*, 17 May. www.gemini.com/cryptopedia/anonymity-vs-pseudonymity-basic-differences#section-what-does-a-pseudonym-mean-in-crypto, accessed 11.04.2022

Cukierman, A. (2019). *Welfare and political economy aspects of a Central Bank digital currency*. Discussion Paper No. 13728. Centre for Economic Policy Research. https://cepr.org/active/publications/discussion_papers/dp.php?dpno=13728

Čuljak, M., Tomić, B., Žiković, S. (2022). Benefits of sectoral cryptocurrency portfolio optimisation. *Research in International Business and Finance*, vol. 60. https://doi.org/10.1016/j.ribaf.2022.101615

Czarny, B. (2010). *Pozytywizm a sądywartościujące w ekonomii*. OficynaWydawnicza SGH.

Dafermos, Y., Gabor, D., Nikolaidi, M., van Lerven, F. (2020). *Decarbonising the Bank of England's pandemic QE: 'Perfectly sensible'*. New Economics Foundation, 04 August.

Dallyn, S. (2017). Cryptocurrencies as market singularities: The strange case of bitcoin. *Journal of Cultural Economy*, pp. 1–12. https://doi.org/10.1080/17530350.2017.1315541, accessed 17.02.2022

Dapp, M. M. (2021). From fiat to crypto: The present and future of money. In M. M. Dapp, D. Helbing, S. Klauser (Eds.), *Finance 4.0 – towards a socio-ecological finance system*. Springer Briefs in Applied Sciences and Technology. Springer. https://doi.org/10.1007/978-3-030-71400-0_1, accessed 29.04.2022

Darbha, S., Arora, R. (2020). *Privacy in CBDC technology*. Staff Analytical Note 2020–9. Bank of Canada. www.bankofcanada.ca/2020/06/staff-analytical-note-2020-9/

Das, K. (2021). *Decoded | What's driving demand for cryptocurrencies in India*. www.livemint.com/market/cryptocurrency/how-indians-invested-in-crypto-in-2021-11640672209795.html, accessed 08.04.2022

Davoodalhosseini, S.M. (2021). Central Bank digital currency and monetary policy. *Journal of Economic Dynamics and Control*. https://doi.org/10.1016/j.jedc.2021.104150

Deardorff, A. (2016). *International economics*. Economics 340, Lecture 15. Fixed versus Floating Exchange Rates. https://fdocuments.in/document/lecture-16-fixed-versus-floating-exchange-rates.html, accessed 10.04.2022

DeFi Llama. (2022). *Defi Llama and our methodology*. https://docs.llama.fi/list-your-project/defillama-and-our-methodology, accessed 19.04.2022

DeFiPrime. (2022). *DeFi and open finance*. https://defiprime.com/

Demirgüç-Kunt, A., Klapper, L., Singer, D., Ansar, S., Hess, J. (2017). *The global findex database: Measuring financial inclusion and fintech revolution*. World Bank Group.

Deutsche Bank Research. (2020). *Das Leben nach Covid-19*, p. 73, 17 June. www.dbresearch.de/PROD/RPS_DE-PROD/PROD0000000000509519/Das_Leben_nach_Covid-19.pdf?undefined&realload=EEv06i~ZPZLXo0HPa7rJRUch4OeXDNmCyIv6VVZE6hLEMuCDqieEZsJ/3MdssqUS, accessed 04.04.2022

Dickey, D. A., Fuller, W. A. (1979). Distribution of the estimators for autoregressive time series with a unit root. *Journal of the American Statistical Association*, vol. 74.

Didenko, A., Buckley, R. (2021). *Central Bank digital currencies: A potential response to the financial inclusion challenge of the Pacific*. Asian Development Bank. www.adb.org/sites/default/files/publication/720016/central-bank-digital-currencies-pacific.pdf

Dikau, S., Robins, N., Täger, M. (2020). *Building a sustainable financial system: The state of practice and future priorities*. Revista de Estabilidad Financiera. Banco de España, p. 37.

Dikau, S., Volz, U. (2021). Central bank mandates, sustainability objectives and the promotion of green finance. *Ecological Economics*, vol. 184. https://doi.org/10.1016/j.ecolecon.2021.107022

Dimitropoulos, G. (2019). Global currencies and domestic regulation: Embedding through enabling?, *SSRN Electronic Journal*. https://10.2139/ssrn.3397521

Draghi, M. (2012). *Introductory statement to the press conference (with Q&A)*. Mario Draghi, President of the ECB, Vítor Constâncio, Vice-President of the ECB, 06 September. www.ecb.europa.eu/press/pressconf/2012/html/is120906.en.html, accessed 29.04.2022

Duncan, C. R. (2007). Mixed outcomes: The impact of regional autonomy and decentralization on indigenous ethnic minorities in Indonesia. *Development and Change*, vol. 38(4), pp. 711–733.

Dunz, N., Naqvi, A., Monasterolo, I. (2021). Climate sentiments, transition risk, and financial stability in a stock-flow consistent model. *Journal of Financial Stability*, vol. 54. https://doi.org/10.1016/j.jfs.2021.100872

Dutkowsky, D. H., VanHoose, D. D. (2018). Breaking up isn't hard to do: Interest on reserves and monetary policy. *Journal of Economics and Business*, vol. 99, pp. 15–27.

Dutkowsky, D. H., VanHoose, D. D. (2020). Equal treatment under the fed: Interest on reserves, the federal funds rate, and the 'third regime' of bank behavior'. *Journal of Economics and Business*, vol. 107, p. 105860.

Dyson, B., Hodgson, G. (2016). *Digital cash: Why central banks should start issuing electronic money. Making money and banking work for society*. https://positivemoney.org/wp-content/uploads/2016/01/Digital_Cash_WebPrintReady_20160113.pdf

EC. (2022). *What is the Euro area?* https://ec.europa.eu/info/business-economy-euro/euro-area/what-euro-area_en, accessed 29.04.2022

ECB & Bank of Japan. (2020). *Balancing confidentiality and auditability in a distributed ledger environment*. STELLA – joint research project of the European Central Bank and the Bank of Japan, European Central Bank, February. www.ecb.europa.eu/paym/intro/publications/pdf/ecb.miptopical200212.en.pdf, accessed 29.04.2022

ECB (2020). *Report on digital euro.*

ECB Statistical Data Warehouse. (2022a). *Total population – Euro area 19* (fixed composition) as of 1 January 2015 – World (all entities, including reference area, including IO), Total economy, Persons, Non transformed data, Neither seasonally adjusted nor calendar adjusted. https://sdw.ecb.europa.eu/home.do, accessed 29.04.2022

ECB Statistical Data Warehouse. (2022b). *Gross domestic product at market prices – Euro area 19* (fixed composition) – Domestic (home or reference area), Total economy, Euro, Current prices, Non transformed data, Calendar and seasonally adjusted data. https://sdw.ecb.europa.eu/home.do, accessed 29.04.2022

ECB, European Central Bank. (2020). *Report on a digital euro*, October 2020. www.ecb.europa.eu/pub/pdf/other/Report_on_a_digital_euro~4d7268b458.en.pdf, accessed 27.01.2022

ECB, European Central Bank. (2021a). *The Eurosystem integrated reporting framework: An overview*. www.ecb.europa.eu/pub/pdf/other/ecb.iref_overview122021~215b23a3fb.en.pdf, accessed 27.01.2022

ECB, European Central Bank. (2021b). *Eurosystem report on the public consultation on a digital euro*, April., www.ecb.europa.eu/pub/pdf/other/Eurosystem_report_on_the_public_consultation_on_a_digital_euro~539fa8cd8d.en.pdf, accessed 04.02.2022

ECB. (2018). *Cyber resilience oversight expectations for financial market infrastructures*. ECB.

ECB. (2020a). *Report on digital euro*. www.ecb.europa.eu/pub/pdf/other/Report_on_a_digital_euro~4d7268b458.en.pdf, accessed 31.01.2022.

ECB. (2020b). *The Eurosystem's analysis of privacy-enhancing techniques in Central Bank digital currencies.* www.ecb.europa.eu/pub/pdf/annex/ecb.sp210414_1_annex~43eee6196e.en.pdf?ed992ba1ebc6915fe12bf5d57013ae54, accessed 29.04.2022

ECB. (2020c). *Study on the payment attitudes of consumers in the euro area (SPACE)*, December. www.ecb.europa.eu/pub/pdf/other/ecb.spacereport202012~bb2038bbb6.en.pdf, accessed 29.04.2022

ECB. (2021a). *Eurosystem report on the public consultation on a digital euro*, April. www.ecb.europa.eu/pub/pdf/other/Eurosystem_report_on_the_public_consultation_on_a_digital_euro~539fa8cd8d.en.pdf, accessed 29.04.2022

ECB. (2021b). *The expanding functions and uses of stablecoins*. Published as part Financial Stability Review. ECB, November.

ECB. (2022a). *An overview of the ECB's monetary policy strategy*. European Central Bank. www.ecb.europa.eu/home/search/review/html/ecb.strategyreview_monpol_strategy_overview.en.html#toc3, accessed 29.04.2022

ECB. (2022b). *The Eurosystem's instruments*. European Central Bank. www.ecb.europa.eu/mopo/implement/html/index.en.html, accessed 29.04.2022

ECB. (2022c). *Asset purchase programmes*. European Central Bank. www.ecb.europa.eu/mopo/implement/app/html/index.en.html, accessed 29.04.2022

Eichengreen, B. (2022). Digital currencies – More than a passing fad?, *Current History*, vol. 121 (831), pp. 24–29. https://doi.org/doi:10.1525/curh.2022.121.831.24. ISSN 0011-3530. S2CID 245436834

Eisenbach, T., Kovner, A., Lee, M. J. (2021). Cyber risk and the U.S. financial system: A pre-mortem analysis. *Journal of Financial Economics*, forthcoming. https://doi.org/10.1016/j.jfineco.2021.10.007

Engert, W., Fung, B. (2017). *Central Bank Digital Currency: Motivations and Implications*, Discussion Papers, Bank of Canada, https://EconPapers.repec.org/RePEc:bca:bocadp, pp. 17–16.

ESRB. (2016). *Macroprudential policy issues arising from low interest rates and structural changes in the EU financial system.* ESRB.

ESRB. (2020). *Systemic cyber risk.* ESRB.

ESRB. (2021). *Lower for longer – macroprudential policy issues arising from the low interest rate environment*. ESRB.

ESRB. (2022). *Mitigating systemic cyber risk.* ESRB.

Esselink, H., Hernández, L. (2017). *The use of cash by households in the Euro area.* Occasional Paper Series No. 201. European Central Bank, November. www.ecb.europa.eu/pub/pdf/scpops/ecb.op201.en.pdf, accessed 29.04.2022

Ethereum Foundation. (2022). *Decentralized finance (DeFi)*. https://ethereum.org/en/defi/, accessed 19.04.2022

EU, Regulation (EU). (2021). 694 of the European Parliament and of the Council of 29 April 2021 establishing the Digital Europe Programme and repealing Decision (EU) 2015/2240. https://eur-lex.europa.eu/legal-content/EN/TXT/?uri=CELEX%3A32021R0694&qid=1643290831066, accessed 27.01.2022

EU. (2014). Directive 2014/65/EU of the European Parliament and of the Council of 15 May 2014 on markets in financial instruments and amending Directive 2002/92/EC and Directive 2011/61/EU (Official Journal of the European Union L 173/349 on 12.06.2014, pp. 349–496).

EU. (2020). The proposal for a regulation of the European Parliament and of the Council on markets in crypto-asset and amending Directive (EU) 2019/1937 (COM(2020)0593 – C9–0306/2020–2020/0265(COD).

European Central Bank. (2020). *Study on the payment attitudes of consumers in the euro area (SPACE)*, December 2020. www.ecb.europa.eu/pub/pdf/other/ecb.spacereport202012~bb2038bbb6.en.pdf, date of accessed: 04.04.2022

European Parliament. (2021). *Central Bank digital currencies: Evolution or revolution?* www.europarl.europa.eu/RegData/etudes/BRIE/2021/698804/EPRS_BRI(2021)698804_EN.pdf, accessed 31.01.2022

Fachverb and Regiogeld. (2022). *Regiogeld.* https://regionetzwerk.blogspot.com/p/blog-page_22.html, accessed 29.04.2022

Fagatelli, P. (2021). *The one trillion euro CBDC: Issuing a digital euro without disrupting the bank lending channel.* Banque centrale du Luxembourg, SUERF Policy Brief, No. 209. The European Money and Finance Forum, October. www.suerf.org/suer-policy-brief/35071/the-one-trillion-euro-cbdc-issuing-a-digital-euro-without-disrupting-the-bank-lending-channel, accessed 03.02.2022

Farras, C., Salmeron, A. M. (2018). *From barter to cryptocurrency, a brief history of exchange.* Caxian Bank Research. www.caixabankresearch.com/en/economics-markets/monetary-policy/barter-cryptocurrency-brief-history-exchange, accessed 16.02.2022

FATF. (2021). *Updated guidance for a risk-based approach to virtual assets and virtual asset service providers.* www.fatf-gafi.org/media/fatf/documents/recommendations/Updated-Guidance-VA-VASP.pdf, accessed 11.04.2022

Fazio, D. M., Tabak, B. M., Cajueiro, D. O. (2015). Inflation targeting: Is IT to blame for banking system instability? *Journal of Banking and Finance*, vol. 59, pp. 76–97. https://doi.org/10.1016/j.jbankfin.2015.05.016

Federal Reserve of the United States. (2022). *Money and payments: The U.S. dollar in the age of digital transformation*, www.federalreserve.gov/publications/files/money-and-payments-20220120.pdf

Fegatelli, P. (2022). A central bank digital currency in a heterogeneous monetary union: Managing the effects on the bank lending channel. *Journal of Macroeconomics*, vol. 71, March. https://doi.org/10.1016/j.jmacro.2021.103392, accessed 29.04.2022

Felber, C. (2017). The basis: The money as a public good. In: *Money – the new rules of the game*. Springer, pp. 29–33. https://doi.org/10.1007/978-3-319-67352-3_4

Feldstein, M. (2002). Argentina's Fall: Lessons from the latest financial crisis. *Foreign Affairs*, vol. 81(2), pp. 8–14.

Fernández-Villaverde, J., Sanches, D., Schilling, L., Uhlig, H. (2021). Central bank digital currency: Central banking for all? *Review of Economic Dynamics*, vol. 41, pp. 225–242, July. https://doi.org/10.1016/j.red.2020.12.004, accessed 29.04.2022

Ferrari, M. M., Mehl, A., Stracca, L. (2020a). *Central bank digital currency in an open economy*. Working Paper Series, No. 2488. European Central Bank, November. www.ecb.europa.eu/pub/pdf/scpwps/ecb.wp2488~fede33ca65.en.pdf, accessed 29.04.2022

Ferrari, M. M., Mehl, A., Stracca, L. (2020b). The international dimension of a Central Bank digital currency. *Vox, CEPR Policy Portal*. https://voxeu.org/article/international-dimension-central-bank-digital-currency

Ferreira de Mendonça, H., de Guimarães e Souza, G. J. (2012). Is inflation targeting a good remedy to control inflation? *Journal of Development Economics*, vol. 98(2), pp. 178–191. https://doi.org/10.1016/j.jdeveco.2011.06.011

Filardo, A., Hofmann, B. (2014). Forward guidance at the zero lower bound. *BIS Quarterly Review*, 37–53, March.

Financial Action Task Force (FATF). (2021). *Second 12-month review of the revised FATF standards on virtual assets and virtual asset providers*, 05 July. www.fatf-gafi.org/

publications/fatfrecommendations/documents/second-12-month-review-virtual-assets-vasps.html, accessed 21.02.2022

FinTech Poland. (2021). *DeFi – zrozumieć zdecentralizowane finanse (DeFi – understand decentralized finance)*, October. https://fintechpoland.com/wp-content/uploads/2022/03/Raport-DeFi-FinTech-1.pdf, accessed 19.04.2022

Fisch, C., Masiak, C., Vismara, S., Block, J. (2021). Motives and profiles of ICO investors. *Journal of Business Research*, vol. 125, pp. 564–576. https://doi.org/10.1016/j.jbusres.2019.07.036

Forexsuggest. (2022). *Transaction speeds: How fast are cryptocurrency transactions and which ones process the most?* https://forexsuggest.com/transaction-speeds/, 04.05.2022

Foster, K., Blakstad, S., Gazi, S., Bos, M. (2021). *Digital currencies and CBDC impacts on least developed countries (LDCs)*. Technical Paper 1.2. UNDP – Dialogue on Global Digital Finance Governance. www.undp.org/sites/g/files/zskgke326/files/2021-06/UNDP-UNCDF-TP-1-2-Digital-Currencies-and-CBDC-Impacts-on-Least-Developed-Countries-LDCs-EN.pdf

Fouejieu, A. (2017). Inflation targeting and financial stability in emerging markets. *Economic Modelling*, vol. 60, pp. 51–70. https://doi.org/10.1016/j.econmod.2016.08.020

Frankovic, I. (2022). *The impact of carbon pricing in a multi-region production network model and an application to climate scenarios*. Paper No. 07/2022. Deutsche Bundesbank.

Friedman, M., Mundell, R. (2001). One world, one money? *Policy Options*, 01 May. https://fdocuments.in/document/lecture-16-fixed-versus-floating-exchange-rates.html, accessed 10.04.2022

Friedrich, C., Hess, K., Cunningham, R. (2019). Monetary policy and financial stability: Cross-country evidence. *Journal of Money, Credit and Banking*, vol. 51, pp. 403–453. https://doi.org/10.1111/jmcb.12526

Fry, J. (2018). Booms, busts and heavy-tails: The story of Bitcoin and cryptocurrency markets? *Economics Letters*, vol. 171, pp. 225–229. https://doi.org/10.1016/j.econlet.2018.08.008

FSB. (2018). *Cyber lexicon*. FSB, 12 November.

Galbraith, J. K. (2009). *The great crash 1929*. Houghton Mifflin Harcourt.

Gambacorta, L., Signoretti, F. M. (2014). Should monetary policy lean against the wind?: An analysis based on a DSGE model with banking. *Journal of Economic Dynamics and Control*, vol. 43, pp. 146–174. https://doi.org/10.1016/j.jedc.2014.01.016

Garcia-Corral, F. J., Cordero-Garcia, J. A., Pablo-Valenciano, J. D., Uribe-Toril, J. (2022). A bibliometric review of cryptocurrencies: How have they grown? *Financial Innovation*, vol. 8, article 2. https://doi.org/10.1186/s40854-021-00306-5

George, B. (2022). *What is governance tokens?* www.coindesk.com/learn/what-is-a-governance-token/, accessed 14.04.2022

Georgiadis, G. (2014). Towards an explanation of cross-country asymmetries in monetary transmission. *Journal of Macroeconomics*, vol. 39(PA), pp. 66–84.

Georgieva, K. (2022). *The future of money: Gearing up for Central Bank digital currency*. Speech. www.imf.org/en/News/Articles/2022/02/09/sp020922-the-future-of-money-gearing-up-for-central-bank-digital-currency

Geršl, A., Jakubik, P., Kowalczyk, D., Ongena, S., Peydró, J.-L. (2015). Monetary conditions and banks' behaviour in the Czech Republic. *Open Economies Review*, vol. 26(3), pp. 407–445, Springer. https://doi.org/10.1007/s11079-015-9355-y

Gilbert, D. (2022). Meet the secretive US company building an 'unbreakable' Internet inside Russia. *Vice*, 24 March 24. www.vice.com/en/article/z3n5e9/russian-internet-lantern, accessed 15.04.2022.

Goetzmann, W. N., Renneboog, L., Spaenjers, C. (2011). Art and money. *American Economic Review*, vol. 101(3), pp. 222–226. https://doi.org/doi:10.1108/ebr.2002.05414fab.004

Goodfriend, M. (2016). The case for unencumbering interest rate policy at the zero bound. *Jackson Hole Economic Policy Symposium*, vol. 26, pp. 127–160.

Goodman, H. (2009). The formation of the Bank of England: A response to changing political and economic climate, 1694. *Penn History Review*, vol. 17(1), article 2.

Gopkumar, B. (2022). *The thriving tribe of Indian retail investors*. www.deccanherald.com/business/the-thriving-tribe-of-indian-retail-investors-1069596.html, accessed 08.04.2022

Greene, M. (2022). King Dollar is not in danger of losing its world financial crown. *Financial Times*, 12 April 12. www.ft.com/content/dec25b43-3548-4be6-9a7c-57286b266dcc, accessed 12.04.2022

Griffoli, T., Peria, M., Agur, I., Ari, A., Kiff, J., Popescu, A., Rochon, C. (2018). *Casting Light on Central Bank Digital Currencies*. Staff Discussion Notes. 18. 1. https://10.5089/9781484384572.006

Grippa, P., Schmittmann, J., Suntheim, F. (2019). Climate change and financial risk. *Finance & Development*, vol. 56(4), pp. 26–29.

Grobys, K., Junttila, J. (2021). Speculation and lottery-like demand in cryptocurrency markets. *Journal of International Financial Markets, Institutions and Money*, vol. 71. https://doi.org/10.1016/j.intfin.2021.101289

Grothoff, C., Moser, T. (2021). *How to issue a privacy-preserving Central Bank digital currency*. SUERF Policy Brief No. 114. SUERF – The European Money and Finance Forum. www.suerf.org/suer-policy-brief/27227/how-to-issue-a-privacy-preserving-central-bank-digital-currency

Grünewald, S., Zellweger-Gutknecht, C., Geva, B. (2021). Digital euro and ECB powers. *Common Market Law Review*, vol. 58(4), pp. 1029–1056. https://kluwerlawonline.com/journalarticle/Common+Market+Law+Review/58.4/COLA2021066, accessed 28.01.2022

Grym, A., Heikkinen, P., Kauko, K., Takala, K. (2017). Central Bank digital currency. *BoF Economics Review, Bank of Finland*. https://helda.helsinki.fi/bof/bitstream/handle/123456789/14952/BoFER_5_2017.pdf

Gu, S., Ślusarczyk, B., Hajizada, S., Kovalyova, I., Sakhbieva, A. (2021). Impact of the COVID-19 pandemic on online consumer purchasing behavior. *Journal of Theoretical and Applied Electronic Commerce Research*. https://mdpi-res.com/d_attachment/jtaer/jtaer-16-00125/article_deploy/jtaer-16-00125.pdf?version=1631081518, date of accessed: 04.04.2022

Gudgeon, L., Perez, D., Harz, D., Livshits, B., Gervais, A. (2020). *The decentralized financial crisis*. arXiv:2002.08099v2 [cs.CR], 27 June.

Gupta, B. C., Shukla, S. K. (2019). *A study of inequality in the Ethereum smart contract ecosystem*. 2019 Sixth International Conference on Internet of Things: Systems, Management and Security (IOTSMS), pp. 441–449. https://doi.org/10.1109/IOTSMS48152.2019.8939257

Gürkaynak, R. S., Levin, A., Swanson, E. (2010). Does inflation targeting anchor long-run inflation expectations? Evidence from the U.S., UK, and Sweden. *Journal of the European Economic Association*, vol. 8(6), pp. 1208–1242. https://doi.org/10.1111/j.1542-4774.2010.tb00553.x

Habibullah, M., Baharumshah, A. (1996). Money, Output and Stock Prices in Malaysia: An Application of the Cointegration Tests. *International Economic Journal*, vol. 10, pp. 121–130. https://10.1080/10168739600080015

Hafid, A., Hafid, A. S., Samih, S. (2020). *Scaling blockchains: A comprehensive survey.* IEEE Access. https://doi.org/10.1109/ACCESS.2020.3007251

Halaburda, H. (2016). Digital currencies: Beyond bitcoin. *Digiworld Economic Journal*, vol. 103, pp. 77–92. https://dx.doi.org/10.2139/ssrn.2865004, accessed 29.04.2022

Handelsblatt. (2021). *BargeldloseZahlungennehmen in Europa zu*, 23 July. www.handelsblatt.com/finanzen/banken-versicherungen/banken/corona-lockdown-bargeldlose-zahlungen-nehmen-in-europa-zu/27447814.html?ticket=ST-12662809-cWDVx24QMV6H1WMXLyst-ap5, accessed 04.04.2022

Harvey, R., Ramachandran, A., Santoro, J. (2020). *DeFi and the future of finance*, 05 April. https://ssrn.com/abstract=3711777 or http://dx.doi.org/10.2139/ssrn.3711777, accessed 18.02.2022

Hayes, A. (2015). *What Factors Give Cryptocurrencies Their Value: An Empirical Analysis*, Working Paper 06/2014, Department of Economics, The New School for Social Research, http://dx.doi.org/10.2139/ssrn.2579445

Hayes, A. (2017). Cryptocurrency value formation: An empirical study leading to a cost of production model for valuing Bitcoin. *Telematics and Informatics,* vol. 34, pp. 1308–1321. http://dx.doi.org/10.1016/j.tele.2016.05.005

Heathcote, J., Perri, F., Violante, G. L. (2010). Unequal we stand: An empirical analysis of economic inequality in the United States, 1967–2006. *Review of Economic Dynamics*, vol. 37.

Heider, F., Saidi, F., Schepens, G. (2019). Life below zero: Bank lending under negative policy rates. *The Review of Financial Studies*, vol. 32(10), pp. 3728–3761. https://doi.org/10.1093/rfs/hhz016.

Heinen, A., Khadan, J., Strobl, E. (2019). The price impact of extreme weather in developing countries. *The Economic Journal*, vol. 129(619), pp. 1327–1342. https://doi.org/10.1111/ecoj.12581

Heinonen, A. (2020). Banknote developments at the global level – Before and after the outbreak of Covid-19. *Currency News, Special Report*, vol. 18(9), pp. 10–12, September.

Hildebrandt, M., Tielmans, L. (2013). Data protection by design and technology neutral law. *Computer Law and Security Review*, vol. 29, pp. 509–521.

Hileman, G., Rauchs., M. (2017). Global cryptocurrency benchmarking study. *SSRN Electronic Journal.* https://doi.org/10.2139/ssrn.2965436

Hoffmann, A. (2013). Did the fed and ECB react asymmetrically with respect to asset market developments? *Journal of Policy Modeling*, vol. 35(2), pp. 197–211. https://doi.org/10.1016/j.jpolmod.2012.09.005

House of Lords. (2022). *Central Bank digital currencies: A solution in search of a problem?* https://publications.parliament.uk/pa/ld5802/ldselect/ldeconaf/131/131.pdf, accessed 31.01.2022

Camilla Russo, Blacki Migliozzi and Cedric Sam. (2018). vol. 18(837), pp. 837–893. https://www.bloomberg.com/graphics/2017-bitcoin-volume/

Huang, R. (2020). The digital Yuan is China's attempt to upend the global financial order. *Forbes*, 27 August. www.forbes.com/sites/rogerhuang/2020/08/27/the-digital-yuan-is-chinas-attempt-to-upend-the-global-financial-order/?sh=682f37e54399, accessed 28.02.2022

Huschka, H. (2013). *Ersatzgeld und geldähnliche Belege in der DDR.* Katalog parallel zur staatlichen Währung umlaufender Ersatzzahlungsmittel in Papierform, Regenstauf.

IMF. (2004). *Classification of exchange rate arrangements and monetary policy frameworks.* www.imf.org/external/np/mfd/er/2004/eng/0604.htm, accessed 02.05.2022.

IMF. (2010). *Working to support a durable global recovery.* International Monetary Fund Annual Report 2010. https://doi.org/10.5089/9781616350154.011.ch03, published in 2010, accessed 11.02.2022

IMF. (2014). *Review of the financial sector assessment program: Further adaptation to the post crisis era*, pp. 1–48, September. www.imf.org/external/np/pp/eng/2014/081814.pdf

IMF. (2020). *Digital money across borders: Macro-financial implications*, September. www.imf.org/external/pp/ppindex.aspx; https://doi.org/10.5089/9781513559209.007.A001, accessed 11.02.2022

IMF. (2021a). *The rise of digital money: A strategic plan to continue delivering on the IMF's mandate*. Policy Papers No. 2021/54, 29 July. https://doi.org/10.5089/9781513589558.007.A001

IMF. (2021c). *2021 financial sector assessment program review – towards a more stable and sustainable financial system*, pp. 1–72. Policy Paper No. 2021/040, 28 May. www.imf.org/en/Publications/Policy-Papers/Issues/2021/05/28/2021-Financial-Sector-Assessment-Program-Review-Towards-A-More-Stable-And-Sustainable-460517, accessed 11.02.2022

IMF. (2021d). *Statement by the managing director on the work program of the executive board – executive board meeting*, pp. 1–4, No. 2021/75, 03 December. https://doi.org/10.5089/9781616354763.007, accessed 11.02.2022

IMF. (2021e). *Global financial stability report, COVID-19, crypto and climate: Navigating challenging transitions*, October. www.imf.org/-/media/Files/Publications/GFSR/2021/October/English/text.ashx, accessed 18.02.2022

IMF. (2022a). *Money and payments: The U.S. dollar in the age of digital transformation, research and analysis*, January. www.federalreserve.gov/publications/files/money-and-payments-20220120.pdf, accessed 11.02.2022

IMF. (2022b). *Behind the scenes of Central Bank digital currency*. FinTech Notes No 2022/004. www.imf.org/en/Publications/fintech-notes/Issues/2022/02/07/Behind-the-Scenes-of-Central-Bank-Digital-Currency-512174

IMF. (2022c). *World economic outlook*. www.imf.org/en/Publications/WEO

Investopedia. (2022a). *Decentralized finance (DeFi) definition*. www.investopedia.com/decentralized-finance-defi-5113835

Investopedia. (2022b). *What is crypto asset management?* www.investopedia.com/tech/why-crypto-asset-management-next-big-thing/

Jetten, J., Mols, F., Selvanathan, H. P. (2020). How economic inequality fuels the rise and persistence of the yellow vest movement. *International Review of Social Psychology*, vol. 33(1), p. 2. https://doi.org/10.5334/irsp.356

Johnson, J., Arel-Bundock, V., Portniaguine, V. (2019). Adding rooms onto a house we love: Central banking after the global financial crisis. *Public Administration*, vol. 97(3), pp. 546–560. https://doi.org/10.1111/padm.12567

Jung, T. (2020). *Covid-19: Auswirkungen auf mobile payments*, 16 October. www.cgi.com/de/de/blog/payments/covid-19-auswirkungen-auf-mobile-payments, accessed 04.04.2022

Kagan, J. (2022). Digital wallet. *Investopedia*. www.investopedia.com/terms/d/digital-wallet.asp, accessed 29.04.2022

Kahler, M. (2021). *The Bretton Woods Moment, Global Governance in a World of Change*. pp. 77–108. https://10.1017/9781108915199.003

Kalecki, M. (1942). A theory of profits. *The Economic Journal*, vol. 52(206–207), p. 258. https://doi.org/10.2307/2225784

Kampf, G., Todt, D., Pfaender, S., Steinmann, E. (2020). Persistence of coronaviruses on inanimate surfaces and their inactivation with biocidal agents. *Journal of Hospital Infection*, vol. 104(3), pp. 246–251, März. www.journalofhospitalinfection.com/article/S0195-6701(20)30046-3/abstractdate of accessed: 04.04.2022

Kapuściński, M., Chmielewski, T., Kocięcki, A., Łyziak, T., Przystupa, Stanisławska, E., Wróbel, E. (2018). Monetary transmission mechanism in Poland. What do we know in 2017?, NBP Working Papers 286, Narodowy Bank Polski, Economic Research Department.

Karaarslan, E., Konacakli, E. (2020). Data storage in the decentralized world: Blockchain and derivatives. In *Who runs the world: DATA*, Istanbul University Press, pp. 37–69, Chapter 3, December. https://doi.org/10.26650/B/ET06.2020.011.03

Kaul, A. (2021). *This is how Indians invested in cryptos during the record rally of 2021*. www.livemint.com/market/cryptocurrency/how-indians-invested-in-crypto-in-2021-11640672209795.html, accessed April 8, 2022

Khan, A., Malaika, M. (2021). *Central Bank risk management, fintech, and cybersecurity*. IMF Working Paper, No. 21/105. IMF.

Khiaonarong, T., Humphrey, D. (2019). Cash use across countries and the demand for central bank digital currency. *Journal of Payments Strategy and Systems*, vol. 13(1). https://10.5089/9781484399606.001

Khudyakova, L. S. (2019). Launching a sustainable financial system in the European Union. *World Economy and International Relations*, vol. 63(7). https://10.20542/0131-2227-2019-63-7-16-22

Kiff, J., Alwazir, J., Davidovic, S., Farias, A., Khan, A., Khiaonarong, T., Malaika, M., Monroe, H. K., Sugimoto, N., Tourpe, H., Zhou, P. (2020). *A survey of research on retail Central Bank digital*. Working Paper No. 20/104, pp. 1–66, June. www.imf.org/en/Publications/WP/Issues/2020/06/26/A-Survey-of-Research-on-Retail-Central-Bank-Digital-Currency-49517, https://doi.org/10.5089/9781513547787.001, accessed 28.01.2022

Kim, E. (2021). *Bitcoin mining consumes 0.5% of all electricity used globally and 7 times Google's total usage, new report says*. www.businessinsider.com/bitcoin-mining-electricity-usage-more-than-google-2021-9?amp, accessed 08.04.2022

Kim, L., Kumar, R., O'Brien, S. (2020). *Consumer payments & the COVID-19 pandemic: A supplement to the 2020 findings from the diary of consumer payment choice*. Federal Reserve Bank of San Francisco Fed Notes.

Klein, T., Thu, H. P., Walther, T. (2018). Bitcoin is not the new gold – A comparison of volatility, correlation, and portfolio performance. *International Review of Financial Analysis*, vol. 59, pp. 105–116. https://doi.org/10.1016/j.irfa.2018.07.010

Knaack, P. (2017). An unlikely champion of global finance: Why is China exceeding international banking standards? *Journal of Current Chinese Affairs*, vol. 46(2). https://10.1177/186810261704600203

Kochergin, D. (2020). Economic nature and classification of stablecoins. *Finance: Theory and Practice*, vol. 24(6). https://10.26794/2587-5671-2020-24-6-140-160

Kool, C. J. M., Thornton, D. L. (2015). How effective is Central Bank forward guidance? *2015 Review*, Fourth Quarter, vol. 97(4), pp. 303–322. http://dx.doi.org/10.20955/r.2015.303-22

Kopp, E., Kaffenberger, L., Wilson, C. (2017). *Cyber risk, market failures, and financial stability*. IMF Working Paper, WP/17/185. IMF.

Korniyenko, Y., Patnam, M., del Rio-Chanon, R., Porter, M. (2018). *Evolution of the Global Financial Network and Contagion: A New Approach*, IMF Working Papers, 18(113). https://10.5089/9781484353240.001

Kothawale, R. (2021). *Digital Euro: Aspirations of a sovereign alternative to crypto-assets*. Observer Research Foundation, July. www.orfonline.org/expert-speak/digital-euro-aspirations-sovereign-alternative-crypto-assets/, accessed 04.02.2022

Kotkowski, R., Polasik, M. (2021). *COVID-19 pandemic increases the divide between cash and cashless payment users in Europe*. NBP Working Paper No. 339. NBP.

Kowalewski, O., Pisany, P. (2021). Different faces of digital financial inclusion across countries. In E. Lechman, A. Marszk (Eds.), *The digital disruption of financial services: International perspectives*. Routledge.

Kowalewski, O., Pisany, P. (2022). Banks' consumer lending reaction to fintech and bigtech credit emergence in the context of soft versus hard credit information processing. *International Review of Financial Analysis*, vol. 81. https://doi.org/10.1016/j.irfa.2022.102116.

KPMG. (2021). *Crypto Insights #1: An introduction to decentralised finance (DeFi)*. KPMG, October.

Kraaijeveld, O., De Smedt, J. (2020). The predictive power of public Twitter sentiment for forecasting cryptocurrency prices. *Journal of International Financial Markets, Institutions and Money*, vol. 65. https://doi.org/10.1016/j.intfin.2020.101188

Kristoufek, L. (2013). BitCoin meets Google Trends and Wikipedia: Quantifying the relationship between phenomena of the Internet era. *Scientific Reports*, vol. 3(1), p. 3415. https://10.1038/srep03415

Kulisz, M., Bojanowska, A., Toborek, K. (2021). Consumer's behaviour regarding cashless payments during the Covid-19 pandemic. *European Research Studies Journal*, vol. XXIV(2). www.ersj.eu/journal/2224/download, accessed 04.04.2022

Kumhof, M., Noone, C. (2021). Central bank digital currencies – design principles for financial stability. *Economic Analysis and Policy*, vol. 71, pp. 553–572, September. https://doi.org/10.1016/j.eap.2021.06.012, accessed 29.04.2022

Kumhof, M., Noone, C. (2018). *Central Bank digital currencies: Design principles and balance sheet implications*. Working Paper No. 725. Bank of England. http://dx.doi.org/10.2139/ssrn.3180713

Kurowski, Ł., Smaga, P. (2018). Monetary policy and cyclical systemic risk – friends or foes? *Prague Economic Papers, Prague University of Economics and Business*, vol. 27(5), pp. 522–540. https://doi.org/10.18267/j.pep.667

Kurowski, Ł., Smaga, P. (2022). *Communicating financial stability in monetary policy reports – a drop in the ocean*. A text-mining experiment in post-communist countries, mimeo. SGH.

Kuzubov, A., Shashlo, N., Rodionov, A. (2018). Cryptocurrency market: Prerequisites of formation, economic features, prospect directions of development. *Espacios*, vol. 39(50), Scopus: 2-s2.0-85058559327

Lahmiri, S., Bekiros, S. (2019). Cryptocurrency forecasting with deep learning chaotic neural networks. *Chaos, Solitons & Fractals*, vol. 118, pp. 35–40. https://doi.org/10.1016/j.chaos.2018.11.014

Laycock, R., Choi, C. (2021). A rising number of Americans own crypto: But adoption is far from widespread. *Finder.com*, 14 June. www.finder.com/how-many-people-own-cryptocurrency, accessed 19.04.2022

Lee, D. K., Yan, L., Wang, Y. (2021). A global perspective on Central Bank digital currency. *China Economic Journal*, vol. 14(1), pp. 52–66. https://doi.org/10.1080/17538963.2020.1870279

Lefranc, A. (2018). Intergenerational earnings persistence and economic inequality in the long run: Evidence from French cohorts, 1931–75. *Economica*, vol. 85(340), pp. 808–845. https://doi.org/10.1111/ecca.12269

Lepcha, M. (2022). The top 5 stablecoins: The bridge between old and new finance. *Capital.com*, 25 January 25. https://capital.com/top-5-stablecoins-by-market-cap, accessed 12.04.2022

Li, S., Huang, Y. (2021). The genesis, design and implications of China's Central Bank digital currency. *China Economic Journal*, vol. 14(1), pp. 67–77. https://doi.org/10.1080/17538963.2020.1870273, accessed 29.04.2022

Li, X., Wang, C. (2017). The technology and economic determinants of cryptocurrency exchange rates: The case of bitcoin. *Decision Support Systems*, vol. 95, pp. 49–60. Elsevier B.V. https://doi.org/10.1016/j.dss.2016.12.001

Lin, S., Ye, H. (2007). Does inflation targeting really make a difference? Evaluating the treatment effect of inflation targeting in seven industrial countries. *Journal of Monetary Economics*, vol. 54(8), pp. 2521–2533. https://doi.org/10.1016/j.jmoneco.2007.06.017

Linis B., Praicheux S. (2021). Digital and blockchain-based legal regimes: An Eea case study based on innovative legislations – Comparison of French and liechtenstein domestic. *Financial Law Review*, vol. 22(2). https://10.4467/22996834flr.21.009.13977

Liu, W. (2018). Portfolio diversification across cryptocurrencies. *Finance Research Letters*, vol. 29, pp. 200–205.

Livieris, I. E., Kiriakidou, N., Stavroyiannis, S., Pintelas, P. (2021). An advanced CNN-LSTM model for cryptocurrency forecasting. *Electronics*, vol. 10(3), p. 287. https://doi.org/10.3390/electronics10030287

Livieris, I. E., Pintelas, E., Stavroyiannis, S., Pintelas, P. (2020). Ensemble deep learning models for forecasting cryptocurrency time-series. *Algorithms*, vol. 13(5), p. 121. https://doi.org/10.3390/a13050121

LLC, Law Library Of Congress, U. S. G. L. R. D. (2021). *Regulation of cryptocurrency around the world Albania, Algeria, Angola, Anguilla, Antigua and Barbuda, Argentina, Australia, Azerbaijan, Bahamas, Bahrain, Bangladesh, Belarus, Belgium*. The Law Library of Congress, Global Legal Research Directorate [Pdf]. Retrieved from the Library of Congress. www.loc.gov/item/2021687419/, accessed 03.03.2022

Lutsyshyn, O. (2020). How fintech changes the world financial order. *World of Finance*, vol. 2(63). https://10.35774/sf2020.02.102

Ma, Y., Zhang, J. (2016). Financial cycle, business cycle and monetary policy: Evidence from four major economies. *International Journal of Finance and Economics*, vol. 21(4), pp. 502–527. https://doi.org/10.1002/ijfe.1566

Mai, H. (2020). Bezahlen in der Krise, Corona, Karten und Bargeld, Deutschland-Monitor, Finanzen der privaten. *Haushalte*, p. 2, 13 May.

Maniff, J. (2020). *Motives matter: Examining potential tension in central bank digital currency designs, payments system research briefing*, Federal Reserve Bank of Kansas City, pp. 1-4, July.

Manimuthu, A., Sreedharan, V. R. G. Marwaha, D. (2019). A literature review on bitcoin: Transformation of crypto currency into a global phenomenon. *IEEE Engineering Management Review*, vol. 47, pp. 28–35. https://doi.org/10.110/EMR.2019.2901431, accessed 18.02.2022

Markowitz, H. (1952). Portfolio selection. *The Journal of Finance*, vol. 7(1), pp. 77–91. https://doi.org/doi:10.2307/2975974

Marr, B. (2017). *A short history of bitcoin and crypto currency everyone should read.* https://www.forbes.com/sites/bernardmarr/2017/12/06/a-short-history-ofbitcoin-and crypto-currency-everyone-should-read, December 6

Mateju, J. (2013). *Explaining the strength and the efficiency of monetary policy transmission: A panel of impulse responses from a time-varying parameter model*, Working Papers IES 2013/18, Charles University Prague, Faculty of Social Sciences, Institute of Economic Studies, revised Nov 2013.

Mattke, J., Maier, C., Reis, L., Weitzel, T. (2021). Bitcoin investment: A mixed methods study of investment motivations. *European Journal of Information Systems*, vol. 30(3), pp. 261–285. https://doi.org/10.1080/0960085X.2020.1787109

Mawhood, P. (1983). *Local government in the third world.* John Wiley.

Mayer, T. (2019). *A digital euro to compete with Libra.* Macroeconomics. Flossbach von Storch Research Institute, pp. 1–9, 2 July. www.flossbachvonstorch-researchinstitute.com/fileadmin/user_upload/RI/Studien/files/study-190702-a-digital-euro-to-compete-with-libra.pdf, accessed 05.02.2022

McBride, N. (2015). *Payments and the concept of legal tender (Bulletin 78(6)).* Reserve Bank of Newzealand. www.rbnz.govt.nz/research-and-publications/reserve-bank-bulletin/2015/rbb2015-78-00-01

Meaning, J., Dyson, B., Barker, J., Clayton, E. (2018). *Broadening narrow money.* Staff Working Paper No. 724. Bank of England. www.bankofengland.co.uk/working-paper/2018/broadening-narrow-money-monetary-policy-with-a-central-bank-digital-currency

Mersch, Y. (2017). *Digital base money – An assessment from the European Central Bank's perspective.* Speech by Mr Yves Mersch, Member of the Executive Board of the European Central Bank, at the Farewell ceremony for Mr Pentti Hakkarainen, Deputy Governor of the Bank of Finland (Suomen Pankki), 16 January. www.ecb.europa.eu/press/key/date/2017/html/sp170116.en.html, accessed 29.04.2022

Mersch, Y. (2018). *Virtual or virtueless? The evolution of money in the digital age.* Lecture by Yves Mersch, Member of the Executive Board of the ECB, Official Monetary and Financial Institutions Forum, 08 February. www.ecb.europa.eu/press/key/date/2018/html/ecb.sp180208.en.html, accessed 29.04.2022

Meunier, S. (2018). Blockchain 101. *Transforming Climate Finance and Green Investment with Blockchains*, pp. 23–34. https://doi.org/10.1016/b978-0-12-814447-3.00003-3

Mishkin, F. (2001). *From monetary targeting to inflation targeting: Lessons from the industrialized countries.* Policy Research Working Paper, No. 2684. World Bank.

Mishkin, F. (2004). *Can inflation targeting work in emerging market countries?* NBER Working Papers, No. 10646. NBER. https://doi.org/10.1596/1813-9450-2684

Monetary Authority of Singapore. (2021). *A retail Central Bank digital currency: Economic considerations in the Singapore context.* www.mas.gov.sg/-/media/MAS/EPG/Monographs-or-Information-Paper/A-retail-CBDC-Economic-Considerations-in-the-Singapore-Context.pdf

Montani, G. (2011). Money and finance as global public goods: Contribution to a supranational macroeconomic theory. *Sage Open*, pp. 1–11. https://journals.sagepub.com/doi/pdf/10.1177/2158244011424175, accessed 15.04.2022.

Mooij, A. (2021). The European Central Bank's monetary policy and Central Bank Digital Currency: Can the ECB lawfully introduce a digital euro under its monetary mandate? *Irish Journal of European Law*, vol. 23, pp. 163–188. https://isel.ie/download/10-the-european-central-banks-monetary-policy-and-central-bank-digital-currency-can-the-ecb-lawfully-introduce-a-digital-euro-under-its-monetary-mandate/, accessed 28.01.2021

Morris, C. (2021). Bitcoin's market cap tops $1 trillion. *Fortune.* https://fortune.com/2021/02/19/bitcoin-market-cap-1-trillion-price-crypto/

Musyaffi, A. M., Sari, D. A. P., Respati, D. K. (2021). Understanding of digital payment usage during COVID-19 pandemic: A study of UTAUT extension model in Indonesia. *Journal of Asian Finance, Economics and Business*, vol. 8(6), pp. 475–482. www.koreascience.or.kr/article/JAKO202115563442861.pdf, accessed 04.04.2022

Nakamoto, S. (2008). *Bitcoin: A peer-to-peer electronic cash system*. https://bitcoin.org/bitcoin.pdf, accessed 29.04.2022

Náñez Alonso, S. L., Jorge-Vazquez, J., Reier Forradellas, R. F. (2021). Central Banks digital currency: Detection of optimal countries for the implementation of a CBDC and the implication for payment industry open innovation. *Journal of Open Innovation: Technology, Market, and Complexity*, vol. 7(1), p. 72. https://doi.org/10.3390/joitmc7010072

Nasir, M. A., Huynh, T. L. D., Nguyen, S. P., Duong, D. (2019). Forecasting cryptocurrency returns and volume using search engines. *Financial Innovation*, vol. 5(1), p. 2. https://doi.org/10.1186/s40854-018-0119-8

National Bank of Poland. (2021). *Pieniądz cyfrowy banku central neg o* [*Central bank digital currency*]. www.nbp.pl/systemplatniczy/cbdc/raport-cbdc.pdf, accessed 31.01.2022.

NFCW. (2021). *Table: Contactless payment transaction limit increases around the world*. www.nfcw.com/2020/03/26/366173/table-contactless-payment-transaction-limit-increases-around-the-world/, accessed 04.04.2022

NGFS. (2020). *Guide to climate scenario analysis for central banks and supervisors*. Technical document. www.ngfs.net/sites/default/files/medias/documents/ngfs_guide_scenario_analysis_final.pdf

Nicolo, G. D., Dell'Ariccia, G., Laeven, L., Valencia, F. (2010). *Monetary policy and bank risk taking*. IMF Staff Position Note, No. 2010/09. IMF.

Niedźwiedzińska, J. (2022). *Inflation targeting and Central Banks: Institutional set-ups and monetary policy effectiveness*. Routledge.

Niedźwiedzińska, J. (2018). *Inflation targeting: Institutional features of the strategy in practice*. NBP Working Paper No. 299. NBP.

Niedźwiedzińska, J. (2021). Initial monetary policy response to the COVID-19 pandemic in inflation targeting economies, Gospodarka Narodowa. *The Polish Journal of Economics*, vol. 308(4), pp. 125–165. https://doi.org/10.33119/GN/144314

Niepelt, D. (2018). *Reserves for All? Central Bank Digital Currency, Deposits, and their (Non)-Equivalence*, (August 08, 2018). CESifo Working Paper Series No. 7176. SSRN: https://ssrn.com/abstract=3254206 or http://dx.doi.org/10.2139/ssrn.3254206

Niepelt, D. (2020a). Reserves for all? Central Bank digital currency, deposits, and their (non)-equivalence. *International Journal of Central Banking*, vol. 62. www.ijcb.org/journal/ijcb20q2a6.pdf, accessed 01.02.2022.

Niepelt, D. (2020b). Digital money and Central Bank digital currency: An executive summary. *Vox, CEPR Policy Portal*. https://voxeu.org/article/digital-money-and-central-bank-digital-currency-executive-summary

Nieto, M. J. (2019). Banks, climate risk and financial stability. *Journal of Financial Regulation and Compliance*, vol. 27(2), pp. 243–262. https://doi.org/10.1108/JFRC-03-2018-0043

Norges Bank. (2021). *Central bank digital currencies: Third report of the working group*. No. 1. www.norges-bank.no/contentassets/554ee1f1ac53417d99d43708f5abbe14/norges-bank-papers-1-2021.pdf?v=05/19/2021132229&ft=.pdf, accessed 01.02.2022

Oates, W. (1993). Fiscal decentralization and economic development. *National Tax Journal*, vol. 46(2), pp. 237–243. https://EconPapers.repec.org/RePEc:ntj:journl:v:46:y:1993:i:2:p:237-43.

Obstfeld, M., Rogoff, K. (1995). The mirage of fixed exchange rates. *Journal of Economic Perspectives*, vol. 9(4), pp. 73–96.

OECD. (2011). *Estonia: Review of the financial system*. OECD. www.oecd.org/finance/financial-markets/49497930.pdf, accessed 27.04.2022.

OECD. (2022a). *Why decentralised finance (DeFi) matters and the policy implications*, 19 January 2022. www.oecd.org/daf/fin/financial-markets/Why-Decentralised-Finance-DeFi-Matters-and-the-Policy-Implications.pdf, accessed 19.04.2022

OECD. (2022b). *Broad money (M3)*. https://data.oecd.org/money/broad-money-m3.htm

Ogachi, D., Mugambi, P., Bares, L., Zeman, Z. (2021). Idiosyncrasies of money: 21st century evolution of money. *Economies*, vol. 9(1), p. 40. https://doi.org/10.3390/economies9010040, accessed 03.03.2022

Ogachi, D., Mugambi, P., Bares, L., Zeman, Z. (2021). *Idiosyncrasies of Money: 21st Century Evolution of Money Economies*, vol. 9(1), p. 40. https://doi.org/10.3390/economies 9010040

Ohtake, F. (2008). Inequality in Japan. *Asian Economic Policy Review*, vol. 3(1), pp. 87–109. https://doi.org/10.1111/j.1748-3131.2008.00093.x

Okoli, T., Tewari, D. (2021). Does the adoption process of financial technology in Africa follow an inverted U-shaped hypothesis? An evaluation of rogers diffusion of innovation theory, *Asian Academy of Management Journal of Accounting and Finance*, vol. 17(1). https://10.21315/aamjaf2021.17.1.10

Ostrom, V. (1989). *The intellectual crisis in American public administration*. University of Alabama Press.

Ostrom, V., Ostrom, E. (1977). Public goods and public choices: The emergence of public economics and industry structures. In E. Savas (Ed.), *Alternatives for delivering public service: Towards improved performance*. Westview Press, pp. 7–49.

Ozili, P. K. (2021a). *A survey of central bank digital currency adoption in African countries*. Working Paper.

Ozili, P. K. (2021b). Central bank digital currency can lead to the collapse of cryptocurrency. SSRN 3850826.

Ozmen, A. (2014). Notes to the concept of decentralization. *European Scientific Journal*, vol. 10(10). https://doi.org/10.19044/esj.2014.v10n10p%25p

Panek, T. (2017). Polaryzacjaekonomiczna w Polsce. *Wiadomości Statystyczne*, vol. 668, pp. 41–61.

Panetta, F. (2020a). *The ECB blog, beyond monetary policy – Protecting the continuity and safety of payments during the coronavirus crisis*, 28 April. www.ecb.europa.eu/press/blog/date/2020/html/ecb.blog200428~328d7ca065.en.html, accessed 04.04.2022

Panetta, F. (2020b). *From the payments revolution to the reinvention of money*. Speech by Fabio Panetta, Member of the Executive Board of the ECB, at the Deutsche Bundesbank conference on the "Future of Payments in Europe", 27 November. www.ecb.europa.eu/press/key/date/2020/html/ecb.sp201127~a781c4e0fc.en.html, accessed 29.04.2022

Panetta, F. (2021). *Evolution or revolution? The impact of a digital euro on the financial system*. Speech by Fabio Panetta, Member of the Executive Board of the ECB, at a Bruegel online seminar, 10 February. www.bis.org/review/r210211d.pdf, accessed 28.01.2022

Pashtova, L., Oseev, V., Klemenov, D. (2021). Financial instrument of the new economy or a pyramid scheme: The issues of cryptocurrency security. *Finance and Credit*, vol. 27(6). https://10.24891/fc.27.6.1395

Payments Canada. (2021). *Central Bank digital currency (CBDC): Retail CBDC global developments*. www.payments.ca/sites/default/files/paymentscanada_centralbankdigitalcurrency_retail_globaldevelopments_2021.pdf, accessed 13.04.2022

Peneder, M. (2021). Digitization and the evolution of money as a social technology of account. *Journal of Evolutionary Economics*. https://doi.org/10.1007/s00191-021-00729-4, accessed 29.04.2022

Perkins, D. W. (2020). *Cryptocurrency: The economics of money and selected policy issues*. Report No. R45427. Congressional Research Service. https://crsreports.congress.gov, accessed 19.02.2022

Petukhina, A., Trimborn, S., Härdle, W. K., Elendner, H. (2021). Investing with cryptocurrencies – evaluating their potential for portfolio allocation strategies. *Quantitative Finance*, vol. 21(11), pp. 1825–1853. https://doi.org/doi:10.1080/14697688.2021.1880023

Phillips, P. C. B., Perron, P. (1988). Testing for a unit root in time series regression. *Biometrika*, vol. 75(2), pp. 335–346.

Piketty, T. (2003). Income inequality in France, 1901–1998. *Journal of Political Economy*, vol. 111(5), pp. 1004–1042. https://doi.org/10.1086/376955

Piketty, T. (2015). *Kapital w XXI wieku*. Wydawnictwo Krytyki Politycznej.

Plantin, J. C., de Seta, G. (2019). We Chat as infrastructure: The techno-nationalist shaping of Chinese digital platforms. *Chinese Journal of Communication*, vol. 12(3), pp. 257–273. https://doi.org/10.1080/17544750.2019.1572633, accessed 29.04.2022

Platanakis, E., Sutcliffe, C., Urquhart, A. (2018). Optimal vs naïve diversification in cryptocurrencies. *Economics Letters*, vol. 171, pp. 93–96. https://doi.org/10.1016/j.econlet.2018.07.020

Polański, Z. (2011). New challenges after the crisis: A monetary policy perspective. *Journal of Management and Financial Sciences*, vol. 4(5), pp. 68–91.

Porfir'ev, B. N. (2016). Green trends in the global financial system. *World Economy and International Relations*, vol. 60(9). https://10.20542/0131-2227-2016-60-9-5-16

Raghavan, M., Dungey, M. (2015). Should ASEAN-5 monetary policy-makers act pre-emptively against stock market bubbles? *Applied Economics*, vol. 47(11), pp. 1086–1105. https://doi.org/10.1080/00036846.2014.990622.

Ramos, D., Zanko, G. (2020). A review of decentralized finance as an application of increasing importance of blockchain technology. *Mobileyour Life*. https://static1.squarespace.com/static/553d790de4b08ceb08ab88fd/t/5f5037549883d84929c20ace/1599092566315/DeFi_SciPaper_Final.pdf, accessed 19.04.2022

Raskin, M., Yermack, D. (2018). Digital currencies, decentralized ledgers and the future of central banking. In *Research handbook on Central Banking*. Edward Elgar Publishing. https://doi.org/10.4337/9781784719227, accessed 19.02.2022

Rauchs, M., Blandine, A., Klein., K., Pieters, G.C. (2019). 2nd global cryptoasset benchmarking study. *SSRN Electronic Journal*, December. https://doi.org/10.2139/ssrn.3306125

Rawls, J. (2013). *Teoria sprawiedliwości*. Wydawnictwo Naukowe PWN.

Read, O., Schäfer, S.(2020). Libra Project: Regulators Act on Global Stablecoins. *Intereconomics*, vol. 55(6). https://10.1007/s10272-020-0936-7

Rennie, E., Steele, S. (2021). Privacy and emergency payments in a pandemic: How to think about privacy and a Central Bank digital currency. *Law, Technology and Humans*, vol. 3(1), pp. 6–17. https://doi.org/10.5204/lthj.1745

Resinek, M. (2019). *Floor versus corridor systems in monetary policy regimes – Overview of the euro area experience and forward-looking issues*. 13th ECB Central Bank seminar ECB. www.ecb.europa.eu/pub/conferences/shared/pdf/20190701_CBS2019/ecb.CBS2019_Resinek_policy_panel_on_monetary_policy_implementation_frameworks_in_evolving_financial_markets_slides.en.pdf, accessed 29.04.2022

Reuters. (2022). China Central Bank launches digital yuan wallet apps for Android, iOS. *Reuters*. www.reuters.com/markets/currencies/china-cbank-launches-digital-yuan-wallet-apps-android-ios-2022-01–04/, accessed 31.01.2022

Reyna, A., Martin, C., Chen, J., Soler, E., Diaz, M. (2018). On blockchain and its integration with IoT: Challenges and opportunities. *Future Generation Computer Systems*, vol. 88, pp. 173–190. https://doi.org/10.1016/j.future.2018.05.046, accessed 20.02.2022

Reznikova, N., Ivashchenko, O. (2018). Sovereign Wealth Funds in the system of global financial imbalances: An analysis of benefits and threads from the perspective of global financial stability. *Actual Problems of International Relations*, (136). https://10.17721/apmv.2018.136.0.60-66

Ribot, J. C. (2004). *Waiting for democracy: The politics of choice in natural resource decentralization*. World Resource Institute.

Ridderstaat, J., Croes, R., Robertico, C. (2017). The link between money supply and tourism demand cycles: A case study of two caribbean destinations. *Journal of Travel Research*, vol. 56(2), pp. 187–205. https://doi.org/doi:10.1177/0047287515619695

Ron, D., Shamir, A. (2013). Quantitative analysis of the full bitcoin transaction graph. *International Conference on Financial Cryptography and Data Security*, pp. 6–24. https://doi.org/10.1007/978-3-642-39884-1_2, accessed 22.02.2022

Rondinelli, D. (1981). Government decentralization in comparative perspective: Theory and practice in developing countries. *International Review of Administrative Science*, vol. 47(2), pp. 133–145.

Rosales, A. (2021). Unveiling the power behind cryptocurrency mining in Venezuela: A fragile energy infrastructure and precarious labor. *Energy Research & Social Science*, vol. 79. https://doi.org/10.1016/j.erss.2021.102167

Rose, A. K. (2014). Surprising similarities: Recent monetary regimes of small economies. *Journal of International Money and Finance*, vol. 49(Part A), pp. 5–27. https://doi.org/10.1016/j.jimonfin.2014.05.004

Rosl, G., Seitz, F. (2021). *Cash and crises: No surprise by the virus*. Working Paper 150. Institute for Monetary and Financial Stability, Goethe University Frankfurt. www.imfs-frankfurt.de/fileadmin/user_upload/IMFS_WP/IMFS_WP_150_web.pdf, accessed 04.04.2022

Rumberger, R. W. (2010). Education and the reproduction of economic inequality in the United States: An empirical investigation. *Economics of Education Review*, vol. 9.

Rusnák, M., Havránek, T., Horváth, R. (2011). *How to Solve the Price Puzzle? A Meta-Analysis*, Working Papers IES 2011/24, Charles University Prague, Faculty of Social Sciences, Institute.

Russo, C., Blacki, M., Cedric S. (2017). *This is where people are buying Bitcoin all over the world*. Bloomberg.com, October 12, 2017, January 11, 2018.

Saez, E., Zucman, G. (2016). Wealth inequality in the United States since 1913: Evidence from capitalized income tax data. *The Quarterly Journal of Economics*, vol. 131(2), pp. 519–578. https://doi.org/10.1093/qje/qjw004

Safiullin, M., Savelichev, M., Elshin, L., Moiseev, V. (2020). Potential of cryptocurrency as global money of the sixth technological mode based on the global financial system. *International Journal of Financial Research*, vol. 11(6). https://10.5430/ijfr.v11n6p296

Salleh, N. H. M., Othman, R., Ramachandran, S. (2007). Malaysia's tourism demand from selected countries: The ARDL approach to cointegration. *International Journal of Economics and Management*, vol. 1(3), pp. 345–363.

Samudrala, R. S., Yerchuru, S. K. (2021). Central Bank digital currency: Risks, challenges and design considerations for India. *CSIT*, vol. 9(4), pp. 245–249. https://doi.org/10.1007/s40012-021-00344-5, accessed 29.04.2022

Sankar, T.R. (2021). *Central bank digital currency – Is this the future money*. Reserve Bank of India. https://rbi.org.in/scripts/BS_SpeechesView.aspx?Id=1111

Schäffler, F. (2022). Der digitale Euro muss nicht von der EZB kommen. *Kolumne*, vol. 11, April. www.frankschaeffler.de/der-digitale-euro-muss-nicht-von-der-ezb-kommen/, accessed 29.04.2022

Schär, F. (2021). Decentralized finance: On blockchain- and smart contract-based financial markets. *Federal Reserve Bank of St. Louis Review*, Second Quarter, pp. 153–174. https://doi.org/10.20955/r.103.153-74

Schellhorn, C. (2020). Financial system stability, the timing of climate change action and the federal reserve. *Journal of Central Banking Theory and Practice*, vol. 9(3). https://10.2478/jcbtp-2020-0035

Schilling, L., Fernández-Villaverde, J., Uhlig, H. (2020). *Central Bank digital currency: When price and bank stability collide*. Working Paper No. 2020–180. Becker Friedman Institute. https://bfi.uchicago.edu/working-paper/central-bank-digital-currency-when-price-and-bank-stability-collide/

Schulz, B. (2021). *Banking sector briefing: COVID-19 alsKatalysator für Innovationen im Zahlungsverkehr?* 18 June. https://www2.deloitte.com/de/de/blog/sector-briefings/2021/banking-sector-briefing-zahlungsverkehr.html, accessed 04.04.2022

Schweik, C. M., Kitsing, M. (2010). Applying Elinor Ostrom's rule classification framework to the analysis of open source software commons. *Transnational Corporations Review*, vol. 2(1), p. 13. https://ssrn.com/abstract=2019697, accessed 15.04.2022

Schweik, C., English, R. (2012). *Internet success: A study of open source software commons*. MIT Press.

SEC. (2018). *Securities and exchange commission administrative proceeding file no. 3–18888 in the matter of Zachary Coburn, order instituting cease-and- desist proceedings pursuant to section 21c of the securities exchange act of 1934, making findings, and imposing a cease- and-desist order*. www.sec.gov/litigation/admin/2018/34-84553.pdf, accessed 15.04.2022

Sen, A. (1979). Equality of what? The Tanner lecture on human values series with a unit root. *Journal of the American Statistical Association*, vol. 74(366), pp. 427–431.

Seth, H., Talwar, S., Bhatia, A., Saxena, A., Dhir, A. (2020). Consumer resistance and inertia of retail investors: Development of the resistance adoption inertia continuance (RAIC) framework. *Journal of Retailing and Consumer Services*, vol. 55. https://doi.org/10.1016/j.jretconser.2020.102071

Shavshukov, V., Zhuravleva, N. (2020). Global economy: New risks and leadership problems. *International Journal of Financial Studies*, vol. 8(1). https://10.3390/ijfs8010007

Siedenbiedel, C. (2021). *Digitaler Euro spätestens in fünf Jahren*. Frankfurter Allgemeine Zeitung, 13 January. www.faz.net/aktuell/finanzen/ezb-praesidentin-lagarde-kuendigt-digitalen-euro-in-fuenf-jahren-an-17144352.html, accessed 29.04.2022

Sielska, A. (2020). Changes in the international monetary system: Opportunities and risks for the US dollar. *Economic Annals-XXI*, vol. 183(5–6). https://10.21003/EA.V183-01

Siklos, P. L., Amand, S. S., Wajda, J. (2018). *The evolving scope and content of Central Bank speeches*. CIGI Paper No. 202. Centre for International Governance Innovation.

Singhal, R., Gupta, A. (2021). Impact of COVID-19 on digital payment services at towns and villages. *International Journal of Creative Research Thoughts (IJCRT)*. https://papers.ssrn.com/sol3/papers.cfm?abstract_id=3947798, accessed 04.04.2022

Sirucek, M. (2014). Impact of money supply on stock bubbles. *Acta Universitatis Agriculturae et Silviculturae Mendelianae Brunensis*, 7. 2835. https://10.11118/actaun201361072835

Slickcharts. (2022). *Cryptocurrency market data*. www.slickcharts.com/currency, accessed 12.04.2022.

Smaga, P. (2021). Are interest rate changes comoving with financial cycle? *Acta Oeconomica*, vol. 71(2), pp. 259–277. https://doi.org/DOI: 10.1556/032.2021.00013

Smith, A. L., Becke, T. (2015). Has forward guidance been effective? *Economic Review, Federal Reserve Bank of Kansas City, Issue Q*, vol. III, pp. 57–78.

Smith, B. C. (1985). *Decentralization: The territorial dimension of the state*. George Allen.

Sobiecki, G. (2021). *Zdecentralizowane finanse (DeFi) (Decentralized finance), in Blockchain w sektorze bankowym (Blockchain in banking sector)*. A report by Związek Banków Polskich (the Union of Polish Banks) and Centrum Prawa Bankowegoi Informacji (the Center for Bank Law and Information). https://alebank.pl/wp-content/uploads/2021/12/Raport_Blockchain-w-sektorze-bankowym.pdf, accessed 19.04.2022

Sovbetov, Y. (2018). Factors influencing cryptocurrency prices: Evidence from bitcoin, ethereum, dash, litcoin, and monero. *Journal of Economics and Financial Analysis*, vol. 2(2), pp. 1–27.

Stacey, K. (2022). Meet the "crypto caucus": The US lawmakers defending digital coins. *Financial Times*, 31 March. www.ft.com/content/29f32905-1933-458e-aa29-7f1685109ea1, accessed 02.05.2022

Steinmetz, F., von Meduna, M., Ante, L., Fiedler, I. (2021). Ownership, uses and perceptions of cryptocurrency: Results from a population survey. *Technological Forecasting and Social Change*, vol. 173. https://doi.org/10.1016/j.techfore.2021.121073

Stepanova, V., Erins, I. (2021). Review of decentralized finance applications and their total value locked. *TEM Journal*, vol. 10(1), pp. 327–333, February. https://doi.org/10.18421/TEM101--41

Stiglitz, J. E. (2013). *The price of inequality*. W. W. Norton & Company.

Stone, D. (1997). *Policy paradox: The art of political decision making*. W.W. Norton and Company.

Strauss-Kahn, M. O. (2021). *A digital Euro*. European Union Focused CBDC Analysis, Atlantic Council, 12 May. www.atlanticcouncil.org/economy-business/a-digital-euro/, accessed 04.02.2022

Suh, H. (2014). Dichotomy between macroprudential policy and monetary policy on credit and inflation. *Economics Letters*, vol. 122(2), pp. 144–149. https://doi.org/10.1016/j.econlet.2013.11.012

Sukmawati, S., Sikora, C.O. (2018). The new era of financial innovation: The determinants of bitcoin's price. *Journal of Indonesian Economy and Business*, vol. 33(1), p. 46. https://doi.org/doi:10.22146/jieb.30646.

Svensson, L. E. O. (2016). Cost-benefit analysis of leaning against the wind: Are costs larger also with less effective macroprudential policy? IMF Working Papers No. 2016/003. IMF. https://doi.org/10.5089/9781498314787.001

SverigesRiksbank. (2017). *The Riksbank's e-krona project*. Report 1. www.riksbank.se/globalassets/media/rapporter/e-krona/2017/rapport_ekrona_uppdaterad_170920_eng.pdf, accessed 31.01.2022

SverigesRiksbank. (2018). *The Riksbank's e-krona project*. Report 2. www.riksbank.se/globalassets/media/rapporter/e-krona/2018/the-riksbanks-e-krona-project-report-2.pdf, accessed 31.01.2022.

SverigesRiksbank. (2020). *Payments in Sweden 2020*. Report. SverigesRiksbank.

Swanson, E. T. (2021). Measuring the effects of federal reserve forward guidance and asset purchases on financial markets. *Journal of Monetary Economics*, vol. 118, pp. 32–53. https://doi.org/10.1016/j.jmoneco.2020.09.003

Swanson, N. R. (1998). Money and output viewed through a rolling window. *Journal of Monetary Economics*, vol. 41(3), pp. 455–474.
Szopa, B. (2005). *Zmianydochodówludności w Polsce na tleuwarunkowańsystemowych.* WydawnictwoAkademiiEkonomicznej w Krakowie.
Talwar, M., Talwar, S., Kaur, P., Tripathy, N., Dhir, A. (2021). Has financial attitude impacted the trading activity of retail investors during the COVID-19 pandemic? *Journal of Retailing and Consumer Services*, vol. 58. https://doi.org/10.1016/j.jretconser.2020.102341
Talwar, S. (2016). *Security analysis and portfolio management* (first ed.). Cengage Learning.
Talwar, S., Gupta-Bhattacharya, N. (2017). Portfolio diversification opportunities across stock markets of Asian tigers. Thailand and India: A vector autoregression approach. *Global Business and Economics Review*, vol. 19(2), pp. 176–193. https://doi.org/10.1504/GBER.2017.082585
Talwar, S., Pansare, J. (2018). Transmission of shock across international stock markets: An econometric analysis. *Economics and Applied Informatics*, vol. 24(1), pp. 110–119.
Talwar, S., Talwar, M., Tarjanne, V., Dhir, A. (2021). Why retail investors traded equity during the pandemic? An application of artificial neural networks to examine behavioral biases. *Psychology & Marketing*, vol. 38(11), pp. 2142–2163. https://doi.org/doi:10.1002/mar.21550
Tauschwiki. (2022). *Tauschring.* https://tauschwiki.de/wiki/Tauschring, accessed 29.04. 2022
Teichmann, F. M. J., Falker, M. C. (2021). Cryptocurrencies and financial crime: Solutions from Liechtenstein. *Journal of Money Laundering Control*, vol. 24(4), pp. 775–788. https://doi.org/10.1108/JMLC-05-2020-0060, accessed 29.04.2022
The World Bank. "GDP (Current US$)." The World Bank, 2021, https://data.worldbank.org/indicator/NY.GDP.MKTP.CD?most_recent_value_desc=true
Thomson Reuters. (2022). *The top 100 global technology leaders.* www.thomsonreuters.com/content/dam/ewp-m/documents/thomsonreuters/en/pdf/reports/thomson-reuters-top-100-global-tech-leaders-report.pdf, accessed 29.04.2022
Tobias, A., Mancini-Griffoli, T. (2019). *The rise of digital money.* International Monetary Fund, IMF Fintech Note 19/01. www.imf.org/-/media/Files/Publications/FTN063/2019/English/FTNEA2019001.ashx, accessed 19.04.2022
Tomeczek, A. F. (2016). ZróżnicowaniesocjoekonomiczneJaponii. In *Zarządzanie i ekonomia: Teraźniejszośćiprzyszłość* (pp. 63–80). WydawnictwoPoltext.
Tomeczek, M. (2017). Nierównościekonomicznejakokategoriaopisowainormatywna. *Studia Ekonomiczne: ZeszytyNaukoweUniwersytetuEkonomicznego w Katowicach*, vol. 334, pp. 7–21.
Töpfer, L. (2018). Inside global financial networks: The state, lead firms, and the rise of fintech. *Dalogues in Human Geography*, vol. 8(3). https://10.1177/2043820618797779
Trimborn, S. (2015). *Towards cryptocurrency index – Analysis of the market.* Master's Thesis. Humboldt-Universit¨atzu.
Trimborn, S., Li, M., Hardle, W. K. (2019). Investing with cryptocurrencies – A liquidity constrained investment approach. *Journal of Financial Economics*, vol. 18(2), pp. 280–306.
Umar, M., Rizvi, S., Naqvi, B. (2021). Dance with the devil? The nexus of fourth industrial revolution, technological financial products and volatility spillovers in global financial system. *Technological Forecasting and Social Change*, vol. 163. https://10.1016/j.techfore.2020.120450

United Nations. (2009). *Report of the commission of experts of the president of the United Nations general assembly on reforms of the international monetary and financial system*. United Nations.

Urbinati, E., Belsito, A., Cani, D., Caporrini, A., Capotosto, M., Folino, S., Galano, G., Goretti, G., Marcelli, G., Tiberi, P., Vita, A. (2021). *A digital euro: A contribution to the discussion on technical design choices*. Banca D'ItaliaEurosystema, pp. 14–16.

van Doremalen, N. (2020). Aerosol and surface stability of SARS-CoV-2 as compared with SARS-CoV-1. *The New England Journal of Medicine*. www.nejm.org/doi/full/10.1056/nejmc2004973, accessed 04.04.2022

Van Hee, K., Wijngaard, J. (2021). A new digital currency system. *Central European Review of Economics and Management, CEREM*, vol. 5(4), pp. 33–60, December. https://doi.org/10.29015/cerem.929

Verona, F., Martins, M. M. F., Drumond, I. (2017). Financial shocks, financial stability, and optimal Taylor rules. *Journal of Macroeconomics*, vol. 54(Part B), pp. 187–207. https://doi.org/10.1016/j.jmacro.2017.04.004

Viñuela, C., Sapena, J., Wandosell, G. (2020). The future of money and the central bank digital currency dilemma. *Sustainability* (Switzerland), vol. 12(22), pp. 1–21. https://10.3390/su12229697

Vitari, C. (2016). *Electronic currencies: A literature review*. Colloque de l'Association Information et management. https://halshs.archives-ouvertes.fr/halshs-01924191/document, accessed 28.01.2022

Vollmer, U. (2005). *Geld- und Währungspolitik*. Vahlens Handbücher der Wirtschafts- und Sozialwissenschaften.

Vovchenko, N., Andreeva, O., Orobinsky, A., Sichev, R. (2019). Risk control in modelling financial management systems of large corporations in the digital economy. *International Journal of Economics and Business Administration*, 7. Scopus: 2-s2.0-85069639905

Vredin, A. (2015). *Inflation targeting and financial stability: Providing policymakers with relevant information*. BIS Working Papers, No. 503. BIS.

Walch, A. (2015). The Bitcoin blockchain as financial market infrastructure: A consideration of operational risk, N. Y. C. *Journal of Legislation and Public Policy*, p. 837.

Waller, C. (2021). Central Bank digital currency: A solution in search of a problem? In D. Niepelt (Ed.), *Central Bank digital currency: Considerations, projects, outlook*. Centre for Economic Policy Research.

Walther, T., Klein, T., Bouri, E. (2019). Exogenous drivers of bitcoin and cryptocurrency volatility: A mixed data sampling approach to forecasting. *Journal of International Financial Markets, Institutions and Money*, vol. 63, pp. 101–133.

Wang, Y. (2020). *Automated market makers for decentralized finance (DeFi)*. arXiv:2009.01676v2 [q-fin.TR], 11 September.

Ward, O., Rochemont, S. (2019). *Understanding Central Bank digital currencies (CBDC)*. Institute and Faculty of Actuaries, March. www.actuaries.org.uk/system/files/field/document/Understanding%20CBDCs%20Final%20-%20disc.pdf, accessed 01.02.2022

Watling, C. (2021). Time for a great reset of the financial system: A 30-year debt super cycle that has fuelled inequality illustrates the need for a new regime. *Financial Times Market Opinions, Financial Times*, 18 March. www.ft.com/content/39c53b9f-f443-4dde-9cdb-07e8999ec783, accessed 18.02.2022

WeChat Pay. (2022). *WeChat pay: Leading mobile payment platform*. https://pay.weixin.qq.com/index.php/public/wechatpay_en, accessed 29.04.2022

WEF, Wharton. (2021). *Decentralized finance (DeFi) policy-maker toolkit*. Whitepaper. WEF, June.

Wharton. (2021). DeFi beyond the hype. *The Emerging World of Decentralized Finance*, May. https://wifpr.wharton.upenn.edu/wp-content/uploads/2021/05/DeFi-Beyond-the-Hype.pdf, accessed 19.04.2022

White, L. (1999). *The theory of monetary* institutions (first ed.). Wiley-Blackwell.

WID. (2022). *World inequality database*. https://wid.world/

Williams, J. C. (2016). *Whither inflation targeting?* Presentation to the Hayek Group, Reno, Nevada, 06 September.

Williamson, S. (2018). Low real interest rates, collateral misrepresentation, and monetary policy. *American Economic Journal: Macroeconomics*, vol. 10, pp. 202–233.

Williamson, S. (2019). Central Bank digital currency: Welfare and policy implications. *The Central Bank Digital Currency Insider*, 12 February. www.cbdcinsider.com/wp-content/uploads/2020/11/paper_386.pdf, accessed 06.03.2022

Wilson, C., Gaidosch, T., Adelmann, F., Morozova, A. (2019). *Cybersecurity risk supervision*, IMF Departmental Paper, No. 19/15. IMF.

Wilson, T. (2021). 10 best fictional currencies in video games. *The Gamer*. 2 December. www.thegamer.com/best-fictional-currency-money-coins-in-video-games/, accessed 15.04.2022.

Wolfson, S. N. (2015). Bitcoin: The early market. *Journal of Business & Economics Research (JBER)*, vol. 13(4), p. 201. https://doi.org/10.19030/jber.v13i4.9452

World Bank. (2005). *What is decentralization?*, Decentralization Thematic Team. World Bank. www.ciesin.org/decentralization/English/General/Different_forms.html, accessed 19.04.2022

Wuermeling, J. (2021). *Exploring DORA – the digital operational resilience act and its impact on banks and their supervisors*. Deutsche Bank, SUERF Policy Brief, No 210, The European Money and Finance Forum, October. www.suerf.org/suer-policy-brief/35145/exploring-dora-the-digital-operational-resilience-act-and-its-impact-on-banks-and-their-supervisors, accessed 03.02.2022

Wullweber, J., Voss, R., Schick, G. (2020). *The covid-19 financial crisis, global financial instabilities and transformations in the financial system*. Finanzwende, Heinrich-Böll-Foundation, p. 63.

Wullweber, J. (2020). The COVID-19 financial crisis, global financial instabilities and transformations in the financial system. *SSRN Electronic Journal*. https://10.2139/ssrn.3688453

Xi, Y., Ng, A. (2021). Disappearing bargain and technical sharing: The sociocultural influence of mobile payment in China. *Chinese Journal of Communication*, vol. 14(1), pp. 40–57. https://doi.org/10.1080/17544750.2020.1814369, accessed 29.04.2022

Yamada, T. (2012). Income risk, macroeconomic and demographic change, and economic inequality in Japan. *Journal of Economic Dynamics and Control*, vol. 36(1), pp. 63–84. https://doi.org/10.1016/j.jedc.2011.07.001

Yao, Q. (2017). Understanding Central Bank digital currency: A systemic framework. *Scientia Sinica Informationis*, vol. 47(11), pp. 1592–1600. https://doi.org/10.1360/n112017-00218

Yefremov, D.(2021). Digital yuan on the foreground: Initial conclusions from the Chinese experiment. *Chinese Studies*, (1). https://10.51198/chinesest2021.01.165

Zamora-Pérez, A. (2021). The paradox of banknotes: Understanding the demand for cash beyond transactional use. *Economic Bulletin*, vol. 2, pp. 121–137. European Central Bank. www.ecb.europa.eu/pub/pdf/ecbu/eb202102.en.pdf, accessed 29.04.2022

Zetzsche, D. et al. (2020). Decentralized finance (DeFi). *Journal of Financial Regulation*, vol. 6, pp. 172–203. https://papers.ssrn.com/sol3/papers.cfm?abstract_id=%203539194, accessed 19.04.2022

Zwiech, P. (2016). *Nierównościekonomiczne w Polsce*. Wydawnictwo Naukowe Uniwersytetu Szczecińskiego.

Index